GREAT LIVES OBSERVED

Lloyd George

Edited by MARTIN GILBERT

*There was no man so gifted, so eloquent,
so forceful, who knew the life
of the people so well.*
—WINSTON CHURCHILL ON LLOYD GEORGE

A SPECTRUM BOOK

PRENTICE-HALL, INC., ENGLEWOOD CLIFFS, N.J.

Current printing (last number):

10 9 8 7 6 5 4 3 2 1

Library of Congress Catalog Card Number: 68–17825

Printed in the United States of America

Prentice-Hall International, Inc. (*London*)

Preface

I would like to thank my wife Helen, who scrutinized the text and made many valuable suggestions; David Hoffman, who gave me the benefit of an American view and was ever ready to advise; Ivor Samuels, whose help was, as always, a great encouragement; and Mrs. Devika Holloway who transformed rough drafts into neat typescript and enabled the book to be written with the minimum of chaos.

MARTIN GILBERT

Contents

PART ONE
LLOYD GEORGE LOOKS AT THE WORLD

1

2

3

PART THREE
LLOYD GEORGE IN HISTORY

Introduction

David Lloyd George was born in 1863, and his youth was spent entirely in Wales. His background was a humble one; he helped in his uncle's shoe shop, searched the neighborhood for firewood, worked in the fields, and listened to the dramatic sermons with which Welsh preachers galvanized their flock. The problems of poverty, the hardships of rural life, and the difficulties of ordinary folk were very much a part of his own experience, as was the Welsh passion for oratory, which was to reach a high point in his own speeches. "Lloyd George never forgot what oratory is really for," wrote one of his biographers, Frank Owen, "—not to please men or to lull them, but to move them,—and if they accepted the message, to make them go out and straightaway do something worthwhile about it."

In Wales Lloyd George came swiftly to hate the arrogance of the land-owning aristocracy and their reliance upon the letter of the law. "Beyond every wood and stream," he once wrote, "there stood the silhouette of a gamekeeper." He was outraged to learn that before the introduction of the secret ballot in 1872 Conservative landlords had gone so far as to evict any tenants who dared to vote Liberal. "They were turned out by the score on to the roadside," he later recalled, "because they had dared to vote according to their consciences." Lloyd George became, through his background and experiences, a champion of conscience, of the un-derprivileged, and of the "little man" whose life was circumscribed by rules and regulations as difficult to explain as to justify.

In 1878, when Lloyd George was fifteen, he became a clerk in a solici-tor's office. When he was eighteen he wrote his first article, for a local Welsh paper, denouncing the Conservatives "for the instigation of foul and atrocious crimes" during the "imperial" war against Afghanistan. It was the Conservatives, he explained in his second article, who "made Afghan mothers husbandless, their children fatherless and both home-less—saturated the Afghan snows with the blood of patriots, and drove hatred of our very name and presence into the heart of the Afghan nation." The young lawyer, who thus took up and echoed William E. Gladstone's anti-imperialist theme with Welsh fury, plunged more and more frequently into political controversy, although he continued to practice as a solicitor until he was twenty-seven. His hero was the radical politician Joseph Chamberlain because, as Lloyd George explained at the time, "he is convinced that the aristocracy stands in the way of de-

velopment of the Rights of Man, and he says so unflinchingly, though he
be howled at as an ill-mannered demagogue by the whole kennelry of
gorged Aristocracy and of their fawning minions."

In 1890, when he was twenty-seven, Lloyd George sought election to
Parliament for the Welsh seat of Caernarvon Boroughs. To those Conservatives who had said that a man born in a cottage should not be a
candidate, he replied: "The Tories have not yet realized that the day
of the cottage-bred man has at last dawned." Lloyd George became an
apostle of the new dawn. He spoke at election meetings with a skillful
mixture of subtle persuasion and violent denunciation. To make a particularly emotional point he would often speak in Welsh. According to
a report by the Conservative Party Agent for Wales, he made in these
speeches "so thrilling and overpowering an appeal to the emotions"
that he would be "invincible in Wales." Lloyd George won the seat, by
only eighteen votes out of a total electorate of 3,908; but he held it
through thirteen general elections, for over fifty years.

Lloyd George brought from rural Wales to parliamentary London a
power to excite men by his words, a power which he knew himself to
possess and which he used to its fullest. As a young Member of Parliament he attacked the Conservatives mercilessly, both in the House of
Commons and at frequent public meetings throughout England. He
wrote articles on parliamentary affairs for the *Manchester Guardian*. He
helped establish a Welsh National Press Company, which bought up a
number of Welsh and English local papers. "The most startling fact
about our country is this," he told his readers, "that you have men who
have accumulated untold wealth living in gorgeous splendour in one
street, and a horde of miserable, poverty-stricken human beings huddled
together in the most abject penury and squalor in the adjoining courts."

From his early experiences Lloyd George sensed that he could captivate
public meetings more easily than he could influence the House of Commons. "These M.P.s are so frightfully decorous and respectable," he wrote
in 1890. "My audience is the country."

For his first five years in Parliament Lloyd George championed the
rights of his fellow Welshmen. He wanted them to be allowed to set up
their own Parliament, to found a University of Wales, and to destroy the
power of the established English Church. He spoke with fervor of the
rights of a small nation to independence. If only, he mocked, an English
statesman could be found "with daring enough to undertake a journey
of exploration" into the Welsh mountains:

> He would discover how backward and primitive are the Welsh. Why,
> would it be believed that we have actually no race-course in the whole
> country, nor even a Stock Exchange? Who would credit the tale that an
> old festival, called the Eisteddfod, a relic of the Middle Ages, where such
> barbaric pastimes as music, poetry and literature are cherished, is still

preferred to horse-racing? Nay, that in some parts the people are so steeped in savagery as to attend preaching meetings on holidays, to the utter neglect of prize-fights?

In 1893 Gladstone's Liberal Government introduced legislation to Parliament which was intended to halt the creation of new Church of England bishoprics in Wales. Here was a step in the direction of destroying the power of the Church establishment, a step which Lloyd George had been urging and which he welcomed enthusiastically. Welsh Disestablishment became his major concern. But the Conservatives were able to defeat the proposed legislation, helped by the former Liberal, Joseph Chamberlain, who now, as a Liberal Unionist, was opposed equally to Home Rule for Ireland or for Wales, and had ceased to be Lloyd George's hero. Lloyd George formed a small pressure group in Parliament and threatened to break away from the Liberal Party if they abandoned Disestablishment. When, in 1895, the Liberals put forward a Welsh Disestablishment Bill, Lloyd George spoke powerfully in its favor. But the Government was defeated before the Bill could become Law, and the Liberals passed into a ten-year period of opposition. While in opposition, Lloyd George became the recognized spokesman for the Welsh Liberals, and the outspoken champion of Welsh nonconformity.

But the battle for Wales was a sideshow to most English politicians. As the advocate of Wales, Lloyd George might arouse sympathy—or annoyance—but he could do little more. The Welsh would support him. They would thrill to hear his praises of their past glories and future "independence." But a wider issue was needed to give him weight and influence in national life.

The Conservative Party was not alone in the late nineteenth century in accepting the need for imperial wars as part of the spread of civilization. Conservative and Liberal Prime Ministers alike were responsible for military expeditions which extended the territory of the British Empire. Few Englishmen learned of the conquest of Burma or the occupation of Egypt with unease or anguish. Two Liberal Prime Ministers, Gladstone and Rosebery, extended the British Empire in Africa by military means. But many Liberals strongly opposed the use of force if its object were annexation. Lloyd George rejected the need for violent imperial expansion. The idea of aggressive war filled him with anger.

It was during the Boer War, when Britain sought to crush the small independent republics of the Transvaal and the Orange Free State, that Lloyd George first publicly and stridently denounced war as an instrument of imperial policy. His speeches in the House of Commons and at public meetings, particularly in Wales, were for the first time widely reported in the national Press. By these speeches he became a public figure. Within three years he made his mark as the champion of small nations and as an opponent of imperial war. By the age of thirty-seven he was recognized as a Liberal politician of stature. He aroused great controversy, even among his fellow Liberals, many of whom disagreed with his denunciation of the war. But he spoke as his conscience dictated, and what he lost in public support—for the "man in the street" can be notoriously bellicose in any war—he gained in reputation. He spoke his mind fearlessly, loudly, and often. He clearly belonged, not to the cyphers, hacks, and shadows who inhabit political life, but to the men of action and passion.

Lloyd George was distressed to find that so many Welshmen supported Britain's war against the Boers. But he refused to modify his views in order to court their approval, even at election time. He thrived on opposition and unpopularity, and though his effigy was burned in his own constituency, he did not waver in his convictions. He answered his critics fiercely and frankly, and was reelected to Parliament in 1900, at the "Khaki election" which confirmed the Conservatives in power, and gave avowed approval to the war itself. "All wars," Lloyd George insisted, "are so horrible in their incidence, and so uncertain in their event, that sensible statesmen recognize that as soon as you can secure the main object of a war and bring it to an end the better it is, even for the victor."

The Boer War ended in 1902. For three more years the Liberal Party remained in opposition. Lloyd George still championed the cause of Wales. But his abilities, which his criticisms of the Boer War had made clear, soon found a wider theme. The Conservative Government began to consider a protectionist policy—the creation of a tariff system which would tax foreign imports and enable home produce to sell more easily. The Liberals believed that the existing Free Trade system was essential; and it was as a champion of Free Trade that Lloyd George now emerged. At this time he made the friendship of Winston Churchill, a young Conservative who also believed strongly in Free Trade and was writing of the Conservatives, "I hate the Tory party, their men, their words and their methods." In 1904 Churchill crossed the floor of the House of Commons to become a Liberal himself, and to champion Free Trade with the same vigor as Lloyd George. These two young men spoke mercilessly against the Tory protectionists. Liberal morale was raised. The chances of a Conservative collapse were increased. Yet neither Churchill nor Lloyd George saw Free Trade as an end in itself, but rather as the foundation stone for social reform at home and international conciliation abroad.

In 1905, when the Liberals came into office, Lloyd George accepted a position in the Cabinet. He became President of the Board of Trade. Behind him lay fifteen years of oratory geared to denunciation. Ahead lay the slow, tedious, constructive tasks of administration. He was forty-two.

For the next nine years, from 1905 until the outbreak of war in 1914, Lloyd George took the initiative in guiding and goading the Liberal

Party into providing Britain with working conditions and government securities adequate for the twentieth century. As President of the Board of Trade he made an immediate reputation as a skillful negotiator. By his personal efforts a national rail strike was averted. He triumphed also as a legislator, both by the detailed excellence of his Bills and by the manner in which he piloted them through the House of Commons. His Merchant Shipping Bill improved the conditions of pay, food, and accommodation for sailors and raised the standard of safety for ships. He established a Census of Production which extracted detailed information about industrial output and served as a necessary base for government economic planning. He set up the Port of London Authority which to this day regulates the complex needs and reconciles the conflicting interests of the world's largest port.

In 1908 Lloyd George became Chancellor of the Exchequer. It was a high reward for two years of legislative activity in a lower sphere. The Chancellor is, by tradition, a close contender for the premiership. He lives and works at 11 Downing Street, most proximate to power. For Lloyd George, at the age of forty-five, this was the promotion whereby his abilities would be tested for the final advance. He had confidence in his abilities, and by them dominated most of his colleagues. He had dreams of a comprehensive scheme of social reform, and by a combination of oratorical skill and administrative effort he intended to change the British way of life.

Lloyd George was Chancellor of the Exchequer in peacetime for six years. His aim during those years was to secure a large revenue for a state-directed social welfare system. He had the support of the Prime Minister, H. H. Asquith, and mobilized the enthusiasm of his colleague Winston Churchill. When the House of Lords used its powers of veto to reject his legislation, Lloyd George and Churchill took a leading part in the agitation which led to the destruction of its veto power. In 1908 Lloyd George piloted Asquith's Old Age Pensions Bill through Parliament. It was a measure long overdue, providing security for those who in their last years would otherwise have been cast into poverty. Both Lloyd George and Churchill used these four years of Liberal parliamentary dominance to emphasize the state's responsibilities to the underdog and to insist on these responsibilities being properly carried out.

In 1909 Lloyd George presented his first budget to Parliament. It became known as the "People's Budget." Its purpose was to finance a radical social reform program, by means of higher income tax, higher death duties, a super-tax on high incomes, and land taxes on large estates which were not put to their full agricultural use. Funds were to be set up from these sources of income to ensure the welfare of miners, agricultural improvement, a new road system, better fisheries, reforestation, and land reclamation.

Lloyd George was not a wrecker, although he seemed like one to the

Conservatives who were frightened by his 1909 budget. He saw his social program as a means of tempering, but not of destroying, the powers of privilege—of raising people up to a higher level of comfort and security, but not of demolishing or humiliating the already rich. The rich could afford the "sacrifices" he demanded of them. He had no intention of reducing them to penury. When, therefore, as a result of his budget, the clash between the Conservatives and Liberals reached its peak, he felt that the two parties should unite in a common program. He envisaged a program of national reconstruction entirely free from the conflicting interests of party politics. It was a bold idea, revealing how little he felt for party ties, which he saw as a shackle in troubled times, when national unity was needed. He regarded the Liberal Party, not as the *sine quâ non* of social reform, but as its vehicle.

In August 1910 Lloyd George, with Churchill's support, proposed to A. J. Balfour, the former Conservative Prime Minister, a Liberal-Conservative Coalition which would launch a mutually acceptable program of social reform. The Coalition would legislate for a housing program, national insurance, widows' and orphans' pensions, technical education, agricultural revival, and other major issues. Balfour was much attracted to the idea, for the Conservative Party as a "sacred organization" meant as little to him as did the Liberal Party to Lloyd George. But party politics had reached too intense a pitch, the "People's Budget" had been too extreme, Liberal aspirations were too imaginative, even revolutionary, for the Conservative rank-and-file to accept any part of them. Lloyd George saw his Coalition plan fade into nothing. He rejoined his Liberal colleagues in the bitter battle which ended in the reduction of the powers of the House of Lords by the Parliament Act of 1911. But the Conservative leaders never forgot that Lloyd George, the scourge of their party, had been willing to join them in a Coalition. However much he attacked their policies, they knew that he had a broad, perhaps even cynical, view of party politics. The Tory rank-and-file might search the dictionaries for rude words to hurl at him, but his action had impressed at least some of the Tory leaders.

Some contemporaries interpreted Lloyd George's plea for a Coalition as a sign of his lack of fixed principles. They saw in him an embryo traitor to the Liberal cause. This was to malign his motives. Lloyd George was maturing with the responsibilities of public office. He believed that social reform should be a national, not a party, issue. He no longer relished harsh political conflict for its own sake. Henceforth, if negotiation, combination, flattery, soothing words, or small concessions could lead to his goal, he accepted them with equanimity. Only when they failed did he resort to oratorical violence, of which he was master.

In May 1911 Lloyd George presented his National Insurance Bill to Parliament. It was the most important piece of social legislation of his career. It contained comprehensive schemes for both health and unemployment insurance. Churchill later described the Bill, in which he too had played an important part, as the first state-conscious effort

> to set a balustrade along the crowded causeway of the people's life, and, without pulling down the structures of society, to fasten a lid over the abyss into which vast numbers used to fall, generation after generation, uncared-for and indeed unnoticed.

Many Conservatives joined the Liberals in supporting and praising Lloyd George for the National Insurance Bill. *The Observer,* a Sunday newspaper devoted to the Conservative cause, wrote:

> He has had an infinitely difficult and intricate task. He has brought to bear upon it exhaustive labour, practical aptitude of the highest kind, thorough moral courage, and with these a certain inimitable reasonableness and skill which are all his own. His exposition on Thursday, devoid of ornament, without a sentence or a syllable of partisanship, was that rarest and almost best thing in Parliamentary politics, a great speech and a quiet speech. Everyone who heard it saw in him a far bigger man when he sat down than he was thought to be, either by friends or by foes, when he rose.

The National Insurance Bill became law before the end of 1911 and established Lloyd George as a great social reformer. He continued also to act as an arbitrator when strike action was imminent. In 1912 he averted a national rail strike which threatened to become the signal for widespread industrial violence. Both political parties praised his sense of moderation and his skill at mediation. But he himself was discontented. Despite his administrative achievements, despite his political prominence, he was still uneasy and frustrated. As he told a colleague in 1911:

> I don't know exactly what I am, but I'm sure I'm not a Liberal. They have no sympathy with the people. . . . All down History, nine-tenths of mankind have been grinding the corn for the remaining one-tenth, been paid with the husks—and bidden to thank God they had the husks. . . . As long as I was settling disputes with their workmen, which they had not got enough sense to settle themselves, these great Business Men said I was the greatest Board of Trade President of modern times. When I tried to do something for the social welfare of their workmen, they denounced me as a Welsh thief.

In 1912 a serious scandal struck the Liberal Party and threatened to destroy the careers of several Cabinet Ministers, including Lloyd George. An anti-Semitic journal accused two Jewish Cabinet Ministers, Rufus Isaacs and Herbert Samuel, of speculating in Marconi Company stocks, and involving other Cabinet colleagues in Marconi purchases. In July

1912 these stocks had, it was alleged, gained in value as the result of a large government contract. In fact, the stocks which the Ministers bought were for the Marconi Company of America, and were not directly affected by any contracts or profits of the British company. The "Marconi" Ministers, who included Lloyd George, denied improper conduct. For over a year they were harried by public abuse and private innuendo. However much they denied that they had misused their ministerial positions in order to make profits, they were disbelieved. An official inquiry absolved Lloyd George of impropriety. "If you will," he told the Commons, "I acted thoughtlessly, I acted carelessly, I acted mistakenly; but I acted innocently, I acted openly and I acted honestly." But henceforth, honesty was a quality which his critics insisted that he lacked. He was deeply affected by the rumors and innuendoes, which followed him for the rest of his career.

In 1913 Lloyd George launched a Liberal Land Campaign aimed at a revolution in farming conditions. Among its proposals were a minimum wage for farm laborers, security of tenure for tenant farmers, and measures to promote efficient farming techniques. But war came before the campaign could get into its stride, nor did it restore the damage done to Lloyd George's reputation by the Marconi scandal.

The coming of war in 1914 found Lloyd George in a strange position. Although in 1911 he had in a public speech warned Germany not to count on British neutrality if her interests were threatened, he was considered one of the Cabinet Ministers most reluctant to commit Britain to war with Germany. Early in 1914 he had challenged Churchill's naval construction program, and urged a big reduction in naval expenditure. As a result, he was looked to by some of his Liberal colleagues as the potential leader of an antiwar group. But he was not a pacifist. When Germany invaded Belgium, whose neutrality both Britain and Germany had guaranteed, Lloyd George accepted the need for war. He saw that Belgium, like Wales, was a small nation in danger. He accepted Britain's Treaty obligations to come to her defense. His public speeches, after the outbreak of war, were passionate and persuasive appeals for national unity and military exertion.

From the outset of the war Lloyd George and Churchill pressed their Cabinet colleagues for a more vigorous prosecution of the war. They both worked with remarkable energy in their respective spheres, conscious of the extra demands which war made on the nation's resources. They both urged action outside the narrow line of trenches in France and Flanders, where the slaughter mounted with no significant territorial gain. Both men argued in favor of an attack on Turkey, Germany's apparently weak and vacillating ally. When the attack came in March 1915 it was Churchill, as First Lord of the Admiralty, who planned it; when it went badly, Churchill took the blame, and in May 1915 was relegated to minor office, against Lloyd George's will.

In May 1915 Asquith formed a Coalition Government, and brought the Conservatives into his Cabinet. Lloyd George left the Treasury to become Minister of Munitions. Churchill's star, which in 1914 had outshone Lloyd George's, now fell with a speed which stunned both himself and his friend. Slowly but perceptibly, and in the public gaze, it was Lloyd George's star which began to rise. Churchill left public life to command a battalion in the trenches of Flanders; Lloyd George became the head of a newly created Ministry of great importance for the successful conduct of the war.

Lloyd George was Minister of Munitions for a year, from June 1915 to June 1916. His task was to supervise and stimulate the manufacture of urgently needed guns and shells. Many munitions factories came under direct government control. At first glance, it might seem that he had been demoted. The new Ministry could hardly be considered as prestigious as the Treasury, which he had held for nearly eight years. But Lloyd George knew the importance, both to the nation and to himself, of organizing munition production so as to break the curse of chronic shortages. He set up departments for every aspect of arms manufacture. He coordinated the demands of the War Office and the Admiralty. He brought women into munition production on a vast scale, giving them a guaranteed minimum wage and piece work at the same rates as men. Thus, under the strain of a war emergency, Lloyd George struck at the scandal of exploited female labor.

In order to manufacture munitions on a massive scale, Lloyd George had to bully other Departments and dragoon reluctant officials. *Action* was his password. "Plant the flag on your workshops!" he exhorted the workers; "Every lathe you have, recruit it! Convert your machinery into battalions!" He was able to persuade the Trade Unions to abandon their restrictions on hours of work. He told the War Office what it should order and the Treasury what it should pay. His successor as Chancellor commented bitterly that Lloyd George was "always running down somebody else's department in order to seize a slice of authority for himself." But his motive was a sound one: to help win the war as quickly and easily as possible.

In June 1916 Lloyd George became Minister of War, and for six months he found himself in a frustrating position. He was revolted by the slaughter of the Somme offensive on the Western Front, where only five miles of territory were gained and over 600,000 Englishmen killed or wounded; but he had no influence over strategic decisions, which were firmly in the hands of the generals. His one noted success was in reorganizing the inefficient transport system behind the lines; he struck without mercy at the existing lethargy and chaos.

In September 1916 a mood of despondency settled upon Britain. There was much talk of a compromise peace. Men were growing weary of the war. Some looked to Woodrow Wilson, the President of the United States, to mediate between Britain and Germany. Lloyd George spoke out against negotiation. He deprecated the belief that a long war would end with an exhausted, crippled Britain: "There is neither clock nor calendar in the British Army today," he said. "Time is the least vital factor. It took England twenty years to defeat Napoleon, and the first fifteen of these years were bleak with British defeat. It will not take twenty years to win this war, but whatever time is required it will be done!"

Lloyd George's dynamism impressed his Cabinet colleagues. Many of them felt that Asquith was not active enough in directing war policy, and even a number of the Conservatives in the Coalition supported the idea of giving Lloyd George greater powers. Their intention was not to remove Asquith, but to widen the scope of Lloyd George's influence. A political crisis arose in December 1916, the workings of which have been described in detail by Cameron Hazlehurst (pages 148–57). Far from intriguing, and seeking power, Lloyd George was reluctant to be pushed into Asquith's place; he wanted responsibility, but not necessarily leadership. It was the Conservatives who urged him on, and, by refusing to serve under Asquith but being willing to support Lloyd George, ensured his premiership. As a result of this crisis, Lloyd George became Prime Minister. The Liberal and Conservative Ministers who continued to serve under him did so because they felt that he was a better man than Asquith to see the war to a victorious end. They welcomed his leadership and accepted his policies.

Lloyd George was responsible as Prime Minister for British policy during two years of war, and then during four years of peacemaking and reconstruction. He proved a vigorous war leader and a constructive peacemaker. But from the day in December 1916 on which he replaced Asquith as Prime Minister, his reputation was persistently and harshly assailed by the Asquith Liberals, who accused him of deliberately and treacherously ousting their leader from power, of cynically cooperating with the Conservatives after the war was over, and of leading a corrupt public and private life. Every lapse which Lloyd George committed was magnified and publicized by newspaper columnists and club gossip. Every mistake was built up into a crime. Lloyd George's many achievements, in war and peace, were denigrated or ignored. His enemies assailed his reputation so successfully that, to this day, his name is for many synonymous with corruption, irresponsibility, and deceit.

Lloyd George was unable to end the war by any sudden stroke. But he succeeded in improving the efficiency of wartime administration, in checking the spread of defeatism, and in coordinating the work of the Allies. When peace came he threw himself into the task of peacemaking with remarkable energy. The records of the years 1914 to 1922 have only just become available to historians. It may therefore be some decades before a full evaluation of them can be made. But the picture is slowly becoming clearer: a picture of Lloyd George as a man of ideals and common sense caught up in an international bog of suspicion and intrigue from which, with all his gifts and determination, even he could not fully or effectively escape.

When peace came Lloyd George had to deal with a succession of vexations and seemingly insoluble problems: peacemaking in Europe and Ireland, the reemergence of Turkey as a strong power, the reconstruction of British life to provide, as he had promised, "homes fit for heroes." He was not always successful. Yet, as A. J. P. Taylor points out (pages 169–74), his achievements were impressive. He thrived on power. It stimulated him to action. Perhaps it also made him too remote, cut him off from the moods and passions of the common man, turned him into a hero without a home.

The most impressive of his achievements were in foreign and imperial affairs. His instinct was as a conciliator. Although he was the leader of a largely Conservative administration, his motives were essentially Liberal and humanitarian. He achieved the miracle of British history, an Irish settlement. The bitterness and bloodshed of many centuries made it appear that the Irish Question was insoluble. Coercion had failed under the Conservatives; Home Rule had proved impossible for the Liberals. Lloyd George inherited the Easter rebellion of 1916 and was caught in the vicious civil war of 1919. He used all his genius to produce a lasting settlement: independence for the Irish Free State, and union with Britain for protestant Ulster. Elsewhere his policies were equally liberal. His policy toward India was that of looking forward to a rapidly increased Indian participation in government, with a view to eventual self-government. He promised the Jews a National Home in Palestine. He opposed a harsh treaty against Germany, and did his utmost to bring about a reconciliation between France and Germany. He also opposed the desire of many of his colleagues, and principally of Churchill, to fight the new Bolshevik regime in Russia; he urged conciliation with the Bolsheviks and persuaded his Cabinet that the urgent need was for trade, not war. The Anglo-Soviet Trade Agreement of 1920 was a triumph for the policy of European reconciliation. By Lloyd George's exertions, Lenin's Russia ceased to be a pariah.

In 1922 Lloyd George was again the center of a major political scandal, reminiscent of the Marconi affair. He was accused of selling peerages and knighthoods for money. The charges were exaggerated, but had a kernel of truth. The sale of "honours" had become a part of the British tradition. But Lloyd George had abused it: some of the "honours" went to those who clearly did not merit them, and the money went, not to Liberal or Conservative funds, as was the normal, accepted procedure, but to Lloyd George's own fund, by which he hoped to build a financially secure Lloyd Georgian or center party. This roused the anger of the existing parties. Lloyd George's private life was also the subject of growing criticism which, even if justified, was both malicious, and irrelevant to politics. Conservatives resented more and more being dominated by his personality and tied to his policies. Many wished to break away from his Coalition and reassert their independence as a party. The Asquith Liberals held aloof, hostile and hoping for his fall. He had bent both parties to his will. Now both were eager to be rid of his control.

Lloyd George's mistake in foreign policy was to champion Greece against Turkey. It was a mistake which had wide repercussions, and precipitated his fall. The Turks, under their military leader Kemal Pasha, drove the Greek invaders, whom Lloyd George had encouraged, into the sea. The Turks were pugnacious nationalists, whose power and zeal Lloyd George had underrated. Yet they were also the persecutors of their Greek minority, and the savage murderers, in 1916, of over a million Armenians. Lloyd George was revolted by Turkish atrocities. His anti-Turk attitude was more Gladstonian than imperialist. When the Turks turned on the British garrison at Chanak, on the Dardanelles, he threatened war if they did not halt. The threat was successful. The Turks withdrew. British lives were saved. Yet this "Chanak" crisis, in which Lloyd George averted a massacre and a war, was seen as a dangerous adventure and provocation. Criticism of "Chanak" became a focal point of anti-Lloyd George feeling.

In October 1922, Lloyd George's former Conservative colleague, Bonar Law, using "Chanak" as his cry, raised the standard of revolt. He was supported by one of the most junior Conservatives from within Lloyd George's Cabinet, Stanley Baldwin. But however much the more senior Conservatives in his Cabinet argued in Lloyd George's favor, the rank-and-file of the party were no longer content to accept his leadership. At a meeting at the Carlton Club on October 19, 1922, the Conservatives, urged on by Baldwin and Bonar Law, resolved to leave Lloyd George's Government. The power of the Coalition was thus broken. Lloyd George resigned. He did not return to power or to office again. "Lloyd George's plan of creating and leading a centre party," wrote his former Liberal colleague Lord Haldane, "has come to nought. He will find his future a difficult one. He has destroyed the Liberal party and Labour won't have him."

For twenty-three years Lloyd George lived in growing political isolation. All efforts to unite his own Liberal followers with the Asquith Liberals failed. The Labour Party grew rapidly in strength; before 1924 it had replaced the Liberals as the opposition, and in that year formed the first Labour Government. Lloyd George's political activity was largely confined to producing plans designed primarily to conquer the serious unemployment. But they were plans without power. His political following dwindled almost to nothing. The accounts of his alleged inconsistency, corruption, and immorality grew and were embedded in people's minds. The discontented and the unemployed looked to the Labour Party, and to the Trade Union movement, to improve their conditions.

In the economic crisis of 1931 Lloyd George would probably have been given a place in the National Government, but he was ill at the time and could not accept. He turned to foreign affairs and in 1936 was widely discredited as a result of a visit to Hitler, to whom he was strongly and immediately attracted. The attraction quickly passed. But Lloyd George's articles and interviews on Hitler's "wisdom" left a sour impression in people's minds which was not easily obliterated.

Within two years, by early 1938, Lloyd George was fully alerted to the Nazi danger. He spoke in Parliament on the need for rapid rearmament and wide alliances, especially with the Soviet Union. He joined Churchill in denouncing the feckless foreign policy of Neville Chamberlain's primarily Conservative Government. When war came he was appalled by what he considered to be the lethargic conduct of affairs. The "Phony War" both angered and depressed him. For a time, it seemed to those who were near him that he was even prepared to put himself at the head of a peacemaking government. It was eighteen years since he had fallen from power; he was seventy-three. His energies were fading, and he had few active supporters.

In May 1940 he made a dramatic appearance in the House of Commons, of which he had been a member for fifty years. He spoke in the debate on the British failure to forestall the German conquest of Norway, and denounced Neville Chamberlain as an incompetent war leader, urging him bluntly to resign. When, two days later, Churchill succeeded Chamberlain as Prime Minister, Lloyd George could feel that he had played his part in this vital transition from lethargy to action. He then saw Churchill, his old and close friend, rouse the very same will to victory that he himself had roused in the First World War, and lead Britain to the threshold of triumph. He died in March 1945, knowing that victory would soon come, but vexed at the policy of unconditional surrender, which he felt to be unwise. To the end, his mind was attracted as much by compromise as by extremes.

What tentative conclusions can one reach about his career? There can be no doubt that David Lloyd George was a leading architect of Britain's most spectacular social revolution, epitomized by his "People's Budget" of 1909 and the National Insurance Act of 1911. He was Prime Minister for the two most strenuous years of the First World War and for the four subsequent years of reconstruction. During these two periods he was both the instigator of policies and the focal point of power. "Lloyd George fed upon power," Professor Gollin has written. "His qualities swelled in the exercise of it. He was a man who dealt in power." Such a man made many enemies, but none of his enemies doubted his remarkable and undeniable abilities. But his powers of work and persuasion contrasted unfavorably with what his critics insisted was an utter lack of principle. "He excited admiration," wrote a contemporary, "but not respect. . . . He really had no principles at all, only emotions."

Lloyd George rose to prominence as a firebrand within the Liberal Party. But his premiership was based upon the loyal support of the Conservatives, against whom, only eight years earlier, he had pitted both his oratorical genius and his legislative ingenuity. He belonged neither to the Liberals, whose radicalism he so enhanced, nor to the Conservatives, without whose support his power would have been impossible.

He was a Welshman, an outsider, a nonconformist, a dreamer. Proud of his national traditions, champion of the underdog, enemy of privilege, master of ridicule, lover of music, he reflected the extraordinary achievements of the Welsh people. When pleased, he could be the warmest of colleagues, suffused with buoyancy and gaiety. When angry, he became a fierce opponent, capable of cruel words and ruthless actions. "I wound where I know I can hurt most," he once said. Yet his humor never left him. "His gaiety was of the essence of his nature," wrote his secretary, Miss Frances Stevenson, whom he married in 1943: "His sense of fun sometimes led him to danger point, for the line between the solemn and the ridiculous was for him very finely drawn." He never became pompous, pedantic, or dull.

Above all, Lloyd George was a man of the people. Snobbery was an attribute he despised. Class distinctions meant nothing to him. Aristocrats could not flatter him. The world of society hostesses and glib conversation bored him. Pomp held no attraction for his unconventional, inquiring mind. "There was no man," said Churchill, "so gifted, so eloquent, so forceful, who knew the life of the people so well." Sometimes he seemed rough, even crude, in his talk and behavior. But in the main his energies, his work, and his emotions were constructively and humanely geared. He strove first to improve the conditions of his compatriots, then to ameliorate international dissensions. He pursued these aims tenaciously, and often with marked success. Yet the cost was high. Political conflicts leave scars no less than the field of battle. A politician cannot expect to be a hero at all times or to all men. "I like Lloyd George," said Bonar Law, when newly elected Conservative leader in 1911. "He is a very nice man. But he is the most dangerous little man that ever lived." Five years later these two rivals became colleagues and worked together closely in war and peace for five years to the national advantage. Lord Beaverbrook has described the violent contrast between these two men, first opponents, then partners (pages 118–20). In this relationship lies the paradox of Lloyd George's career.

The Oxford historian Robert Blake has asked: "Was he a man of principle pursuing by devious means a consistent end, or was he an opportunist who relied on his intuition to gratify at every turn his love of power and office?" In my opinion the former view is the true one. But the reader must try, from the extracts presented here, and from the volumes to which I refer, to come to his own conclusions about Lloyd George's character and achievements.

Chronology of the Life of Lloyd George

1863 (January 17) Born in Manchester, son of a schoolmaster.

1864 Death of his father. Brought up in Wales with his uncle, a shoemaker.

1878 Becomes a solicitor's clerk in North Wales.

1884 Passes Law Society Examination. Practices law in Wales.

1888 Marries Margaret Owen, a farmer's daughter.

1890 Elected to Parliament as a Liberal for Caernarvon Boroughs. Remains its Member of Parliament for fifty-four years.

1891 Becomes political correspondent of Y Genedl Cymreig (the Welsh Nation).

1899–1902 A leading critic of the Conservative Government's Boer War policy.

1905 President of the Board of Trade in Campbell-Bannerman's Liberal Government.

1908 Chancellor of the Exchequer in Asquith's Liberal Government.

1909 Introduces his first budget—"The People's Budget."

1910 Active in campaign to reduce the power of the House of Lords.

1913 Cleared of impropriety in the "Marconi Scandal."

1914 (November) First war budget doubles income tax.

1915 (May) Minister of Munitions in Asquith's Coalition Government.

1916 (June) Secretary of State for War in Asquith's Coalition Government.

1916 (December 7) Age 53. Prime Minister. Replaces Cabinet of 23 Ministers by a War Cabinet of five for formulating war policy. Leads Coalition of all parties.

1918 General Election confirms Lloyd George's Coalition in power after end of war with 478 seats out of 707.

1919 (January–June) At the Paris Peace Conference. Principal British negotiator and signatory of the Treaty of Versailles.

1920 Inaugurates two years of "diplomacy by conference" in attempt to reduce postwar tensions; attends conferences at London, San Remo, Lympne, Cannes, and Genoa.

1921 Signs Irish Treaty.

1922 (October) Conservatives withdraw support from Coalition. Lloyd George resigns. At General Election only 54 Lloyd George and

60 Asquith Liberals elected to Parliament. Conservatives, with 344 seats, return to power. Labour with 142 seats replaces Liberals as the principal opposition Party.

1923	Lecture tour in the United States.
1924	At General Election, Conservatives 413, Labour 151, Liberals 40 seats.
1925	Proposes that the State should buy up all landlords to provide security for tenants.
1926	Leader of the Liberal Party (until 1931).
1929	Fights General Election on slogan "We can conquer Unemployment." Labour 288, Conservatives 260, Liberals 59 seats.
1931	National Government of all parties established. Lloyd George not included. At General Election Lloyd George Liberals reduced to four seats—including himself and two members of his family.
1935	Fights General Election on a "New Deal" policy of economic expansion. Lloyd George Liberals remain with only four seats.
1936	Visits Hitler at Berchtesgaden.
1937–1939	Criticizes Neville Chamberlain's reluctance to prepare for war with Germany. Urges alliance with Soviet Union.
1940	(May) Speaks against Chamberlain in debate before Chamberlain's resignation.
1940	(June) Invited by Churchill to join all-party Coalition Government, but declines.
1940	(December) Offered Washington Embassy by Churchill but declines on health reasons.
1941	(January) Death of his wife Margaret.
1941	(May) Criticizes Churchill's conduct of the war in Parliament.
1943	Marries Frances Stevenson, who had joined his staff as personal secretary in 1913.
1944	Created Earl Lloyd-George of Dwyfor.
1945	(March 26) Dies in Wales, aged 82.

PART ONE

LLOYD GEORGE
LOOKS AT THE WORLD

1
War

You hear sneers and jibes at conscience. Take this warning. Never trust an individual, never trust a party, whose stock jest is a jibe at conscience. I say it in all solemnity, it is God's greatest gift to the human mind, the propeller and the rudder of human progress.

—LLOYD GEORGE

Lloyd George first became a national figure by denouncing Britain's Boer War policy. He believed that, in seeking to defeat the two independent Boer Republics—the Transvaal and the Orange Free State—Britain was primarily motivated by financial greed. He put himself forward as a champion of the two small Republics, denouncing both the aims and the methods of British policy. It was not a popular stance, for even Liberals were divided in their attitude toward the war. But it was an uncompromising and an outspoken one.

"A WAR OF EXTERMINATION" [1]

The Colonial Secretary, Joseph Chamberlain, defended British policy toward the Boers in the House of Commons. He insisted that the war was not a war of annexation or conquest, but a war to force President Kruger to treat the non-Boer immigrants fairly. Lloyd George challenged Chamberlain in the House of Commons.

[1] From *Hansard*, July 25, 1900. Reprinted by permission of the Controller of Her Majesty's Stationery Office.

He had led us into two blunders. The first was the war. But worse than the war is the change that has been effected in the purpose for which we are prosecuting the war. We went into the war for equal rights; we are prosecuting it for annexation. That is a most serious change in the tactics of the Government from any point of view. There may be something to be said for a war so long as it is entered upon for an unselfish purpose. The influence of a war must always be brutalising, at best; but still if you enter upon it for an unselfish purpose, there is something which almost consecrates the sacrifices, bloodshed, and suffering endured. But when you enter upon a war purely and simply for the purposes of plunder, I know of nothing which is more degrading to the country or more hideous in its effects on the mind and character of the people engaged in it. Any one who looks at the illustrated papers must see the horrible presentment given of incidents which were formerly relegated to prints like the "Police Gazette"—details which I cannot give to the House without a gross breach of good taste. Incidents of that kind are not given for the purpose of producing any disgust in the minds of the people, but with every circumstance of indication that they are there to invoke admiration. And all these are circulated broadcast in every household throughout the country. The right hon. gentleman the Colonial Secretary, in a speech . . . said that a war in order to impose internal reforms upon President Kruger would be an immoral war. If that be so, I ask the right hon. gentleman or any of his friends to find an adjective sufficiently expressive of the character of a war entered upon for the purposes of annexation. The right hon. gentleman admitted that we had no right to meddle in the affairs of the Transvaal, and that there was only one possible justification for it—that our motive was an unselfish one. We have thrown that justification away now. It is exactly as if you had entered into a man's house to protect the children, and started to steal his plate. You entered into these two Republics for philanthropic purposes and remained to commit burglary. In changing the purpose of the war you have made a bad change. That is the impression you are creating abroad. Our critics say you are not going to war for equal rights and to establish fair play, but to get hold of the goldfields; and you have justified that criticism of our enemies by that change. But, worst of all, a change has been effected in the character of the war. Up to a certain point it was conducted with considerable chivalry, with apparent good temper on both sides. A war of annexation, however, against a proud people, must be a war of extermination, and that is unfortunately what it seems we are now committing ourselves to—burning homesteads and turning men and women out of their homes. The telegram received from Pretoria, which had passed the military censor, stated that fact, and I do not think he would have let it come unless it was true. It is also confirmed from Lourenco Marques by information that 600 women and children have been turned out and sent to the hills. There has been the burning of the homesteads of the rebels, and this war will brutalise the people, and the savagery which must necessarily follow will stain the name of this country. It seems to me that in this war we have gradually followed the policy of Spain in Cuba. The action of the Spaniards in Cuba produced such a feeling in America that they could not tolerate it, and we know how that war degraded the name of Spain. This is the state of things into which the right hon. gentleman has brought us.

"IT IS TIME TO STOP THE SLAUGHTER" 2

In the General Election of 1900 the issue of the rights and wrongs of the Boer War played a significant part. The ruling Conservative Party was returned to power and the war went on. The following extract is typical of Lloyd George's powerful antiwar speeches during the election campaign.

All wars are so horrible in their incidence, and so uncertain in their event, that sensible statesmen recognize that as soon as you can secure the main object of a war and bring it to an end the better it is, even for the victors. . . .

In May, this year, the Boer Army was so discomfited and disheartened by Field-Marshal Lord Robert's daring strategy that their generals utterly failed to induce them to make a stand anywhere. They were nothing but a demoralized rabble of peasants. They had been swept out of Natal. There was not a Boer in uniform left in Cape Colony, nor a single Boer Commando to be found anywhere south or east of the Orange Free State. De Wet was the only Boer leader who could persuade his followers to make even a show of fighting.

That was the time to make peace! General Sir Redvers Buller, with his downright British common sense, was of that opinion and he advised in May that terms be offered. What did Headquarters reply? "Nothing but Unconditional Surrender!" And what was the outcome of the foolish decision? It drove the Boers to despair! They listened again to the fighting men in their own ranks, and they plucked up new courage. They went on fighting, and the war is not over yet. I say that it is time to stop the slaughter in the African sand of brave soldiers on either side.

[Lloyd George paused. Then he added in Welsh:]

2 Speech delivered by Lloyd George during the General Election of 1900. The speech was made at Nevin, the district in his constituency most hostile to his "pro-Boer" policy. Quoted in Frank Owen, *Tempestuous Journey* (London, 1954), p. 105. Reprinted by permission of the Hutchinson Publishing Group Ltd. For a discussion of the Liberal Party and the Boer War, see Robert Rhodes James, *Lord Rosebery* (London, 1963).

Five years ago, the electors of the Caernarvon Boroughs gave to me my strip of blue paper, the certificate of my election, to hand to the Speaker of Parliament as your accredited representative. If I never again represent the Caernarvon Boroughs in the House of Commons, I shall at least have the satisfaction of handing back to you that blue paper with no stain of human blood upon it.

"WE HAVE NOW TAKEN TO KILLING BABES" [3]

Lloyd George became a national figure as a result of his strident and passionate opposition to the methods and aims of the Boer War. By the third year of the war many Liberals had grown weary of what had originally appeared to be only another brief and easy colonial war. This extract shows Lloyd George's antiwar oratory at its height.

I have seen it said—in fact, it is one of the commonplaces of the war—that never in the history of the world has there been such quixotic tenderness displayed towards an enemy as to feed and care for his women and children whilst he was engaged in shooting down our men. Now what are the real facts? They are carefully suppressed in the Unionist and Jingo Press. In order to render the country absolutely untenable by the Boer commandos, and to force them into surrender by sheer starvation, it was decided to go in for what was called denuding the country. What did that mean? The villages were burnt to the ground; all the farmhouses were blown up, so that there should be no shelter from one end of the country to the other for a single rover; the cattle were swept away, such of the grain as could not be carried away was burnt. Thousands of tons have been burnt. So determined were the military authorities that there should be nothing left for either man or beast that they destroyed all the agricultural implements, all the mills, and broke open the irrigation dams, so that the territory over which our armies had trodden was left a blackened, devastated wilderness. I am not criticising that policy for the moment. It may be said that it was a purely military operation, and the only comment I offer upon it is that the event has proved it to be, like every other measure of harshness, an acknowledged failure. But what was to be done with the women and children who dwelt in those villages and farmhouses? Is it suggested that they should be left in this barren wilderness created by ourselves, without shelter or sustenance, to die of famine and cold? And if the military authorities took the view that it was their bounden duty not to commit such a monstrosity, where was the excessive mercifulness of the proceeding which herded them in the

[3] From a speech at Pwllheli, October 23, 1901. Quoted in Herbert du Parcq, *Life of David Lloyd George* (London, 1912), II, 253–54.

depths of winter in thin, leaky tents, surrounded by barbed wire, where thousands of them have died from the privations they unnecessarily suffered? If this conduct is to be defended on the ground of military tactics, let them do so, but at any rate do not let them add hypocrisy to the other crimes of this war. How did this mistaken leniency work for its victims? Since the month of June we have been furnished with official figures showing the mortality in the camps. A good deal has been said about the splendid way these people were cared for. The answer to that is the number of deaths.[4] . . .

If I were to despair for the future of this country it would not be because of trade competition from either America or Germany, or the ineffectiveness of its army, or anything that might happen to its ships; but rather because it used its great, hulking strength to torture the little child. Had it not been that this Ministry has shown distinct symptoms of softening of the brain, I would call the torpor and indifference they are showing in face of all this criminal. It is a maddening horror, and it will haunt the Empire to its dying hour. What wonder is it that Europe should mock and hiss at us? Let any honest Britisher fearlessly search his heart and answer this question: Is there any ground for the reproach flung at us by the civilised world that, having failed to crush the men, we have now taken to killing babes?

"HOW TO PREVENT WAR" [5]

As a result of his many speeches opposing the Boer War, Lloyd George established himself not only as a political orator of the first rank but also as a man to whom antiwar and pacifist forces looked for leadership. Although the Liberal Party was still in opposition, it was assumed that the Liberals must soon return to political power, and that Lloyd George would play an important part in their future policy. A speech which he made a year after the Boer War had ended showed the lesson which he had drawn from it and helps to explain why people looked to him with such hope.

We are spending forty millions a year more now than we did four years ago on the weapons of human slaughter, and every country in the world is increasing its armaments. Three or four hundred millions a year are being spent in Europe on these terrible machines of murder, and

[4] Over 9,000 Boer women and children died in British camps. Only 4,000 Boer soldiers were killed in action. The Liberal leader, Campbell-Bannerman, accused the British Government of resorting to "methods of barbarism."
[5] From a speech at Deganwy, September 28, 1903. Quoted in Herbert du Parcq, *Life of David Lloyd George* (London, 1912), III, 439.

we seem to be on the point of flying at each other's throats. Argument has failed to break down the mad competition in armaments. We cannot get these men to meet at the same altar, and the world is divided into its Protestants, its Roman Catholics, its Greek Church, its Mahomedans, its Buddhists and its followers of Confucius. There is one thing that will help. Get them to meet in the market place. They may come to the same mart, and men who have met each other in honest trade respect and honour each other. It is the next approach to friendship. With an open door to the trade of all the world we shall gradually help to break down the terrible system which is crushing industry in Europe. I am a hopeful man, and I feel that the time will come when, in spite of the armaments, the swords will be beaten into ploughshares and the spears into pruning-hooks, and there will be no more war. When that time comes the name of Britain will be blessed as the country which, in spite of all the inducements of false statesmen, stood up against the world for a free mart for all.

"NO MORE MURDER" [6]

The Liberals formed a Government in 1905 and were given a large electoral mandate in 1906. Lloyd George turned to social reform. His hostility to war was confirmed, for he saw the extent to which money spent on armaments cut into the money needed for State contributions to social welfare. In a speech which he delivered when he was Chancellor of the Exchequer, and responsible for allocating the money both to armaments and social projects, he stressed his belief in the absurdity of war between civilized states. Although he appealed for "no more murder" and insisted that Britain and Germany did not wish to kill each other, these two civilized nations were at war nine months later.

Since I have been at the Exchequer it has been my misfortune to have to provide twenty millions a year more money for armaments than my predecessor had to find the year he left office. Twenty millions a year! Do you know what that means in rates? Supposing you inoculated the nations of the world with a little sanity, with a little common sense, and they suddenly thought what all this foolish, wild, mad competition meant, and they said, "Let us stop it, let us go back to what we were five years ago." If I got the twenty millions without putting an additional penny on anything I could next year take eighteenpence in the pound off

[6] From a speech at Middlesbrough, November 8, 1913. Published as a Liberal Party pamphlet, *The Urban Land Problem: Housing, Wages* (London, 1913). Reprinted by permission of the Liberal Publication Department.

the rates of everybody in the United Kingdom. But I would not do it, and I will tell you why. There are some people who are not paying their fair contribution. There are some who are paying their fair contribution, and there are some who are paying more than their fair contribution, and I would relieve these first. I think cottages are paying far more than their fair contribution. If you are going to tax people according to their means I think business premises are paying far more than their fair contribution. I think machinery is certainly paying more than it ought; I am not at all sure that it ought to be rated at all, but it is paying too much. I am perfectly certain that there are many owners of land who are not paying anything like their fair share. It means that you could take a third off the rates on some of the property that is over-burdened if you only had this twenty millions. Do let me say this. It would be better for Germany and Great Britain, and France, and Russia if they agreed to drop it in the German Ocean—than that you should spend it on this hideous machinery and mechanism of human slaughter.

I do not shirk the consideration of armaments, but I do say one nation cannot do it alone. I do say it is about time the whole of these countries should take counsel together. We really do not want to kill each other. I have never met a German yet who was anxious to kill any Britisher whom he knew, and I have never met a decent Britisher yet who was really anxious to murder the first German he met in the street. What they do is to conjure up some sort of monster in their minds, and they say, "That is Germany, let us spend seventy millions to blow it up," and the Germans do the same thing with us. This is lunacy. The nations are suffering from the spasms of epilepsy; you want to inoculate them with a little common sense. We would soon bring down the rates and taxes, build houses, we would sweep away slums, we could make a really new land in Britain if you could only grip these countries frankly by the hand and say, "No more murder."

"PATRIOTISM HAS LOST ITS REASON" [7]

Lloyd George's aversion to war was strengthened by the excesses of the First World War. In 1934 he spoke passionately to a Welsh audience.

England's most promising young poet fell in the War, so did the brilliant young Merionethshire shepherd who was awarded the Chair of the Birkenhead Eisteddfod in 1917 for the poem he had sent

[7] From a speech delivered by Lloyd George on August 9, 1934, at the National Eisteddfod at Neath. I am grateful to the Countess Lloyd-George of Dwyfor for permission to use this speech, a copy of which, with corrections in Lloyd George's handwriting, she kindly made available to me.

in a few weeks before he was killed at the Somme. Forty thousand young Welshmen were slain in the last War. This number constituted a greater army than Llewelyn or Glendower ever had under their banners and represented a larger contingent than all the English troops which Wellington had under his command at Waterloo. Many of them fell before they ever came in sight of the land of their promise. What was their quality? Who can tell? They would find the names of hundreds of them engraved on the tablets of the fallen in Colleges, Public Schools, and thousands in the churches of the land. Had they survived they would now be in the prime of their manhood, with their varied gifts developed. How many poets fell on these battlefields? Were there not some whose powers would have enabled them to take rank with the brilliant Bards of the pre-war period? Might there not peradventure have been one or two who possessed even greater gifts?

One of the greatest losses of war to a nation is the extinction of great potential capacity—possibly great genius—which the country needs to guide the coming generation. Britain is suffering today from this gash in her young leadership in every branch of initiative. Nine hundred thousand of the young men of this Empire fell in the War with their infinite possibilities. This constitutes the incalculable loss which war inflicts on nations.

You can estimate something of the damaging possibilities of War to a nation if you imagine Shakespeare, Milton, Shelley, Byron or Keats having fallen as young conscripts in the Wars of their time. What would have been the loss to Wales if Williams Pantycelyn, Howell Harries and Daniel Rowlands, or the loss to Britain if John Wesley had been slain in the French Wars? Can you estimate it? If this country had been robbed of such careers the intellectual and spiritual currency of the race would have been lower than it is today.

Have we seen the last of these devastating frenzies called "WAR"? It is 16 years since I presided over an Eisteddfod at Neath. It was the last year of the Great War. I told you then that we saw light at the end of the tunnel. We emerged soon afterwards. Nevertheless, we are still travelling in the shadows of overhanging precipices. The light of peace is not yet shining on the permanent way of the nations. We have wars and rumours of wars. Worst of all, we have preparations for more destructive wars than the world has yet seen. And these preparations are growing each year. Everybody is afraid of war and everybody is preparing for it. The nations are spending £1,000,000,000 each year on the forging of weapons for human slaughter, and on training for the most effective use of them. And women and children are now to be included in the sacrifice. The last thing the British Parliament did was to approve of spending an additional £25,000,000 on the most horrible of all the destructive machines. I cannot here discuss the question of whether it was necessary, but if it is, then the more terrible and imminent the prospect. Patriotism has lost its reason in all lands. It is raving and raging with suspicion and downright fear of the very evils it is helping to create. The old German warrior Hindenburg, some time ago predicted that Europe would once more become a greater furnace than ever; and he pleaded with his countrymen to keep Germany out of the flames. Let us keep Britain out of the flames and keep mankind out of the flames.

Since love of country is becoming demented and developing homicidal mania, there are millions who believe that patriotism is an evil spirit which ought to be suppressed in the interests of our common humanity. It is a spirit and it cannot be annihilated. You must put up with it and make the best of it whether you like it or not. Every passion is injurious if it ceases to be under the control of reason. The problem for all men who still believe that love of your native land is a beneficent impulse is to reconcile patriotism and peace. Demonstrate that they can live in harmony on the same earth and work together for the advancement of mankind. That is the aim of the Eisteddfod. It has been the basis and guarantee of its activity through the ages. The national fervour it has engendered has built our fine Colleges and Public Schools and in half a century transformed the educational outlook and equipment of Wales. The Eisteddfod is the temple of peace. During the many centuries of its existence it has never had a stain of human blood on its altars. There is a great rebuilding task awaiting patriotism in all lands. First to rebuild and then to go on building. You have here at hand a devastated and distressed area that needs restoring. There are many such districts in Britain.

Restoration can only be accomplished if we devote the whole of our mind and strength to it. You may achieve something when one hand is working and the other is grasping the sword. But not so much as if you were to devote both hands to your tasks. And, unfortunately, today, the right hand is on the sword. More than half of our enormous national revenue goes to pay for past wars and to prepare for future wars, and essential human services are starved. The other method distracts our thoughts, scatters our energies, divides our zeal and wears down our nerves.

Let the nations agree to keep patriotism out of the field of blood. There are other battlefields where it can render greater service and win higher renown. Let it fight disease, poverty, ignorance, disorganisation, waste and all the myriad human wrongs and oppressions. Fight them with the weapons of humanity and freedom. Then mankind in every land will advance—to use a phrase from the great Eisteddfod prayers—under the protection of God and His peace, to higher realms of happiness and achievement.

2
Social Justice

I hold the doctrine that the men who work and toil, the men upon whose labour the wealth, the greatness and the very existence of the community depend, ought to enjoy at any rate equal privileges and opportunities with those whose sole service to their generation lies in the direction of the consumption of the good things produced by the exertions of others.

—LLOYD GEORGE (*in 1895*)

This is a rich country. It is the richest country under the sun; and yet in this rich country you have hundreds and thousands of people living under conditions of poverty, destitution and squalor that would, in the words of an old Welsh poet, make the rocks weep. This is the stain upon the flag.

—LLOYD GEORGE (*in 1908*)

By the end of the nineteenth century it was clear that successive Conservative and Liberal Governments had failed to deal with the problem of social inequality. Working-class poverty was acute in both industrial and rural areas, and it was spreading. The rigid class structure of society gave little scope for the workingman in his search for self-advancement. The State played no part in creating opportunities for those who were underprivileged, nor did it provide security for those who had fallen upon hard times. Lloyd George entered politics with a deep anger against privilege. He was determined to be personally involved in a series of significant measures of State initiative aimed at spreading social justice and accelerating social improvement. These were political objectives. But they had a strong emotional origin. Lloyd George had a pugnacious sympathy for the underdog. He also knew what could be done by a combination of zeal and ruthlessness. With the political support of the Prime Minister, H. H. Asquith, and the oratorical and administrative alliance of Churchill, Lloyd George launched the Liberal Party upon a revolutionary social policy, and laid the foundations of the welfare state which, since 1945, has been the principal feature of British social policy, both Labour and Conservative.

26

THE HOUSE OF LORDS: "A LUMBER ROOM OF MUSTY PREJUDICE"[1]

Lloyd George's first published article, written when he was only eighteen, was an attack on privilege.

That the opinions of minorities should be taken into account I fully grant; but that in their consideration anything else should be included than the arguments advanced in support of those opinions, I think is a little preposterous, for if the opinions of the minority are to outweigh those of the majority it is not only a subversion of an established rule of government that the majority is to sway, but also a subversion of all reason as substituting for it something else which must thereby be unreasonable. It is true that the House of Lords forms a component part of the State; it is quite as true that it is to be a servant of the State. Founded for the public interest, it is a traitor to the public if it diverts its power to the injury of those interests. Are we going to connive at an oligarchy here? And if we are, should we entrust our destinies to the hands of men whose judgments are like the institution which they constitute—a lumber-room of musty prejudice—an asylum of hereditary delusion? Not that Peers are a race of intellectual Hottentots, but more resembling the Red Indian, who in accordance with a custom of their race, by an aduncous process form—or rather deform —their skulls "into the same image." So these Peers, however noble their dispositions may be by nature (and I believe some of them are naturally noble), are bent by their education to take an artificial, fashionable, ignoble ply. Well, considering their education, their conduct may be an unenviable selfishness, but certainly it is not an insuperable difficulty. Statesmen should provide for the wants of a people before respecting the urbanity of a class; they should alleviate the misery of the poor before pandering to the vanity of the rich. It is something worse than ridiculous—it is criminal—to send a punt to save a ship's crew because the lifeboat is wanted for a pleasure trip. Keep your family from starving, and then you can apply what remains of your income to luxuries.

MONEY MISSPENT[2]

In one of his earliest Parliamentary speeches Lloyd George attacked what he considered to be unnecessary inequalities beween rich and poor.

[1] From an article by Lloyd George published in the *North Wales Express*, February 19, 1881. Quoted in Herbert du Parcq, *Life of David Lloyd George* (London, 1912), I, 55.

[2] From *Hansard*, August 13, 1890. Reprinted by permission of the Controller of Her Majesty's Stationery Office.

With regard to the first payment, namely £439 3s. 4d., fees paid on the Installation of H.R.H. Prince Henry of Prussia as a Knight of the Garter, I wish to point out that dignity is, as a general rule, granted for some signal service rendered to the country; but what service has Prince Henry of Prussia ever rendered to this country? He has not yet rendered any service to his own country, to say nothing of service to Great Britain. When this honour is conferred upon people here, they have to pay their own installation fees, but that is not so in the case of a foreign prince. Although it may be argued that diplomatic considerations should weigh in these cases, I hold that that argument should only be valid in cases where these honours are bestowed upon persons of distinction. But when they are conferred upon people who have never done anything to deserve attention, these interchanges of courtesies become empty expressions of diplomacy without any real meaning in them.

With regard to the second item, £2,769 4s. 8d. Equipage money on appointment to the Earl of Zetland Lord Lieutenant of Ireland, I think it is generally admitted that that office is a sinecure. (No, no.) Well, there is nothing which the Lord Lieutenant is supposed to do which is not better done already by his subordinates. We have been frequently reminded by the Chief Secretary that he is the real governor of Ireland. The Lord Lieutenant is simply a man in buttons, who wears silk stockings and has a coat of arms on his carriage. (Cries of "Order!")

The Chairman: Order, order! The salary of the Lord Lieutenant is not placed upon the Consolidated Fund, in order that he may be criticised in this style. The only question into which the hon. gentleman can enter is that of the adequacy of this expenditure.

Mr. Lloyd George: I only wish to point out to this House that this sum of £3,000 is thrown away upon a sinecure. I find that a sum of about £3,000 appears in the estimates under the head of Dublin Metropolitan Police, a force which is as necessary to the present system of government as the Lord Lieutenant is unnecessary.

Well, then comes a sum of £180 in respect of the funeral of the Duchess of Cambridge. Such items are not calculated to produce sentiments of loyalty; on the contrary, they cause irritation and provoke an amount of criticism and inquiry which otherwise would be absent. The result of the inquiry promoted by this item is to show that the family of the Duke of Cambridge has from first to last received something like £3,000,000 out of the Exchequer. I think it positively monstrous that we should be paying these sums for what is absolutely worthless to this country, when there is so much suffering, so much absolute penury and want among our working classes.

Shortly before this Supplementary Estimate was issued the report of the Sweating Committee appeared and what a ghastly comment are the main features of that report upon this expenditure! The report shows that thousands of hard-working, thrifty men are living a life of hopeless, ceaseless toil, and yet we are asked to spend hundreds in decorating a foreign prince and thousands in adorning a mere supernumerary. These items represent principles of expenditure which do a vast amount of harm in this country. Others are induced by this extravagance to spend a vast amount of money on what is perfectly superfluous, and the result is this monstrous sweating system that is a blot on our civilisation. I do not believe that this gorgeousness, and this ostentation of wealth, is necessary in order to maintain the Constitution. On the contrary, I think it does far more to repress than to promote sentiments of loyalty.

"THINGS MUST BE EQUALISED" [3]

Lloyd George's impact on his audiences can be understood from the following extract from a speech in which he told his listeners what he considered to be the basis of the power of the ruling Conservative Party.

What are the components of the Tory party in this country? It contains practically the whole of the members of the privileged classes. Their numbers, and far more their wealth and their influence, constitute the chief ingredients of its power. They must therefore wield its policy. Now, what are the privileged classes? They are all those who squander the resources of a community without helping to produce them. Landlords consume millions of the wealth of the land of this country, without turning a sod to create it. There are monopolists who spend untold millions of the products of our mines and manufactures without blasting a rock, handling a machine, or even wielding a pen to build up that wealth. These are the governing forces of the Tory party. . . .

The most startling fact about our country is this—that you have men who have accumulated untold wealth living in gorgeous splendour in one street and a horde of miserable, poverty-stricken human beings huddled together in the most abject penury and squalor in the adjoining courts. Incalculable wealth and indescribable poverty dwell side by side. Why, in this very Bangor union, where you have noblemen and squires enjoying riches which they are at their wit's end to know how to squander and commanding such amplitude of resources that they are absolutely running to waste for want of use, I was startled to observe

[3] From a speech at Bangor, North Wales, May 21, 1891. Quoted in Herbert du Parcq, *Life of David Lloyd George* (London, 1912), I, 130–32.

in the last return of pauperism that on January 1 last 1 out of every 20 of the population was in receipt of parish relief. In London, with all its deplorable poverty, the paupers constituted but 1 out of every 39 of the population. And it is not that the country around Bangor is barren and desolate. On the contrary, it is rich in agricultural and mineral wealth. But these riches, intended by Providence for the people, are intercepted ere they reach them. It is a matter which is notorious to all of you that there is not one of the horses of these high-born gentlemen that is not better fed, better housed, and less worked than thousands of working-men in this very union. Things must be equalised. This deplorable state of things cannot go on for ever. But let no working-man make a mistake: the party which is dominated by these plutocrats and millionaires is not the one which is likely to assist them in attaining such a desirable consummation.

"ABUNDANT WEALTH . . . HIDEOUS POVERTY"

During 1903 the Conservatives began to discuss the need for a protectionist policy. Joseph Chamberlain was particularly anxious to impose tariffs on imported goods. He argued that foreign produce must be taxed so that home production could flourish. Lloyd George was among the leading Liberal critics of the tariff reformers. But he saw Free Trade as more than a political slogan with which to chastise the Conservatives; for him it had an even more important, constructive aspect.

Speaking at Hanley on June 19, 1903, Lloyd George said:
I am all for encouraging home production, but I will tell you how I would do it. I would have better land laws in this country: I would give security of tenure and fair rent, so that the people might put all they could into the land with confidence. I would have cheaper transit, for it should not cost as much, and more, to carry your goods from one part of the United Kingdom to the other as it costs you to transport them across the ocean to New York. Above all, I would have a fuller, freer, and better education—it means everything for the people. That is where Germany is beating us, if she is beating us at all. . . . What we want is to improve the quality of the brains of the people, and send them into life not with the blunt weapon of unhammered iron, but with the fine weapon of tempered steel. . . . No poor man can afford to be ignorant—leave that to the rich.

And shortly afterwards, at Manchester:

There is abundant wealth in this country, and by its side there is hideous poverty. If the Cabinet want an inquiry, let them inquire into that. Mr. Chairman, I also am a protectionist. I avow myself a man who believes in protecting industry. Yes, I would protect people—not from honest labour abroad—I would protect the agricultural industry from the extortion that confiscates its improvements. I would protect the education of the sons and daughters of the people from the black sceptre of the priest. I would protect labour from the unconscionable tyranny and oppression of men of the type of Lord Penrhyn. And above all I would protect industry from that terrible evil which is worse here than in any land, that ill which is enfeebling the health, the strength, the intelligence, which oppresses the people in their effort not merely in the struggle with foreign foes, but in that nobler struggle to rise up to a healthier, a purer and a nobler zone of life.[4]

Speaking at Manchester on April 21, 1908, Lloyd George said:

Well, I am standing for Britain—Britain and the flag of freedom in her markets. That flag has stood for Free Trade for fifty years, and the results are superb. If, with England's magnificent results in shipping, in machinery, in the cost of food, in the hours of labour, in wages, in textiles, yes, and not merely that, in the security which is given for the peace of the world—if all this is not worth fighting for, then all I can say is that I wonder what is. It is better worth fighting for than an excess of public-houses, than for keeping miners underground to work under conditions where hundreds of them meet their death every year; it is better worth fighting for than bigotry in the schools; it is the flag of freedom and fair play.

Before I abandon this question of Free Trade, will you allow me to say one other thing? It is not merely in the interests of trade alone that I would have you stand by freedom in our markets. Free Trade is a great pacificator. We have had many quarrels, many causes of quarrels, during the last fifty years, but we have not had a single war with any first-class Power. Free Trade is slowly but surely cleaving a path through the dense and dark thicket of armaments to the sunny land of brotherhood amongst the nations. We buy largely from nations. We sell largely to nations. We fetch here, we carry there, and we traffic everywhere. It is their interest to be on good terms with us. It is our interest to be on good terms with them. Our trade, our commerce, our shipping—they are

[4] Quoted in Herbert du Parcq, *Life of David Lloyd George* (London, 1914), pp. 422–23.

weaving "the silken strands of peace that bind the nations to us in the bonds of a commercial fraternity."

Let me tell you this, the day will come when a nation that lifts up the sword against a nation will be put in the same felon category as the man who strikes his brother in anger. I know not how many generations, maybe centuries, it will take before swords are beaten into ploughshares, and spears into pruning-hooks. But of this I feel assured, that when that day dawns it will be reckoned as one of the greatest and noblest achievements in the story, in the wonderful story, of the human race, that the men and women that dwelt in this little island, standing alone against a world armed with tariffs—valiantly, triumphantly defended the paths along which humanity eventually marched into the realm where the Prince of Peace reigneth for ever.[5]

THE FUTURE OF LIBERALISM [6]

Shortly after the Liberals had come to power Lloyd George laid down what he considered to be the objectives of Liberalism. Many Liberals were not prepared to go as far as he was. But he wished to set the pace and broaden the political scope of Liberal activity. He was determined that the young Labour Party should not outstrip the Liberals as a result of any Liberal neglect of a comprehensive social policy.

If at the end of an average term of office it were found that a Liberal Parliament had done nothing to cope seriously with the social condition of the people, to remove the national degradation of slums and widespread poverty and destitution in a land glittering with wealth; that they had shrunk from attacking boldly the main causes of this wretchedness, notably the drink and this vicious land system; that they had not arrested the waste of our national resources in armaments, nor provided an honourable sustenance for deserving old age; that they had tamely allowed the House of Lords to extract all the virtue out of their Bills, so that the Liberal statute book remained simply a bundle of sapless legislative faggots fit only for the fire; then would a real cry arise in this land for a new party, and many of us here in this room would join in that cry. But if a Liberal Government tackle the landlords, and the brewers, and the peers, as they have faced the

[5] Quoted in Herbert du Parcq, *Life of David Lloyd George* (London, 1914), IV, 635–36. Lloyd George was speaking in support of Winston Churchill at a by-election. Churchill was defeated.
[6] From a speech at Cardiff, South Wales, October 11, 1906. Published as "Liberalism and the Labour Party" in D. Lloyd George, *Better Times* (London, 1910), pp. 36–39.

parsons, and try to deliver the nation from the pernicious control of this confederacy of monopolists, then the Independent Labour party will call in vain upon the working men of Britain to desert Liberalism that is so gallantly fighting to rid the land of the wrongs that have oppressed those who labour in it.

The election of 1906 not only brought the Liberals back into office, but saw the emergence of a strong Labour Party, obviously attractive to the working-class voters, and potentially more radical in its social program. Lloyd George shared the fears of his shrewder Liberal colleagues that Labour might one day gain the allegiance of the middle classes and threaten the foundations of Liberal electoral strength. But in the same speech at Cardiff he tried to minimize the seriousness of the Labour challenge.

How does this new Labour agitation affect us in the capacity of British Liberals? Frankly I don't believe there is the slightest cause for alarm. Liberalism will never be ousted from its supremacy in the realm of political progress until it thoroughly deserves to be deposed for its neglect or betrayal of the principles it professes. As long as the Liberals go on as they have done this Session, showing that they are not afraid of their professions when they are reduced to practice, then their trust will never be transferred to a new party. The working man is no fool. He knows that a great party like ours can, with his help, do things for him which he could not hope to accomplish for himself without its aid. It brings to his assistance the potent influences drawn from the great middle classes of this country, which would be frightened into positive hostility by a purely class organisation to which they did not belong.

No party could ever hope for success in this country which does not win the confidence of a large portion of this powerful middle class. That is an asset brought by Liberalism to the work of progress which would never be transferred to a Progressive party constructed on purely Labour lines, and I would strongly urge the importance of this consideration upon those who wish to drive Liberalism out in order to substitute another organisation. You are not going to make Socialists in a hurry out of the farmers and traders and professional men of this country, but you may scare them into reaction. They are helping us now to secure advanced Labour legislation; they will help us later on to secure land reform and other measures for all classes of wealth producers, and we need all the help they give us. But if they are threatened with

a class war, then they will surely sulk and harden into downright
Toryism. What gain will that be for Labour?

Of course if the Labour leaders could ever hope to detach every working man through the country from both political parties and recruit
them into a Labour combination, then I agree such a party might be
all-powerful. But those who know anything about political history
can tell you that this is an impossible feat. There are hundreds and
thousands of working men who never under any pressure or provocation
quit the parties that they join any more than they leave the churches
of which they become members for any new-fangled religious organisation.

THE AIM OF THE BUDGET

*In 1909 Lloyd George, as Chancellor of the Exchequer in charge
of the nation's finances, introduced his "People's Budget" to Parliament. It taxed the rich more severely than before in order to
establish a State welfare system hitherto unknown in Britain. The
speech itself was long and detailed, and should be read in full in
Hansard. Having explained his proposals to Parliament, Lloyd
George proceeded to address the people directly throughout the
country. The cold logic of his Parliamentary statistics was then
replaced by the passion of popular oratory. The Baron de Forest,
a Liberal Member of Parliament, who often heard him speak
at this time recalled that:*

In his particular art of rhetoric the absence of pomposity and the familiar
touch he knew so well how to impart had a most convincing effect on his
audience, and this was especially the case when accompanied by a gesture
I remember that consisted in raising his right hand above his head and
bringing it down before him with a contracted spiral wriggle of his hand
and fingers that lent an almost spectacular emphasis to the point he was
making.

At the close of his Budget speech in Parliament Lloyd George said:

What the Government have to ask themselves is this: Can the whole
subject of further social reform be postponed until the increasing demands made upon the National Exchequer by the growth of armaments
has ceased? Not merely *can* it be postponed, but ought it to be postponed? Is there the slightest hope that if we deferred consideration of
the matter, we are likely within a generation to find any more favourable

moment for attending to it? And we have to ask ourselves this further question: If we put off dealing with these social sores, are the evils which arise from them not likely to grow and to fester, until finally the loss which the country sustains will be infinitely greater than anything it would have to bear in paying the cost of an immediate remedy? There are hundreds of thousands of men, women, and children in this country now enduring hardships for which the sternest judge would not hold them responsible; hardships entirely due to circumstances over which they have not the slightest command; the fluctuations and changes of trade—even of fashions; ill-health and the premature breakdown or death of the breadwinner. Owing to events of this kind, all of them beyond human control—at least beyond the control of the victims— thousands, and I am not sure I should be wrong if I said millions, are precipitated into a condition of acute distress and poverty. How many people there are of this kind in this wealthy land the figures of old age pensions have thrown a very unpleasant light upon. Is it fair, is it just, is it humane, is it honourable, is it safe to subject such a multitude of our poor fellow-countrymen and countrywomen to continued endurance of these miseries until nations have learnt enough wisdom not to squander their resources on these huge machines for the destruction of human life? . . .

I have to thank the House for the very great indulgence which they have extended to me, and for the patience with which they have listened to me. The task has been an extraordinarily difficult one. It has been as disagreeable a task as could well have been allotted to any Minister of the Crown. But there is one element of supreme satisfaction in it. That is to be found in contemplating the objects for which these new imposts have been created. The money thus raised is to be expended, first of all, in insuring the inviolability of our shores. It has also been raised in order not merely to relieve but to prevent unmerited distress within those shores. It is essential that we should make every necessary provision for the defence of our country. But surely it is equally imperative that we should make it a country even better worth defending for all and by all. And it is that this expenditure is for both those purposes that alone could justify the Government. I am told that no Chancellor of the Exchequer has ever been called on to impose such heavy taxes in a time of peace.

This is a War Budget. It is for raising money to wage implacable warfare against poverty and squalidness. I cannot help hoping and believing that before this generation has passed away we shall have advanced a great step towards that good time when poverty and wretchedness and human degradation which always follow in its camp will be as remote to the people of this country as the wolves which once infested its forests.[7]

[7] From *Hansard*, April 29, 1909. Reprinted by permission of the Controller of Her Majesty's Stationery Office.

Three months later Lloyd George told a London audience:

It is rather a shame that a rich country like ours—probably the richest in the world, if not the richest the world has ever seen—should allow those who have toiled all their days to end in penury and possibly starvation. It is rather hard that an old workman should have to find his way to the gates of the tomb, bleeding and footsore, through the brambles and thorns of poverty. We cut a new path for him—an easier one, a pleasanter one, through fields of waving corn. We are raising money to pay for the new road—aye, and to widen it so that 200,000 paupers shall be able to join in the march. There are many in the country blessed by Providence with great wealth, and if there are amongst them men who grudge out of their riches a fair contribution towards the less fortunate of their fellowcountrymen they are very shabby rich men.

We propose to do more by means of the Budget. We are raising money to provide against the evils and the sufferings that follow from unemployment. We are raising money for the purpose of assisting our great friendly societies to provide for the sick and the widows and orphans. We are providing money to enable us to develop the resources of our own land. I do not believe any fair-minded man would challenge the justice and the fairness of the objects which we have in view in raising this money.[8]

"THEY ARE FORCING A REVOLUTION"

The House of Lords, which was overwhelmingly Conservative, decided to assert its Constitutional powers to reject Lloyd George's Budget. The Liberal Prime Minister, H. H. Asquith, led his colleagues in determination to support Lloyd George, even if it meant challenging the powers of the House of Lords. This was a bitter time in British politics. The forces of privilege and reaction appeared to be mobilizing against those of Liberalism and progress; seldom did a political issue seem more clear-cut to those who took part in the battle. Lloyd George was foremost in the attack on the powers of the House of Lords.

Who talks about altering and meddling with the Constitution? The Constitutional party—the great Constitutional party. As long as the

---

[8] From a speech delivered at Limehouse, east London, July 30, 1909. Reprinted as "The Land and the People" in D. Lloyd George, *Better Times* (London, 1910), pp. 144–56.

Constitution gave rank and possession and power to the Lords it was not to be interfered with. As long as it secured even their sports from intrusion and made interference with them a crime; as long as the Constitution enforced royalties and ground rents and fees and premiums and fines, and all the black retinue of exaction; as long as it showered writs and summonses and injunctions and distresses and warrants to enforce them, then the Constitution was inviolate. It was sacred. It was something that was put in the same category as religion, that no man should with rude hands touch, something that the chivalry of the nation ought to range itself in defence of. But the moment the Constitution looks round; the moment the Constitution begins to discover that there are millions of people outside park gates who need attention, then the Constitution is to be torn to pieces.

Let them realise what they are doing. They are forcing a revolution and they will get it. The Lords may decree a revolution, but the people will direct it. If they begin, issues will be raised that they little dream of. Questions will be asked which are now whispered in humble voices, and answers will be demanded then with authority. The question will be asked whether five hundred men, ordinary men chosen accidentally from among the unemployed, should override the judgment—the deliberate judgment—of millions of people who are engaged in the industry which makes the wealth of the country.

That is one question. Another will be, Who ordained that a few should have the land of Britain as a perquisite? Who made ten thousand people owners of the soil, and the rest of us trespassers in the land of our birth? Who is it who is responsible for the scheme of things whereby one man is engaged through life in grinding labour to win a bare and precarious subsistence for himself, and when, at the end of his days, he claims at the hands of the community he served a poor pension of eightpence a day, he can only get it through a revolution, and another man who does not toil receives every hour of the day, every hour of the night, whilst he slumbers, more than his poor neighbour receives in a whole year of toil? Where did the table of that law come from? Whose finger inscribed it? These are the questions that will be asked. The answers are charged with peril for the order of things the Peers represent; but they are fraught with rare and refreshing fruit for the parched lips of the multitude who have been treading the dusty road along which the people have marched through the dark ages, which are now emerging into the light.[9]

[9] From a speech at Newcastle, October 9, 1909. Quoted in D. Lloyd George, *Better Times* (London, 1910), pp. 157–75. Lloyd George denounced the House of Lords as "Mr. Balfour's poodle. It fetches and carries for him. It barks for him. It bites anybody that he sets it on to!" For a full account of the Lords' crisis, see Roy Jenkins, *Mr. Balfour's Poodle* (London, 1954).

When the Lords voted against the Budget, Lloyd George rose to the challenge:

They have slain the Budget. In doing so they have killed the Bill which if you will permit me to say so, had in it more promise of better things for the people of this country than most Bills that have been submitted to the House of Commons. It made provision against the inevitable evils which befall such large masses of our poor population— their old age, infirmity, sickness, and unemployment. The schemes of which it was the foundation would, in my judgment, if they had been allowed to fructify, have eliminated at least hunger from the terrors that haunt the workman's cottage.

And yet here you have an order of men blessed with every fortune which Providence can bestow on them grudging a small pittance out of their super-abundance in order to protect those who have built up their wealth against the haunting terrors of misery and despair. They have thrown out the Budget, and, in doing so, have initiated one of the greatest, gravest, and most promising struggles of the time. Liberty owes as much to the foolhardiness of its foes as it does to the sapience and wisdom of its friends. I wish for no better illustration of that than this incident.

Here, for years, for generations, Liberal statesmen have striven to bring to an issue these great forces. Their Bills were mutilated, torn, and devitalised by this machine, and they were never able to bring the cause to any sort of decision. It has been done at last, and I am proud that I have had a small share in it. At last the cause between the Peers and the people has been set down for trial in the great assize of the people, and the verdict will soon come. The Assembly which has delayed, denied, and mutilated justice for so long has at last been brought to justice.

Well, now, we are on the eve of a General Election, which will decide this great question. There may be the usual attempt to divert the attention of the jury by turning their minds on to other and irrelevant questions. I have no doubt the stale old question of Protection will be brought up. Any one who has read carefully the modern political history of this country can recall many instances where the Tory party, hard pressed, has always resorted to Protection. They will try it again. It will fail. It is not that we are afraid of them. In fact, it raises in a very clear way the issue which we will be delighted to get the mind of the country upon: whether the service of the country, whether the money for the service of the country is to be raised by taxing the unearned increment upon land and by taxing luxuries, or by taxing the bread and meat of the people.

But, after all, there will be one great dominant question submitted to the electors, one that will absorb all others. What is that? [A Voice: "The

House of Lords."] That's it—the question which was put by the Prime Minister in his great speech yesterday. Here are you a nation of nearly 45 millions, one of the greatest nations the world has ever seen, a nation whose proficiency in the art of government is unrivalled, a nation which has no superior in commerce or in industry. It has established the greatest merchant fleets that ever rode the waves. It has got the greatest international commerce in the world. It has founded the greatest and the most extensive empire the world has ever witnessed.

And yet we are told that this great nation, with such a record of splendid achievements in the past and in the present, is unfit to make its own laws, is unfit to control its own finance, and that it is to be placed as if it were a nation of children or lunatics, under the tutelage and guardianship of some other body—and what body? Who are the guardians of this mighty people? Who are they? With all respect—I shall have to make exceptions; but I am speaking of them as a whole, and I shall come to the analysis later on. They are men who have neither the training, the qualifications, nor the experience which would fit them for such a gigantic task. They are men whose sole qualification—speaking in the main, and for the majority of them—they are simply men whose sole qualification is that they are the first born of persons who had just as little qualifications as themselves.

To invite this Imperial race; this, the greatest commercial nation in the world; this, the nation that has taught the world the principles of self-government and liberty; to invite this nation itself to sign the decree that declares it unfit to govern itself without the guardianship of such people, is an insult which I hope will be flung back with ignominy. This is a great issue. It is this: Is this nation to be a free nation and to become a freer one, or is it for all time to be shackled and tethered by tariffs and trusts and monopolies and privileges? That is the issue, and no Liberal will shirk it.[10]

We have found them out in time. What they wanted were "the good old days," that the rich might be made richer, that the fat rent rolls might become fatter. But the bare cupboard of the poor would become barer. It is the spirit of reaction, the spirit which takes you back sixty years to the days of the Corn Laws, a spirit that would take you still further back to the days when the Commons were still struggling for the right to grant supplies to secure redress; still further back to the days when the barons ruled the land.

[10] From a speech at the National Liberal Club, London, December 3, 1909. Quoted in Herbert du Parcq, *Life of David Lloyd George* (London, 1913), V, 697.

Our policy is the policy of forward progress. They say, "Let us go back." Never! The Budget found them out, found them out in time to stop the conspiracy. And now they are worrying about their land and they are anxious about their privileges. They are unhappy about their general position. And I am glad to see anxieties for once flitting from the cottage to the castle. It is a good omen. I come from a part of the country where we have some very fine mountains, and I tell you how we who never could afford a weather-glass used to know what kind of weather was coming there We used to look at the hills, and if we saw the clouds hanging heavily in the valleys and on the lower ridges of the hills, we knew there was bad weather coming. But if we saw the clouds lifting and gathering round the summits we knew there was going to be fine weather in front of us.

Today the clouds are lifting from the valleys, from the lowly and humble homes of the people, and they are gathering round the tops. There is a fine day coming.[11]

LANDLORDISM: "THE GREATEST OF ALL MONOPOLIES"

The House of Lords lost its power to reject legislation passed by the House of Commons. Any Parliamentary Bill could henceforth become law, even if rejected by the Lords, provided it obtained majorities in three consecutive years in the House of Commons. This triple assent overruled all adverse votes in the House of Lords. Thus Lloyd George's social legislation could and did become part of the established fabric of British social life. It was accepted by successive Conservative Governments. In 1913 Lloyd George returned to the attack against the power of the landed aristocracy. Having destroyed their political influence as asserted through the House of Lords he now determined to break the basis of their wealth and power, their control over the land. War came before he could introduce legislation. But extracts from two of his speeches give a clear picture of what he had in mind. Most of his proposals were acted upon in some way by the Labour Governments of Clement Attlee (1945–1951) and Harold Wilson (1964–   ).

. . . For every man, from the beginning of his life to the end—the cradle is rocked on the land, and the grave is sunk in the land. Land enters into everything. You cannot raise an issue which is more important for us to consider, and to consider thoroughly, to consider intelligently, and, having considered, to act boldly in reference to, than the question of the land.

[11] From a speech at Walworth, December 17. 1909. Quoted in Herbert du Parcq. *Life of David Lloyd George* (London, 1913), IV, 730–31.

Most of the land of Britain is in the hands of very few persons. I should say it is in the hands of something like one-half of the population of Bedford. There was a great, a prominent Unionist the other day making a speech. He said one-third of the land of England belonged to the House of Lords. Well, what use do they make of it? Their powers are great, their authority is extensive. If they mishandle that power and authority the effect is disastrous to the community as a whole. We are therefore entitled to examine the way they exercise their influence. Their powers are terrible.

Landlordism is the greatest of all monopolies in this land. Not only is it the greatest of all monopolies, it is the least controlled of all monopolies. I want to know the reason why, and I think the time has come to inquire. I want you to follow me whilst I am making an examination of the use which has been made of these great powers, and the effect it has had upon the welfare of the community. I wonder how many people there are who realise what gigantic powers those who own the land possess upon the life of the nation. The Sovereign of this Empire has no power over his subjects comparable to the power which the landowner has over his subjects. What can he do? The landowner can devastate the countryside. He can sweep every cottage away and convert it into a wilderness. He can do what no foreign invader is permitted to do now by the laws of civilised warfare—destroy cottages and drive the peasantry away to exile, convert the land into a desert. He can do more than a foreign enemy. Even in the old barbarous days of warfare, the moment the invader had retired the peasants returned to their homes, rebuilt their cottages, tilled their land, and the country assumed its normal appearance of industry and of thrift. Landlordism can by legal process not merely ordain a wilderness, it can maintain a wilderness.

You may say those are purely imaginary powers they have got by law. Not at all. If anyone doubts it he has simply to take his next holiday in the Highlands of Scotland, where he will find millions of acres which formerly maintained the sturdiest, the bravest, the most gallant race under the sun—a desert. What has become of the inhabitants? Whilst their sons were maintaining the glory of Britain on continental fields their parents were having their cottages burnt down and they were being driven away homeless. Go to the north of Scotland, and you will find still the remains of the old crofts, but the crofters are not there. The land is trodden by deer. Those are legal powers.

The workman is worse off than he used to be. . . . There was a time when he had an interest of his own in the land—a freehold interest. The labourer was a freeholder in the land. He had his commons. There he could graze a cow to give him butter and milk for himself and his children. There was a little patch where he could raise corn to feed them. There he had his poultry, his geese, his pigs—a patch of land where he could raise green produce for the table. He was a gentleman. He was independent. He had a stake in the country. His title was as ancient and apparently as indefeasible as that of the lord of the manor. Where has it gone to? Stolen! Landlord Parliaments have annexed Naboth's vineyard. There is now occasionally a little garden. Sometimes, as a matter of grace, he has a little row of potatoes, but he has no longer a right in the soil as his fathers had. He has been converted from a contented, well-fed, independent peasant to a hopeless, underpaid, landless drudge on the soil.[12]

We have therefore come to the conclusion that a man who likes to go to the country to live should be encouraged whatever his work. There has been too much discouraging of people to come and live in the villages. You find the landlord with his blunderbuss turning a man out whom he does not know by face, because they are strangers. No man is a stranger if he is of British blood in England. The last thing of all we have got proposals on is with regard to the most important thing of all, the price of land. You cannot have those great schemes if the price which is charged is a prohibitive one. Up to the present almost every housing scheme has been crippled by the extravagant price paid for land, and I will tell you where the harm is done. It is not so much that it goes into the rent, but it goes upon the land which is available for the house. There is less land attached to the house because the price of the land is so high. That accounts for this sort of cramming and crowding and pressing houses into an acre of land—as many as it will hold—with miserable little backyards. If you want air, light, space, breathing room, something to fill the lungs, you must not treat the land as if it were radium.

Why is the price extravagant? I will tell you why. Whenever land is required for a public purpose, you always pay more for it than it is worth. Every great public project has been oppressed, injured, handicapped in that way. Railways pay for the land for their lines of rails, for their sidings, for their stations, for their workshops—they pay three, four, and five times as much as the land is worth. Do you think they pay? It is passed on to you. Waterworks, gasworks, schools, cemeteries, houses, every public need is made the excuse for charging extravagant prices. Why is it? The reason is this: you generally hand over the determination of the price to arbitrators, who have been trained in the old methods of the Lands Clauses Acts—Acts passed by Parliament which were pre-

[12] From a speech at Bedford, October 11, 1913. Published as a Liberal Party pamphlet, *The Rural Problem: What It Is* (London, 1913), pp. 4, 9–11, 21–24. Reprinted by permission of the Liberal Publication Department.

dominantly landlord. The men who set the precedents under these Acts were men who had been valuing under the old traditions before compulsion. They are steeped in them. In addition to that, arbitrators, as a rule, are men who are only occasionally employed by the municipalities, and the bulk of whose business comes afterwards through the landowning class, so that their bias is unconsciously in favour of putting up the price. It is a perfectly honourable profession, but every profession is very conservative, and the result is this—that, somehow or other, they have got into the marrow of their bones, that whenever land is required for a public purpose you ought to pay more for it and charge more for it than if it were required as between two men who are bargaining with each other. It is a vicious principle. It is unjust. It is unpatriotic. It is inhuman. And we have decided to put an end to it. The comparative restriction of small holdings comes through that, and the first thing we have to do is this. We have decided that the Commissioners shall be the body who will fix the price of land when there is a compulsory acquisition for any public purpose. . . . It is a great undertaking, it is a gigantic one, but we mean to put it through. It is one that may take time, it is one that may involve us in a struggle with great interests; we are accustomed to that. We have beaten interests before, and we will do it again. But it is a task, which, when it is accomplished, will bring Britain in our judgment a long march nearer the dawn. I believe it will have the effect not merely of filling the countryside with a happy, prosperous, contented peasantry, but it will do more than that—it will free the towns from the nightmares of unemployment and sweating and slums. Then we shall have a Motherland that its children can rejoice in, and one that the Empire to the ends of the earth can be proud of.[13]

"WE CAN CONQUER UNEMPLOYMENT" [14]

Lloyd George held no political office after 1922. But he continued to be a fertile source of political proposals relating to the social field. In particular, he turned his mind and pen to the problem of unemployment, and was an early advocate of urgent direct Government involvement in the creation of public works projects which could absorb the unemployed. Although he led only a handful of Members of Parliament, his ideas on how to solve the growing and pressing problem of unemployment encouraged coordination between politicians and economists in the inter-war years. He foreshadowed both Hitler's massive program of public works and

[13] From a speech at Swindon, October 18, 1913. Published as a Liberal Party pamphlet, *The Rural Land Problem: The Remedy* (London, 1913). Reprinted by permission of the Liberal Publication Department.

[14] From the Liberal Party booklet, *We Can Conquer Unemployment* (London, 1929). Reprinted by permission of Cassell & Co. Ltd. and the Beaverbrook Library.

Franklin D. Roosevelt's New Deal. He formed local "Councils of Action" to serve as a base for political power, but failed to reestablish himself or the Liberal Party as a political force. From 1922 to 1939 his was a lone voice, loud but powerless to affect the march of events.

The Liberal Party, for their part, have no need to conjure with rabbits or with words. Their proposals are fully developed. Their pledge to reduce unemployment to normal proportions is specific. Their record will bear the closest scrutiny. It was the Liberal Party which twenty years ago established the Road Fund and included in it a specific provision for its use in accordance with the needs of unemployment. It was the Liberal Party which first introduced unemployment insurance. It was the Liberal Industrial Enquiry which formulated that Policy of National Development, which is the only workable alternative to another five years of grim despair for a great section of our countrymen.

Finally, and of the most vital importance (as will be realised by those who have some conception of the difficulties, the obstruction and the prejudice to be faced in the execution of such a policy as this) the work must be placed in the hands of men who have demonstrated their ability to deal with a big and difficult situation in a big way. The situation cannot wait while Ministers learn the A B C of administration. It is too urgent. It must be handled by men who have won their spurs; who have the experience and the driving force required to achieve what is declared to be impossible. What party is there who has amongst its leaders men who can compare with the Liberal Party in this respect?

We finish as we began: what is wanted to conquer unemployment is the belief that it can be conquered; the determination to attack it in the same spirit as the emergencies of the war; a policy calculated to secure success; and a capacity to carry that policy through to a conclusion. These things the Liberal Party possess in unique degree.

The Liberal Policy is Work for the Workless, now. We can conquer Unemployment.

3
Patriot and War Leader

We shall need all our qualities . . . prudence in counsel, daring in action, tenacity in purpose, courage in defeat, moderation in victory.

—Lloyd George in 1914

We are not an infantile nation, and it is not necessary to withhold unpleasant facts from us, so as not to frighten us. This is not a nation easily frightened . . . Therefore I beg the Government to let us know the facts.

—Lloyd George in 1941

It was as "the man who won the war" that Lloyd George was remembered by most of his contemporaries. Up to 1914 he had used his oratorical genius and administrative acumen to promote social change. From 1914 to 1918 he transformed himself into a man of war. He spoke bluntly of the dangers, but confidently of the final result. In 1916 he became Prime Minister. He filled the people of Britain with a determination to see the difficult, costly, heartrending struggle through to a victorious end. He worked at fever pitch to coordinate the work of his Ministers and his Allies. He traveled to inter-allied Conferences, to the front line, and to the factories. He brought the imperial governments of Canada, Australia, India, South Africa and New Zealand into direct contact with his policy-making machinery. "In the day of our dire need," wrote Lord Beaverbrook,

when the blast of the terrible one was against the wall, a strange figure sprang into the arena to do battle . . . The sword looked as fragile as a rapier, and yet smote with the impact of a battle-axe. As it was held on high, so was the hope of Britain. And when the swordsman stumbled, anxiety filled the breasts of the multitude.

BRITAIN'S PLACE IN THE WORLD [1]

Before 1914 Lloyd George was widely considered to be ignorant of foreign affairs. He had visited Germany in 1908 to study German

[1] From a speech at the Mansion House, London, July 21, 1911. Widely reproduced in British and German newspapers at the time. I am most grateful to Count de Bendern (formerly the Baron de Forest) for his recollections of Lloyd George before 1914.

*insurance schemes, but this was not thought to have awakened his
interest in European problems. His friend Baron de Forest recalled
discussing the Balkan War of 1912 with him:*

We spoke together on the subject when our talks revealed that Lloyd
George's information on the questions at issue, as also on the political
problems involved in that part of Europe, were singularly vague. He spoke
of the "Boolgars" and made inquiries from me as to the precise location of
their country and their national aspirations of which he professed ignorance, as also of the personality of the monarch then known as "Foxy
Ferdinand" with whom I had been acquainted.

*Yet three years before the war Lloyd George had revealed to a
surprised audience in the City of London that he was certainly not
the out-and-out pacifist many assumed him to be.*

I am bound to say this, that I believe it is essential in the highest
interests, not merely of this country, but of the world, that Britain should
at all hazards maintain her place and prestige amongst the Great
Powers. Her potent influence has many a time in the past, and may
yet in the future, be invaluable to the cause of human liberty. It has more
than once in the past redeemed Continental nations—who are sometimes
too apt to forget that service—from overwhelming disaster and national
extinction. I would make great sacrifices to preserve peace. I can conceive of nothing that could justify disturbance of international good-
will except questions of the greatest national moment, but if a situation
were to be forced upon us, in which peace could only be preserved by
the surrender of the great and beneficent position which Britain has
won by centuries of heroism and achievement by allowing Britain to be
treated, where her interests are vitally affected, as if she were on no
account in the Cabinet of nations, then I say emphatically that peace at
that price would be a humiliation intolerable for a great country like
ours to endure.

"THROUGH TERROR TO TRIUMPH" [2]

*Immediately before the outbreak of war Lloyd George had been
thought of as a potential leader of the antiwar group in the Cabinet.
He quickly redressed the balance in a speech which marked him out
as a potential war leader.*

[2] From a speech delivered on September 19, 1914, at the Queen's Hall, London.
Reprinted in numerous pamphlets during the first months of the war under the
titles *Through Terror to Triumph* and *Honour and Dishonour*. The clash between
Lloyd George and Churchill seven months before the outbreak of war over naval construction is dealt with fully in Randolph S. Churchill, *Winston S. Churchill* (London,
1967), Vol. 2, Chap. 17.

There is no man in this room who has always regarded the prospect of engaging in a great war with greater reluctance and with greater repugnance than I have done throughout the whole of my political life. There is no man either inside or outside of this room more convinced that we could not have avoided it without national dishonour. I am fully alive to the fact that every nation which has ever engaged in any war has always invoked the sacred name of honour. Many a crime has been committed in its name; there are some being committed now. All the same, national honour is a reality, and any nation that disregards it is doomed. Why is our honour as a country involved in this war? Because in the first instance, we are bound by honourable obligations to defend the independence, the liberty, the integrity, of a small neighbour that has always lived peaceably. She could not have compelled us; she was weak; but the man who declines to discharge his duty because his creditor is too poor to enforce it is a blackguard. We entered into a treaty—a solemn treaty—two treaties—to defend Belgium and her integrity. Our signatures are attached to the documents. Our signatures do not stand alone there; this country was not the only country that undertook to defend the integrity of Belgium. Russia, France, Austria, Prussia—they are all there. Why are Austria and Prussia not performing the obligations of their bond? . . .

Lloyd George then discussed the German attack on Belgium and the Austrian attack on Serbia:

This is the story of two little nations. The world owes much to little nations—and to little men! This theory of bigness, this theory that you must have a *big* Empire, and a *big* nation, and *big* men—well, long legs have their advantage in a retreat. Frederick the First chose his warriors for their height, and that tradition has become a policy in Germany. Germany applies that ideal to nations, and will only allow 6-foot-2 nations to stand in the ranks. But ah! the world owes much to the little 5-foot-5 nations. The greatest art in the world was the work of little nations; the most enduring literature of the world came from little nations; the greatest literature of England came when she was a nation of the size of Belgium fighting a great Empire. The heroic deeds that thrill humanity through generations were the deeds of little nations fighting for their freedom. Yes, and the salvation of mankind came through a little nation. God has chosen little nations as the vessels by which He carries His choicest wines to the lips of humanity, to rejoice their hearts, to exalt their vision, to stimulate and strengthen their faith; and if we had stood by when two little nations were being crushed and broken by the brutal hands of barbarism, our shame would have rung down the everlasting ages.

It is the interest of Prussia to-day to break the treaty, and she has done it. She avows it with cynical contempt for every principle of justice. She says: "Treaties only bind you when it is your interest to keep them." "What is a treaty?" says the German Chancellor: "A scrap of paper." Have you any £5 notes about you? I am not calling for them. Have you any of those neat little Treasury £1 notes? If you have, burn them; they are only scraps of paper. What are they made of? Rags. What are they worth? The whole credit of the British Empire. Scraps of paper! I have been dealing with scraps of paper within the last month. One suddenly found the commerce of the world coming to a standstill. The machine had stopped. Why? I will tell you. We discovered—many of us for the first time, for I do not pretend that I do not know much more about the machinery of commerce to-day than I did six weeks ago, and there are many others like me—we discovered that the machinery of commerce was moved by bills of exchange. I have seen some of them—wretched, crinkled, scrawled over, blotched, frowsy, and yet those wretched little scraps of paper move great ships laden with thousands of tons of precious cargo from one end of the world to the other. What is the motive power behind them? The honour of commercial men. Treaties are the currency of International statesmanship. Let us be fair: German merchants, German traders, have the reputation of being as upright and straightforward as any traders in the world; but if the currency of German commerce is to be debased to the level of that of her statesmanship, no trader from Shanghai to Valparaiso will ever look at a German signature again. This doctrine of the scrap of paper, this doctrine which is proclaimed by Bernhardi, that treaties only bind a nation as long as it is to its interest, goes under the root of all public law. It is the straight road to barbarism. It is as if you were to remove the Magnetic Pole because it was in the way of a German cruiser. The whole navigation of the seas would become dangerous, difficult and impossible; and the whole machinery of civilisation will break down if this doctrine wins in this war. We are fighting against barbarism, and there is only one way of putting it right. If there are nations that say they will only respect treaties when it is to their interest to do so, we must make it to their interest to do so for the future. . . .

Have you read the Kaiser's speeches? If you have not a copy I advise you to buy one; they will soon be out of print, and you will not have many more of the same sort. They are full of the glitter and bluster of German militarism—"mailed fist," and "shining armour." Poor old mailed fist! Its knuckles are getting a little bruised. Poor shining armour! The shine is being knocked out of it. There is the same swagger and boastfulness running through the whole of the speeches. . . .

I do not believe he meant all these speeches; it was simply the martial straddle he had acquired. But there were men around him who meant every word of them. This was their religion. Treaties? They tangle the feet of Germany in her advance. Cut them with the sword! Little nations? They hinder the advance of Germany. Trample them in the mire under the German heel! The Russian Slav? He challenges the supremacy of Germany and Europe. Hurl your legions at him and massacre him! Britain? She is a constant menace to the predominancy of Germany in the world. Wrest the trident out of her hand! Christianity? Sickly sentimentalism about sacrifice for others! Poor pap for German digestion! We will have a new diet. We will force it upon the world. It will be made in Germany—a diet of blood and iron. What remains? Treaties have gone. The honour of nations has gone. Liberty has gone. What is left? Germany. Germany is left!—"Deutschland über Alles!"

That is what we are fighting—that claim to predominancy of a material, hard civilisation, a civilisation which if it once rules and sways the world, liberty goes, democracy vanishes. And unless Britain and her sons come to the rescue it will be a dark day for humanity.

Have you followed the Prussian Junker and his doings? We are not fighting the German people. The German people are under the heel of this military caste, and it will be a day of rejoicing for the German peasant, artisan, and trader when the military caste is broken. You know its pretensions. They give themselves the air of demi-gods. They walk the pavements, and civilians and their wives are swept into the gutter: they have no right to stand in the way of a great Prussian soldier. Men, women, nations—they all have to go. He thinks all he has to say is, "We are in a hurry." That is the answer he gave to Belgium—"Rapidity of action is Germany's greatest asset," which means "I am in a hurry; clear out of my way." You know the type of motorist, the terror of the roads, with a 60-horse-power car, who thinks the roads are made for him, and knocks down anybody who impedes the action of his car by a single mile an hour. The Prussian Junker is the road-hog of Europe. Small nationalities in his way are hurled to the roadside, bleeding and broken. Women and children are crushed under the wheels of his cruel car, and Britain is ordered out of his road. All I can say is this: if the old British spirit is alive in British hearts, that bully will be torn from his seat. Were he to win, it would be the greatest catastrophe that has befallen democracy since the day of the Holy Alliance and its ascendancy.

They think we cannot beat them. It will not be easy. It will be a long job. It will be a terrible war. But in the end we shall march through terror to triumph. We shall need all our qualities—every quality that Britain and its people possess—prudence in counsel, daring in action, tenacity in purpose, courage in defeat, moderation in victory; in all things faith. . . .

The people in all lands will gain more by this struggle than they comprehend at the present moment. It is true they will be free of the greatest menace to their freedom. That is not all. There is something infinitely greater and more enduring which is emerging already out of this great conflict—a new patriotism, richer, nobler, and more exalted than the old. I see amongst all classes, high and low, shedding them-selves of selfishness, a new recognition that the honour of the country does not depend merely on the maintenance of its glory in the stricken field, but also in protecting its homes from distress. It is bringing a new outlook for all classes. The great flood of luxury and sloth which had submerged the land is receding, and a new Britain is appearing. We can see for the first time the fundamental things that matter in life, and that have been obscured from our vision by the tropical growth of prosperity.

May I tell you in a simple parable what I think this war is doing for us? I know a valley in North Wales, between the mountains and the sea. It is a beautiful valley, snug, comfortable, sheltered by the mountains from all the bitter blasts. But it is very enervating, and I remember how the boys were in the habit of climbing the hill above the village to have a glimpse of the great mountains in the distance, and to be stimulated and freshened by the breezes which came from the hilltops, and by the great spectacle of their grandeur. We have been living in a sheltered valley for generations. We have been too comfortable and too indulgent —many, perhaps, too selfish—and the stern hand of fate has scourged us to an elevation where we can see the great everlasting things that matter for a nation—the great peaks we had forgotten, of Honour, Duty, Patriotism, and, clad in glittering white, the great pinnacle of Sacrifice pointing like a rugged finger to Heaven. We shall descend into the valleys again; but as long as the men and women of this generation last, they will carry in their hearts the image of those great mountain peaks whose foundations are not shaken, though Europe rock and sway in the convulsions of a great war.

"THE MOCKING SPECTRE OF TOO LATE!" [3]

As a member of the War Council Lloyd George shared respon-
sibilities with his colleagues for the conduct of the war. But he
never disguised in his public speeches the dangers and setbacks.

. . . I have a very remarkable photograph of the battlefield of Loos; taken immediately after the battle. There is barbed wire which had not been destroyed. There is one machine-gun emplacement intact —only one! The others had been destroyed. There, in front of the

[3] From *Hansard*, December 20, 1915. Reprinted by permission of the Controller of Her Majesty's Stationary Office.

barbed wire, lie hundreds of gallant men. There was one machine gun —one!

These are the accidents you can obviate. How? Every soldier tells me there is but one way of doing it. You must have enough ammunition to crash in every trench wherein the enemy lurks, to destroy every concrete emplacement, to shatter every machine-gun, to rend and tear every yard of barbed wire, so that if the enemy want to resist they will have to do it in the open, face to face with better men than themselves. That is the secret—plenty of ammunition. I hope that this idea that we are turning out too much will not enter into the mind of workman, capitalist, taxpayer, or anybody until we have enough to crash our way through to victory. You must spend wisely; you must spend to the best purpose; you must not pay extravagant prices; but, for Heaven's sake, if there are risks to be taken, let them be risks for the pocket of the taxpayer, and not for the lives of the soldiers!

There is only one appeal to employer and employed; it is the appeal to patriotism! The employer must take steps. He is loth to do it. It is a sort of inertia which comes to tired and overstrained men—as they all are. They must really face the local trade unions, and put forward the demand, because until they do so the State cannot come in. We have had an Act of Parliament, but the law must be put into operation by somebody. Unless the employer begins by putting on the lathes unskilled men and women we cannot enforce that Act of Parliament. The first step, therefore, is that the employer must challenge a decision upon the matter. He is not doing so because of the trouble which a few other firms have had. But victory depends upon it! Hundreds of thousands of precious lives depend upon it! It is a question of whether you are going to bring this war victoriously to an end in a year or whether it is going to linger on in bloodstained paths for years. Labour has the answer. The contract was entered into with labour. We are carrying it out. It can be done. I wonder whether it will not be too late! Ah! fatal words of this war! Too late in moving here! Too late in arriving there! Too late in coming to this decision! Too late in starting with enterprises! Too late in preparing! In this war the footsteps of the Allied forces have been dogged by the mocking spectre of "Too Late"; and unless we quicken our movements damnation will fall on the sacred cause for which so much gallant blood has flowed. I beg employers and workmen not to have "Too Late" inscribed upon the portals of their workshops! . . .

"WHY SHOULD WE NOT SING?" [4]

Lloyd George was not a pessimist; he deprecated gloom and struck at despondency. He learned, as Churchill was to learn in the

[4] From a speech at the Aberystwyth National Eisteddfod, August 17, 1916. Quoted in W. H. Beable, ed. *Celebrated and Historical Speeches* (London, 1933), pp. 203–204.

*Second World War, the importance of optimism, humor and the
human touch, in rallying the nation to the cruel demands which
war inevitably makes upon soldiers and civilians alike.*

Why should we not sing during the war? Why especially should we
not sing at this stage of the war? The blinds of Britain are not down yet,
nor are they likely to be. The honour of Britain is not dead, her
might is not broken, her destiny is not fulfilled, her ideals are not
shattered by her enemies. She is more than alive; she is more potent, she
is greater than she ever was. Her dominions are wider, her influence
is deeper, her purpose is more exalted than ever. Why should her
children not sing? I know war means suffering, war means sorrow.
Darkness has fallen on many a devoted household, but it has been
ordained that the best singer amongst the birds of Britain should give
its song in the night, and according to legend that sweet song is one
of triumph over pain. There are no nightingales this side of the Severn.
Providence rarely wasted its gifts. We do not need this exquisite
songster in Wales; we can provide better. There is a bird in our villages
that can beat the best of them. He is called Y Cymro. He sings in joy,
he sings also in sorrow; he sings in prosperity, he sings also in adversity.
He sings at play, he sings at work; he sings in the sunshine, he sings
in the storm; he sings in the daytime, he sings also in the night; he
sings in peace; why should he not sing in war? Hundreds of wars have
swept over these hills, but the harp of Wales has never yet been
silenced by one of them, and I should be proud if I contributed something to keep it in tune during the war by the holding of this
Eisteddfod to-day.

But I have another and even more urgent reason for wishing to
keep this Eisteddfod alive during the war. When this terrible conflict is
over, a wave of materialism will sweep over the land. Nothing will
count but machinery and output. I am all for output, and I have done
my best to improve machinery and increase output. But that is not
all. There is nothing more fatal to a people than that it should narrow
its vision to the material needs of the hour. National ideals without imagination are but as the thistles of the wilderness, fit neither for
food nor fuel. A nation that depends upon them must perish. We
shall need at the end of the war better workshops, but we shall
also need more than ever every institution that will exalt the vision
of the people above and beyond the workshop and the counting
house. We shall need every national tradition that will remind them that
men cannot live by bread alone.

I make no apology for advocating the holding of the Eisteddfod in
the middle of this great conflict, even although it were merely a

carnival of song as it has been stigmatized. The storm is raging as fiercely as ever, but now there is a shimmer of sunshine over the waves, there is a rainbow on the tumult of surging waters. The struggle is more terrible than it has ever been, but the legions of the oppressor are being driven back, and the banner of right is pressing forward. Why should we not sing? It is true there are thousands of gallant men falling in the fight—let us sing of their heroism. There are myriads more standing in the battle lines, facing the foe, and myriads more behind ready to support them when their turn comes. Let us sing of the land that gave birth to so many heroes.

"VIGOUR AND VISION ARE THE SUPREME NEED" [5]

By the end of 1916 the war was going badly for Britain. The numbers of those killed or maimed in the struggle rose swiftly, but no significant gains of territory were made. There seemed to the public, as well as to the politicians, no end to the slaughter. Lloyd George put himself at the head of those who criticized the Prime Minister, Asquith, for his lack of dynamism. In a letter to Asquith on December 5, 1916, Lloyd George offered to resign his position as Minister of War:

As all delay is fatal in war, I place my office without further parley at your disposal.

It is with great personal regret that I have come to this conclusion. In spite of mean and unworthy insinuations to the contrary—insinuations which I fear are always inevitable in the case of men who hold prominent but not primary positions in any administration—I have felt a strong personal attachment to you as my chief. As you yourself said, on Sunday, we have acted together for ten years and never had a quarrel, although we have had many a grave difference on questions of policy. You have treated me with great courtesy and kindness; for all that I thank you. Nothing would have induced me to part now except an overwhelming sense that the course of action which has been pursued has put the country—and not merely the country, but throughout the world, the principles for which you and I have always stood throughout our political lives—in the greatest peril that has ever overtaken them.

[5] From a letter dated December 5, 1916. Quoted in Roy Jenkins, *Asquith* (London, 1964), p. 452. Copyright © 1964 by Roy Jenkins. Reprinted by permission of Chilmark Press, Inc. and Wm. Collins Sons & Co. Ltd. For other letters written to Asquith at this time, see p. 101 of this volume. The details of this crisis are documented in Lord Beaverbrook, *Politicians and the War 1914–1916* (London, 1966).

As I am fully conscious of the importance of preserving national unity, I propose to give your Government complete support in the vigorous prosecution of the War; but unity without action is nothing but futile carnage, and I cannot be responsible for that. Vigour and vision are the supreme need at this hour.

WAR LEADER

Two days later, Lloyd George became Prime Minister, supported by most Conservatives and by many Liberals. Men and women of all parties looked to him to pursue the war with vigor. Although he was deeply involved in the many daily problems of war administration, Lloyd George did not neglect, as Asquith had done, to keep in contact with the people. He spoke frequently, and with zest.

What is the urgent task in front of the Government? To complete and make even more effective the mobilisation of all our national resources, so as to enable the nation to bear the strain, however prolonged, and to march through to victory, however lengthy and however exhausting may be the journey. It is a gigantic task, and let me give this word of warning: If there be any who have given their confidence to the new Administration in expectation of a speedy victory, they will be doomed to disappointment. I am not going to paint a gloomy picture of the military situation—if I did, it would not be a true picture—but I must paint a stern picture, because that accurately represents the facts. I have always insisted on the nation being taught to realise the actual facts of this war. I have attached enormous importance to that at the risk of being characterised as a pessimist. I believe that a good many of our misunderstandings have arisen from exaggerated views which have been taken about successes and from a disposition to treat as trifling real set-backs. To imagine that you can only get the support and the help, and the best help, of a strong people by concealing difficulties is to show a fundamental misconception. The British people possess as sweet a tooth as anybody, and they like pleasant things put on the table, but that is not the stuff that they have been brought up on. That is not what the British Empire has been nourished on. Britain has never shown at its best except when it was confronted with a real danger and understood it.[6]

6 From Hansard, December 19, 1916. Reprinted by permission of the Controller of Her Majesty's Stationery Office.

There are some people engaged in a constant and systematic grumble. The peace propaganda is fed with grumbles. These people are anxious to break down the national nerve and then to rush us into a premature and disastrous peace. Let us beware of playing their game. We have challenged a sinister power which is menacing the world with enslavement. It would have been better never to have issued the challenge unless we meant to carry it through. A challenged power which is not overthrown always becomes stronger for the challenge. The people who think that they can begin a new era of peace while the Prussian military power is unbeaten are labouring under a strange delusion. We have all been dreaming of a new world to appear when the deluge of war has subsided. Unless we achieve victory for the great cause for which we entered this war the new world will simply be the old world with the heart out of it.

The old world, at least, believed in ideals. It believed that justice, fair play, liberty, righteousness must triumph in the end; that is, however you interpret the phrase, the old world believed in God, and it staked its existence on that belief. Millions of gallant young men volunteered to die for that divine faith. But if wrong emerged triumphant out of this conflict, the new world would feel in its soul that brute force alone counted in the government of man; and the hopelessness of the dark ages would once more fall on the earth like a cloud. To redeem Britain, to redeem Europe, to redeem the world from this doom must be the settled purpose of every man and woman who places duty above ease. This is the fateful hour of mankind. If we are worthy of the destiny with which it is charged, untold generations of men will thank God for the strength which He gave us to endure to the end.[7]

THE FAILURE OF THE GENERALS [8]

Over a million British and Empire troops had been killed during the war. It was a bitter reflection for Lloyd George that more men had died during his two years as Prime Minister than in the first two years of the war when Asquith was in power. In his war memoirs Lloyd George sought to lay the responsibility for the high death rate upon the Commander-in-Chief, General Sir Douglas Haig, over whom Lloyd George had been unable to exercise any significant influence, and toward whom he had developed a bitter hostility.

[7] From a speech delivered at Gray's Inn, London, on December 14, 1917. Published in D. Lloyd George, *The Great Crusade*. (London, 1918).

[8] From David Lloyd George, *War Memoirs* (London, 1938), pp. 1322–24, 2013–15. Reprinted by permission of Beaverbrook Newspapers Ltd. For Lloyd George's relations with Haig, see Duff Cooper, *Haig* (London, 1935), and Robert Blake, ed., *The Private Papers of Douglas Haig 1914–1919* (London, 1952).

Those who were responsible for planning and persisting in the plan when it had failed, were not men of imagination. All that quality was concentrated in the information bureau. The planning department were conspicuously devoid of it. In the absence of this rare gift there ought to have been a meticulous examination of the ground and a careful and honest survey of the enemy's resources in men and munitions. Unfortunately, the General Officer who prepared the plans for attack after attack across kilometres of untraversable quagmire, and the General who had control of what was by a strange irony called "Intelligence," and whose business it was to sift all the information that came in, and to prepare the reports upon which plans were based, never themselves got near enough to the battlefield to see what it was like. They worked on the basis of optimistic reports in the shelter of a remote chateau, out of sight of the mud and far from the sound of the deadly clatter of the machine-guns. Where draft plans had been submitted, received and approved, the fatal ink, which in a few days would be converted into blood, set forth orders and instructions which were not smudged by a drop of the devastating rain that drowned the wounded warriors who fell in a vain attempt to realise these paper dreams. If General Headquarters received any reports as to the conditions under which the men were asked to attack, those reports were never passed on to the War Council. Were they presented to the Commander-in-Chief? Gough told him something of the realities. But Haig was not a man to encourage discouraging reports.

A great deal of the catastrophe is due to the change effected by modern methods of warfare in the opportunities and therefore in the personal risks and responsibilities of Commanders. At Waterloo, Napoleon and Wellington could see the whole battlefield with their eyes, and with the help of field-glasses almost every hump and hollow. Even then Napoleon overlooked the sunken road.

But in modern warfare, the more important the General, the less he feels it to be his duty to see for himself what the battlefield is like. Wellington's Generals were on the field amongst their troops. No General in this war—and these remarks apply to every army in the field on both sides—was expected to visit no-man's-land until the battleground had been made safe for "brass hats" by retreat of the enemy to an invisible distance. Some of them courted danger to inspire their troops and to view the ground for themselves, and in doing so, several fell. But the rule was that Generals no longer led but sent their troops into action. This transformation may have been inevitable owing to the magnitude and the character of the operations and also owing to the increased power and range of the weapons used. But the increase in the danger factor cannot be pleaded in defence of so revolutionary a change. Admirals share risks with their sailors in a sea-fight. The departure from time-honoured ideas as to the duty of personal observation is due either to an exaggerated estimate of the importance of the individual General, or to an under-estimate of the qualities of the officers available to take the place of superiors in rank who have fallen. The price paid in this War for immunity to Generals was prodigious. No one suggests that it is the duty of Generals to lead their men up to the barbed wire, through the mud, whilst machine-guns are playing upon them. But, had men high up in military rank, ordering or continuing an offensive, been obliged by the exigencies of duty to view for themselves something of the character of the terrain of attack and the nature of the operation they were ordering their officers and men to undertake, the fatuous assaults of the Somme, Monchy, Bullecourt, the Chemin des Dames and Passchendaele would never have occurred; or at any rate one such experience would have been enough.

It is not for me to express an opinion as to whether the change which has taken place in the duties and dangers of Generals is justified. This comment, however, I am entitled to make. If Generals are no longer under any necessity to join their men in an attack or even to go within the zone of fire, it is more incumbent upon them than ever to exercise the greatest care in ascertaining the kind of task they call upon their officers and men to carry through. Apart from good generalship, the obligations of comradeship and of common decency demand it. The men who persisted in the Passchendaele assaults could not have known the conditions under which their orders had to be executed. It is an insult to their intelligence, let alone their humanity, to believe otherwise. I have quoted reputable evidence to prove that some of them had no idea of the actual state of the ground which they commanded tanks and troops to cross. Gough knew and passed his knowledge on to Haig. It seems to have made no impression on the latter's obsessed mind. His apologists quote his obduracy as a proof of the sublime courage that disdained obstacles and dangers. The fact that they were obstacles and dangers which had to be faced only by others and not himself would not, I feel sure, weigh with him. Had he been a humble officer he would have faced them without quaking. No one ever cast a doubt on his personal courage. But it demanded a much higher courage to own up that he had been guilty of a grave error of judgment— that the operation he had planned was an impossible one—that, in fact, he had been wrong and the subordinate generals and interfering politicians had been right.

Thus G.H.Q. never witnessed, not even through a telescope, the attacks it ordained, except on carefully prepared charts where the advancing battalions were represented by the pencil which marched with ease across swamps and marked lines of triumphant progress without the loss of a single point. As for the mud, it never incommoded the movements of this irrestible pencil.

No wonder that nothing daunted a Staff working under such conditions. They could afford to be the very incarnation of ruthlessness and vicarious heroism: the gods of war, not on the battlefield, but in their temple.

I was privileged, whilst this horrible battle was proceeding, to have a talk with one of Haig's most prominent military advisers, who afterwards owned that he had no idea of the conditions under which the battle was fought. I entreated him once more to reconsider the prospects of this venture in the light of what had actually happened. But he also was imbued with the relentlessness of his Chief. He treated me as a stupid civilian who knew nothing of war. When I alluded to the terrible casualties, he reminded me in Hotspur strain that you could not expect to make war without death and wounds. When I pointed to the wet season which had soaked the ground and made it unfit for the passage of tanks, artillery, or men, he said: Battles could not be stopped like tennis matches for a shower. Here again was Mars, but, I thought, Mars under an umbrella.

                                    *   *   *

I had no reason to believe that Haig was in the least interested in the conflict of parties, as such. He preferred Asquith's method of dealing with Generals to mine. After Asquith made an appointment in any Department he was always inclined not to concern himself with what occurred in that Department unless and until Parliamentary trouble was threatened over some of its operations. The less he heard from or of a Department the better he was pleased. He exercised no close supervision over the doings of his Ministers or Generals. His easy-going temperament suited both much better than mine or Mr. Winston Churchill's! No wonder that both Haig and Robertson preferred him and his methods. During the critical days of the War, when it was important not to undermine public confidence in the Commander-in-Chief of our own Army, I made no public attack on his personal fitness for so immense a responsibility, but I never concealed from myself or my colleagues that I thought Sir Douglas Haig was intellectually and temperamentally unequal to the command of an Army of millions fighting battles on fields which were invisible to any Commander.

In substance Mr. Duff Cooper admits that I was justified in my estimate of Haig's mental equipment for such a task. According to him, Haig was as good a soldier as a man can be who did not possess genius—that means he was a second-rate Commander in unparalleled and unforseen circumstances, where the resources of even a first-rate leader like Foch were only just adequate to pull us through. He had a long training on lines which were irrelevant to the experiences and exigencies of this War. That was not his fault. There never had been such a war, and the narrow and rigid system which he had learnt and taught made it difficult for so unsupple a mind to adapt himself readily to any other ideas. He was above the average of his profession in intelligence and industry—perhaps more in industry than intelligence. He was always a steady and conscientious worker. No one could impute to him indolence or slackness in the discharge of his duty. He possessed an untiring tenacity of purpose. But Mr. Duff Cooper's appreciation of his gifts acknowledges in effect that he was not endowed with any of the elements of imagination and vision which determine the line of demarcation between genius and ordinary capacity. And he certainly had none of that personal magnetism which has enabled great leaders of men to inspire multitudes with courage, faith and a spirit of sacrifice. I was not thinking of the great gods of war like Alexander, Hannibal, Caesar or Napoleon. It would be unfair to challenge a comparison between them and any of the Generals of the Great War.

Haig was not endowed with the magnetic qualities and the discerning eye of a Cromwell, a Marlborough or a Stonewall Jackson. I had once the unforgettable privilege of conversing with a number of Confederate officers and men who had taken part in the American Civil War. They had fought, some under Lee, others under Jackson, Beauregard and Jeb Stuart. The personality that had made the deepest impression on these survivors of a hundred battles was Stonewall Jackson. I asked one of the veterans what was the secret of his hold on his soldiers. "Well," he said, "all I can tell you is that once when we were given what seemed to us an impossible position to storm the men were reluctant to advance in face of fire until an officer went up to them and said to them: 'We must do it—these are the orders of General Jackson.' Upon which they cried out: 'Oh, it is Old Jack! Why didn't you tell us that before?' They all leapt up and swept along through bullets and shells. They knew that he never gave them an impossible task. He never ordered an attack until he was convinced by a careful survey of the ground that its capture was attainable by brave and resolute men."

The only Army Commander in France who commanded that kind of confidence in his men was Plumer. Haig never inspired that feeling in his army. His name never sent a thrill through the ranks on the eve of a battle—his presence he never vouchsafed on these occasions. I have spoken to hundreds who fought in his battles from Festubert to Passchendaele and they all testify to that absence of inspiration which flows from the words, presence or personality of a great leader. That is why the appointment of Foch as Generalissimo was hailed with such relief and delight throughout the British Army. Haig undoubtedly lacked those highest qualities which were essential in a great Commander in the greatest war the world has ever seen. He was incapable of planning vast campaigns on the scale demanded on so immense a battle area. The problem set before a Commander of two million men on a hundred-mile battle front was one which needed capacity of a very high order.

No British General was ever given so gigantic an undertaking. It was far beyond his mental equipment.

Serving under Marlborough, Wellington or Cromwell, he would have been a highly competent leader in a field every acre of which was visible to his own eyes. But when he had to fight battles in quagmires he had never seen and over an area extending to a hundred miles which he never did or could personally inspect, he was lost. He did not possess that eye within an eye which is imagination. He was like the blind King of Bohemia at Crecy. He was entirely dependent on others for information essential to judgment, and those he chose to enlighten and guide him were not only just as devoid of vision as he was himself, but were not his equals in experience, intelligence or conscience. When, in addition to all that, he was called upon in his computations to visualise other battle fronts in far lands or in other continents, some of them hundreds and some thousands of miles away, his mind could not range over such distances, and he felt that to devote any of our resources to assist in these enterprises was like expending explosive energy on flights to the moon, when he needed every kilowatt to drive a few yards at a time over obstacles placed along the bit of earth which was in front of him.

4
Peacemaking and Diplomacy

No quarrel ought ever to be converted into a policy.
                                    —LLOYD GEORGE (*in 1922*)

Injustice, arrogance, displayed in the hour of triumph will never be forgotten or forgiven.
                                    —LLOYD GEORGE (*in 1919*)

Nations, like dogs, are always convinced that the other dog is out to steal their bone.
                                    —LLOYD GEORGE (*in 1932*)

During his social reform days Lloyd George had revealed many unexpected streaks of moderation. In industrial disputes he had triumphed, not in the role of militant strikebreaker, but in that of conciliator. Between 1918 and 1922, while peacetime Prime Minister, he showed this same zeal for compromise in his dealings with the defeated nations. After the Allied victory he did not seek to crush Germany into a permanent, embittered submission. His aim became the reconciliation of the former combatants. He hoped to supervise the gradual whittling away of international hatreds. He knew that a smoldering desire for revenge must lead, in a short time, to new wars. He felt strongly that statesmanship consisted in bringing the victors and the vanquished together as soon as possible, at a conference table where enmity would give way to mutual confidence. Even at the Paris Conference, within a few months of the end of the war, his was increasingly the voice of moderation.

THE SEARCH FOR A JUST PEACE [1]

During the Paris Peace Conference Lloyd George was made aware of the extent to which national ambitions and fears

---

[1] From the final draft of The Fontainebleau Memorandum. Quoted in Martin Gilbert, *The Roots of Appeasement* (New York, 1967), Appendix I, pp. 189–96. Reprinted by permission of the author and The New American Library, Inc. This volume contains a full account of Lloyd George's diplomatic activity from 1919 to 1922.

*distorted the judgment of the peacemakers. One weekend he left
Paris for the country and wrote down his troubled thoughts.*

When nations are exhausted by wars in which they have put forth
all their strength and which leave them tired, bleeding, and broken,
it is not difficult to patch up a peace that may last until the generation
which experienced the horrors of the war has passed away. Pictures of
heroism and triumph only tempt those who know nothing of the
sufferings and terrors of war. It is therefore comparatively easy to
patch up a peace which will last for 30 years.

What is difficult, however, is to draw up a peace which will not
provoke a fresh struggle when those who have had practical experience
of what war means have passed away. History has proved that a peace
which has been hailed by a victorious nation as a triumph of diplomatic
skill and statesmanship, even of moderation, in the long run has proved
itself to be short-sighted and charged with danger to the victor. The
peace of 1871 was believed by Germany to ensure not only her security
but her permanent supremacy. The facts have shown exactly the
contrary. France itself has demonstrated that those who say you can
make Germany so feeble that she will never be able to hit back are
utterly wrong. Year by year France became numerically weaker in
comparison with her victorious neighbour, but in reality she became
ever more powerful. She kept watch on Europe; she made alliance
with those whom Germany had wronged or menaced; she never ceased
to warn the world of its danger and ultimately she was able to secure
the overthrow of the mightier power which had trampled so brutally
upon her. You may strip Germany of her colonies, reduce her armaments
to a mere police force and her navy to that of a fifth rate power; all
the same in the end if she feels that she has been unjustly treated in
the peace of 1919 she will find means of exacting retribution from her
conquerors. The impression, the deep impression, made upon the
human heart by four years of unexampled slaughter will disappear with
the hearts upon which it has been marked by the terrible sword of the
great war. The maintenance of peace will then depend upon there
being no causes of exasperation constantly stirring up the spirit of
patriotism, of justice or of fair play to achieve redress. Our terms may
be severe, they may be stern and even ruthless, but at the same time they
can be so just that the country on which they are imposed will feel in
its heart that it has no right to complain. But injustice, arrogance, displayed in the hour of triumph will never be forgotten or forgiven.

For these reasons I am, therefore, strongly averse to transferring more
Germans from German rule to the rule of some other nation than can
possibly be helped. I cannot conceive any greater cause of future war

than that the German people, who have certainly proved themselves one of the most vigorous and powerful races in the world, should be surrounded by a number of small states, many of them consisting of people who have never previously set up a stable government for themselves, but each of them containing large masses of Germans clamouring for reunion with their native land. The proposal of the Polish Commission that we should place 2,100,000 Germans under the control of a people which is of a different religion and which has never proved its capacity for stable self-government throughout its history must, in my judgment, lead sooner or later to a new war in the East of Europe. . . .

If we are wise, we shall offer to Germany a peace, which, while just, will be preferable for all sensible men to the alternative of Bolshevism. I would, therefore, put it in the forefront of the peace that once she accepts our terms, especially reparation, we will open to her the raw materials and markets of the world on equal terms with ourselves, and will do everything possible to enable the German people to get upon their legs again. We cannot both cripple her and expect her to pay.

Finally, we must offer terms which a responsible Government in Germany can expect to be able to carry out. If we present terms to Germany which are unjust, or excessively onerous, no responsible Government will sign them; certainly the present weak administration will not. If it did, I am told that it would be swept away within 24 hours. Yet if we can find nobody in Germany who will put his hand to a peace treaty, what will be the position? A large army of occupation for an indefinite period is out of the question. Germany would not mind it. A very large number of people in that country would welcome it as it would be the only hope of preserving the existing order of things. The objection would not come from Germany, but from our own countries. Neither the British Empire nor America would agree to occupy Germany. France by itself could not bear the burden of occupation. We should therefore be driven back on the policy of blockading the country. That would inevitably mean spartacism from the Urals to the Rhine, with its inevitable consequence of a huge red army attempting to cross the Rhine. As a matter of fact I am doubtful whether public opinion would allow us deliberately to starve Germany. If the only difference between Germany and ourselves were between onerous terms and moderate terms, I very much doubt if public opinion would tolerate the deliberate condemnation of millions of women and children to death by starvation. If so the Allies would have incurred the moral defeat of having attempted to impose terms on Germany which Germany had successfully resisted.

From every point of view, therefore, it seems to me that we ought to endeavour to draw up a peace settlement as if we were impartial arbiters, forgetful of the passions of the war. This settlement ought to have three ends in view. First of all it must do justice to the Allies, by taking into account Germany's responsibility for the origin of the war, and for the way in which it was fought. Secondly, it must be a settlement which a responsible German Government can sign in the belief that it can fulfil the obligations it incurs. Thirdly, it must be a settlement which will contain in itself no provocations for future wars, and which will constitute an alternative to Bolshevism, because it will commend itself to all reasonable opinion as a fair settlement of the European problem.

AVOIDING "THE SCOURGE AND AGONY OF WAR" [2]

Before the Treaty was completed, Lloyd George was strongly criticized in Parliament and in the British press for undue leniency toward Germany (a leniency which historians have until recently almost entirely ignored) and for many points of detail (on which historians have ever since laid stress). He made his own defense at the time to those M.P.s who had sent a telegram to Paris criticizing his leniency and urging both a harsh and a speedy peace.

The task with which the Peace Delegates have been confronted has indeed been a gigantic one. No Conference that has ever assembled in the history of the world has been confronted with problems of such variety, of such complexity, of such magnitude, and of such gravity. The Congress of Vienna was the nearest approach to it. You had then to settle the affairs of Europe. It took eleven months. But the problems at the Congress of Vienna, great as they were, sink into insignificance compared with those which we have had to attempt to settle at the Paris Conference. It is not one continent that is engaged—every continent is affected. With very few exceptions, every country in Europe has been in this War. Every country in Asia is affected by the War, except Tibet and Afghanistan. There is not a square mile of Africa that has not been engaged in the War in one way or another. Almost the whole of the nations of America are in the War, and in the far islands of the Southern Seas there are islands that have been captured, and there are hundreds of thousands of men who have come to fight in this great world struggle. There has never been in the whole history of this globe anything to compare to it. Ten new States have sprung into existence, some of them independent, some of them semi-independent, some of them may be Protectorates, and, at any rate, although you

[2] From *Hansard*, April 16, 1919. Reprinted by permission of the Controller of Her Majesty's Stationery Office.

may not define their boundaries, you must give indications of them. The boundaries of fourteen countries have to be re-cast.

That will give some idea of the difficulties, purely of a territorial character, that have engaged our attention. But there are problems, equally great and equally important, not of a territorial character, but all affecting the peace of the world, all affecting the well-being of men, all affecting the destiny of the human race, and every one of them of a character where, if you make blunders, humanity may have to pay. Armaments, economic questions, which are the life of commerce and trade, questions of international waterways and railways, the question of indemnities—not an easy one, and not going to be settled by telegram—and international arrangements for labour practically never attempted before! . . . And there is that great organisation—a great experiment, but an experiement upon which the whole future of the globe for peace hangs—the Society of Nations.

All, and each of them separately, would occupy months. A blunder might precipitate universal war—it may be near, it may be distant. And all nations, almost every nation on earth, engaged in the consideration of all these problems! We were justified in taking some time. In fact, I do not mind saying that it would have been imperative in some respects that we should have taken more time but for one fact, and that is that we are setting up a machinery which is capable of readjusting and correcting possible mistakes. That is why the League of Nations, instead of wasting time, has saved the time of the Conference. We had to shorten our labours and work crowded hours, long and late, because, whilst we were trying to build, we saw in many lands the foundations of society crumbling into dust, and we had to make haste. I venture to say that no body of men ever worked harder, and that no body of men have ever worked in better harmony. I am doubtful whether any body of men with a difficult task have worked under greater difficulties —stones clattering on the roof, and crashing through the windows, and sometimes wild men screaming through the keyholes. . . .

When enormous issues are depending upon it, you require calm deliberation. I ask it for the rest of the journey. The journey is not at an end. It is full of perils, perils for this country, perils for all lands, perils for the people throughout the world. I beg, at any rate, that the men who are doing their best should be left in peace to do it, or that other men should be sent there.

Those are merely artificial difficulties. They are difficulties that are more trying to the temper than to the judgment. But there are intrinsic difficulties of an extraordinary character. You are dealing with a multitude of nations, most of them with a problem of its own, each and every one of them with a different point of view, even where the problems are common, looking from a different angle at questions—sometimes, perhaps, with different interests; and it requires all the tact, all the patience, and all the skill that we can command to prevent different interests from developing into conflicting interests. I want the House and the country to bear that in mind. I believe that we have surmounted those difficulties, but it has not been easy. There were questions one never heard of which have almost imperilled the peace of Europe while we were sitting there.

I should like to put each Member of this House under an examination. I am certain that I could not have passed it before I went to the Peace Conference. How many Members have heard of Teschen? I do not mind saying that I had never heard of it, but Teschen very nearly produced an angry conflict between two Allied States, and we had to interrupt the proceedings to try and settle the affairs at Teschen. There are many questions of that kind where commissions have had to be sent, and where we have had to smooth difficulties, in order to enable us to get on with the bigger problems of the War. And those questions are important. They are questions of small States. It was the quarrel for small States that made the great War. The difficulties of the Balkans —I believe they disturbed Europe, they created the atmosphere of unrest which began the trouble, they aroused the military temper, and I am not at all sure they did not excite the blood lust in Europe. One of the features of the present situation is that, owing to the break-up of great Empires, Central Europe is being broken into small States, and the greatest care must be taken that no cause of future unrest shall be created by the settlements which we make. . . .

We want peace. We want a peace which will be just, but not vindictive. We want a stern peace, because the occasion demands it. The crime demands it. But its severity must be designed, not to gratify vengeance, but to vindicate justice. Every clause and term in those conditions must be justified on that ground. Above all, we want to protect the future against a repetition of the horrors of this War, by making the wrongdoer repair the wrong and the loss which he has inflicted by his wanton aggression, by punishing any individual who is responsible, by depriving the nations that have menaced the peace of Europe for half a century with a flourishing sword—by depriving them of their weapon . . . by avoiding conditions which would create a legitimate sense of wrong, which would excite national pride needlessly to seek opportunities for redress, and by giving the most permanent security to the nations of the earth to federate for a firm purpose of maintaining right. . . .

One of the most beneficent results of peace, in my judgment, will be that the great continental menace of armaments will be swept away. The country that has kept Europe armed for forty years is to be reduced to an army which is just adequate to police her cities and her villages, and with her fleet, which was a sort of terror to us—a hidden terror— she will now have just enough to protect her commerce, and no more. We must profit by that. Europe must profit by it, and not Germany alone. I know there is a good deal of talk about the recrudescence of the military power of Germany, and you get paragraphs about what Germany is going to do—she is going to release her fleet, and she is going to have great armies. That is not the danger. The fact is that, with difficulty, can she gather together 80,000 armed men to preserve order. Her guns have been taken away from her—her weapons of offence on the sea, on the land, and in the air.

That is not the danger. The world is going to pieces. A very keen observer who has just come from Central Europe said to me, "I have seen a world going to pieces—men helpless, half-starved, benumbed; no fight in them, no revolution, because the men have no heart." Two British soldiers crossing a square in Vienna saw a hungry child. They took out a biscuit, and cast it to the child. You have seen when you throw a bit of bread on the ground how birds flock from every part, birds that you have never seen before. Well, hundreds of children came from nowhere; they clawed for that food, and it was with difficulty that these two British soldiers escaped with their lives! . . .

That which I have described is the real danger. The gaunt spectre of hunger is stalking throughout the land. The Central Powers and Russia have overtaxed their strength in the conflict. They are lying prostrate, broken, and all these movements of Spartacists, and Bolsheviks, and revolutionaries in each of these countries are more like the convulsions of a broken-backed creature, crushed in a savage conflict. It is in these conditions, and with this material, that we are making peace. Nations with military ambitions have received a cruel lesson, nay, Europe itself has suffered more in the last five years than ever in the whole of its past history. The lesson has been a sharper one than ever. It has been administered to vaster multitudes of human beings than ever. The people have a more intelligent appreciation of what it means than ever. For that reason the opportunity of organising the world on the basis of peace is such a one as has never been presented to the world before, and in this fateful hour it is the supreme duty of statesmen in every land— of the Parliaments upon whose will statesmen depend, of those who guide and direct the public opinion which is the making of all—not to soil this triumph of right by indulging in the angry passions of the moment, but to consecrate the sacrifices of millions to the permanent redemption of the human race from the scourge and agony of war.

NO WAR WITH RUSSIA[3]

After the Bolshevik revolution of 1917 Lloyd George had sent British troops to Russia to protect Allied military stores and to
[3] From the previously unpublished Minutes of a Meeting of the Imperial War Cabinet held at 10 Downing Street, London, on December 31, 1918. Public Record

prevent any further German advance into Russia. When the European war ended, the British troops, together with American, Japanese, Serbian, Italian, French and Czechoslovak units, remained in Russia and helped the anti-Bolshevik "white" Russians in their attempt to destroy Bolshevism by force. Some of Lloyd George's colleagues, especially Churchill, Curzon and Birkenhead, believed that Britain had a moral duty to overthrow the Bolshevik tyranny. Lloyd George disagreed with them, as he explained to the Imperial War Cabinet:

He was definitely opposed to military intervention in any shape. In the first place, it appeared to him a tremendously serious undertaking. The Germans, who had occupied only a relatively small part of Russia, within striking distance of Petrograd and with practically nothing in front of them, had found themselves unable either to go to Petrograd or to save the situation in the west, while all the time they and the Austrians had something like a million men stuck in that morass, the greater part of whom they had not even yet succeeded in disentangling. In our case the Allies were on the mere fringe of Russia, with less than 100,000 troops. The Bolsheviks had raised their forces to 300,000, which might exceed 1,000,000 by March, and had greatly improved their organisation. Where were we to find the troops with which to march into the heart of Russia and occupy the country? We already had to find troops for Germany, Palestine, Mesopotamia, and the Caucasus. He asked what contribution Australia, Canada, or South Africa were prepared to furnish to the task of conquering and keeping down Russia? No British troops could be found for the purpose without conscription, and if Parliament endorsed conscription for that purpose he doubted whether the troops would go. Our citizen army were prepared to go anywhere for liberty, but they could not be convinced that the suppression of Bolshevism was a war for liberty.

A further reason which weighed with him was the danger that military intervention would only strengthen the very force which we set out to destroy. It was impossible to ignore the parallel of the French Revolution. There, too, there had been horrors as bad as, or worse than, those of the Bolsheviks, perpetrated by a small fraction which had secured the control of France. There, too, we were invited to help.

Office reference Cab 23/42. Among those present were the Prime Ministers of Canada, Australia, and South Africa, as well as Churchill and Curzon. Reprinted by permission of the Controller of Her Majesty's Stationery Office. Lloyd George's Russian policy is discussed in detail in Richard M. Ullman, *Intervention and the War* (Princeton and London, 1961). His clashes with Churchill are documented in Winston S. Churchill, *The Aftermath* (London, 1929).

Toulon and La Vendee corresponded to Riga and the Ukraine. But the very fact that we intervened enabled Danton to rally French patriotism and make the terror a military instrument. When the revolution was suppressed we were no better off. France became organised as a great military machine imbued with a passionate hatred against us. Were we prepared to face a revolutionary war against a population of over 100,000,000, associating ourselves in this intervention with allies like the Japanese, against whom feeling in Russia was so passionately strong? He knew of no authority on the strength of which we could be justified in hypothecating our resources and our manhood in the belief that the Russians would regard us as deliverers. For Russia to emancipate herself from Bolshevism would be a redemption, but the attempt to emancipate her by foreign armies might prove a disaster to Europe as well as to Russia. The one thing to spread Bolshevism was to attempt to suppress it. To send our soldiers to shoot down the Bolsheviks would be to create Bolsheviks here.

THE WORLD AND THE JEWS 4

Lloyd George never lost his basic concern for human justice. But it seemed often to be submerged during the troubled period from 1918 to 1922 when, as a peacetime Prime Minister, he had to deal with the contentious problems of civil war in Ireland, the extension and maintenance of British power in the Middle East, military intervention against Russian Bolshevism, and the domestic curses of slum housing, unemployment and industrial unrest. Shortly after he fell from power he wrote in his old, humanitarian vein on the Jewish question. It was his own wartime Government which, in 1917, had promised the Jews a national home in Palestine.

Of all the bigotries that savage the human temper there is none so stupid as the anti-Semitic. It has no basis in reason; it is not rooted in faith; it aspires to no ideal; it is just one of those dank and unwholesome weeds that grow in the morass of racial hatred. How utterly devoid of reason it is may be gathered from the fact that it is almost entirely confined to nations who worship Jewish prophets and apostles, revere the national literature of the Hebrews as the only inspired mes-

---

4 From an article entitled "Palestine and the Jews," first published in July 1923, and later in David Lloyd George, *Is It Peace?* (London, 1923), pp. 246–53. Reprinted by permission of Beaverbrook Newspapers Ltd. See also Lloyd George's speech on Jewish affairs published in Philip Guedalla, *Napoleon and Palestine* (London, 1925). Lloyd George's part in the making of the Balfour Declaration is described in Leonard Stein, *The Balfour Declaration* (London, 1961).

sage delivered by the Deity to mankind, and whose only hope of salvation rests on the precepts and promises of the great teachers of Judah. Yet, in the sight of these fanatics the Jews of today can do nothing right. If they are rich they are birds of prey. If they are poor they are vermin. If they are in favour of a war it is because they want to exploit the bloody feuds of the Gentiles to their own profit. If they are anxious for peace they are either instinctive cowards or traitors. If they give generously—and there are no more liberal givers than the Jews—they are doing it for some selfish purpose of their own. If they do not give—then what could one expect of a Jew but avarice? If labour is oppressed by great capital, the greed of the Jew is held responsible. If labour revolts against capital—as it did in Russia—the Jew is blamed for that also. If he lives in a strange land he must be persecuted and pogrommed out of it. If he wants to go back to his own he must be prevented. Through the centuries in every land, whatever he does, or intends, or fails to do, he has been pursued by the echo of the brutal cry of the rabble of Jerusalem against the greatest of all Jews—"Crucify Him!"

No good has ever come of nations that crucified Jews. It is poor and pusillanimous sport, lacking all the true qualities of manliness, and those who indulge in it would be the first to run away were there any element of danger in it. Jew-baiters are generally of the type that found good reasons for evading military service when their own country was in danger.

The latest exhibition of this wretched indulgence is the agitation against settling poor Jews in the land their fathers made famous. Palestine under Jewish rule once maintained a population of 5,000,000. Under the blighting rule of the Turk it barely supported a population of 700,000. The land flowing with milk and honey is now largely a stony and unsightly desert. To quote one of the ablest and most far-sighted business men of today,

> It is a land of immense possibilities, in spite of the terrible neglect of its resources resulting from Turkish misrule. It is a glorious estate let down by centuries of neglect. The Turks cut down the forests and never troubled to replant them. They slaughtered the cattle and never troubled to replace them.

It is one of the peculiarities of the Jew-hunter that he adores the Turk.

If Palestine is to be restored to a condition even approximating to its ancient prosperity, it must be by settling Jews on its soil. The condition to which the land has been reduced by centuries of the most devastating oppression in the world is such that restoration is only possible by a race that is prepared for sentimental reasons to make and endure sacrifices for the purpose. What is the history of the Jewish settlement in Palestine? It did not begin with the Balfour Declaration. A century ago there were barely 10,000 Jews in the whole of Palestine. Before the War there were 100,000. The War considerably reduced these numbers, and immigration since 1918 has barely filled up the gaps. At the present timorous rate of progress it will be many years before it reaches 200,000.

Jewish settlement started practically seventy years ago, with Sir Moses Montefiore's experiment in 1854—another War year. The Sultan had good reasons for propitiating the Jews in that year, as the Allied had in 1917. So the Jewish resettlement of Palestine began. From that day onwards it has proceeded slowly but steadily. The land available was not of the best. Prejudices and fears had to be negotiated. Anything in the nature of wholesale expropriation of Arab cultivators, even for cash, had to be carefully avoided. The Jews were, therefore, often driven to settle on barren sand dunes and malarial swamps. . . .

Everywhere the Jew cultivator produces heavier and richer crops than his Arab neighbour. He has introduced into Palestine more scientific methods of cultivation, and his example is producing a beneficent effect on the crude tillage of the Arab peasant. It will be long ere Canaan becomes once more a land flowing with milk and honey. The effects of the neglect and misrule of centuries cannot be effaced by the issue of a Declaration. The cutting down of the trees has left the soil unprotected against the heavy rains and the rocks which were once green with vineyards and olive groves have been swept bare. The terraces which ages of patient industry built up have been destroyed by a few generations of Turkish stupidity. They cannot be restored in a single generation. Great irrigation works must be constructed if settlement is to proceed on a satisfactory scale. Palestine possesses in some respects advantages for the modern settler which to its ancient inhabitants were a detriment. Its one great river and its tributaries are rapid and have a great fall. For power this is admirable. Whether for irrigation, or for the setting up of new industries, this gift of nature to Palestine is only rendered capable of exploitation by the scientific discoveries of the last century. The tableland of Judea has a rainfall which if caught in reservoirs at appropriate centres would make of the "desert of Judea" a garden. If this be done Arab and Jew alike share in the prosperity.

There are few countries on earth which have made less of their possibilities. Take its special attractions for the tourist. I was amazed to find that the visitors to Palestine in the whole course of a year only aggregate 15,000. It contains the most famous shrines in the world. Its history is of more absorbing interest to the richest peoples on earth, and is better taught to their children, than even that of their own country. Some of its smallest villages are better known to countless millions than many a prosperous modern city. Hundreds of thousands ought to be treading this sacred ground every year. Why are they not doing so? The answer is: Turkish misrule scared away the pilgrim. Those who went there came back disillusioned and disappointed. The modern "spies" on their return did not carry with them the luscious grapes of Escol to thrill the multitude with a desire to follow their example. They brought home depressing tales of squalor, discomfort, and exaction which dispelled the glamour and discouraged further pilgrimages. Settled government gives the Holy Land its first chance for 1900 years. But there is so much undeveloped country demanding the attention of civilisation that Palestine will lose that chance unless it is made the special charge of some powerful influence. The Jews alone can redeem it from the wilderness and restore its ancient glory.

In that trust there is no injustice to any other race. The Arabs have neither the means, the energy, nor the ambition to discharge this duty. The British Empire has too many burdens on its shoulders to carry this experiment through successfully. The Jewish race with its genius, its resourcefulness, its tenacity, and not least its wealth, can alone perform this essential task. . . .

There are fourteen millions of Jews in the world. They belong to a race which for at least 1900 years has been subjected to proscription, pillage, massacre and the torments of endless derision—a race that has endured persecution, which for the variety of torture, physical, material and mental, inflicted on its victims, for the virulence and malignity with which it has been sustained, for the length of time it has lasted, and more than all for the fortitude and patience with which it has been suffered, is without parallel in the history of any other people. Is it too much to ask that those amongst them whose sufferings are the worst shall be able to find refuge in the land their fathers made holy by the splendour of their genius, by the loftiness of their thoughts, by the consecration of their lives, and by the inspiration of their message to mankind?

"A BAD OUTLOOK FOR EUROPE"

Between the wars Lloyd George saw two interrelated solutions to the problem of European peace. The first was the need for France to accept Germany as a powerful neighbor and to discard the anti-German passions which the war had understandably created. The second was for America to relieve Europe of the burden of war debts and to play a more positive and constructive part in European affairs than she was willing to do. Neither came to pass. France continued to be deeply suspicious of even a democratic and disarmed Germany. American isolationist sentiment survived even beyond the beginning of the Second World War in 1939.

What a muddle it all is! France and Germany are both anxious to settle in the Ruhr, but are too proud to admit it. The struggle, therefore, goes on, and will continue to the detriment of both. Belgium is sorry she ever entered the Ruhr, but cannot get out of it. Every time she tries to get away France pulls her back roughly by the tail of her coat, so she has to do sentry-go at Essen whilst her franc is leading a wild life at home. Italy has forgotten that she ever sanctioned the occupation, and her moral indignation is mounting rapidly, although it has not yet risen to a height which is visible across the Alps. Great Britain is growling futile notes of dissatisfaction with everybody—France and Germany alike. The confusion of tongues is deafening and paralysing, and no one is quite happy except the spirit of mischief who is holding his sides with ghoulish laughter. He never had such a time—not since the Tower of Babel. And this time it may end in a second deluge.

The horror of the Great War seems to have unhinged the European mind. Nations do not think normally. The blood pressure is still very high. The excitement over the Ruhr does not tend to improve it. When some of the articles written and speeches delivered today come to be read by the diligent historian a generation hence, he will recognise there the ravings of a continent whose mental equilibrium has been upset by a great shock. The real issue involved in all this struggle is a comparatively simple one. How much can Germany pay and in what way can she pay? America, Britain, Italy and Germany are all agreed that the only way to settle that question is to appoint competent experts to investigate and report upon it. The Pope also has blessed this reasonable suggestion. France, on the contrary, says it is a question to be determined by guns and generals—both equally well fitted for that task. Germany must present her accounts to the mitrailleuse and argue her case before the soixante-quinze. It is a mad world.

Frenchmen are now sowing the same seeds of anger in the German breast. Hatreds are bad negotiators. That is why I despair of a real settlement.

But Germany may collapse. She might even break up, temporarily. The authority of the Central Government has already largely disappeared. There is practically no collection of taxes. The mark has gone down in a little over a week from 1,000,000 to the £ to 27,000,000. How can any Government collect taxes in such a fugitive and attenuated currency? You might as well try to collect land taxes on the tail of a comet. The state of the currency is but a symptom of the general disintegration. Berlin has ceased to wield any influence in Bavaria, and the Monarchy might be restored in that Province at no distant date. There is a movement in the Rhineland to set up a Republic freed from the dominion of Prussia. This movement is fostered by French agencies and financed by French subventions. If it is declared Prussia will not be allowed to suppress it. We may, therefore, soon witness a Rhineland Republic whose glorious freedom and independence will be jealously guarded against internal as well as external foes by the coloured warriors of Senegal and Cochin-China. Saxony might be captured by Communists and Prussia be torn between Monarchist and Communist. These are not unlikely happenings. Is it too much to say they are not altogether out of the computation of French statesmanship? If Germany dissolves, then the Rhineland and the Ruhr would remain under the dominion of France. France would not secure Reparations, but she would enjoy security, and she would, so it is conjectured, enormously enhance her power in the world. An old French dream would be realised. The work of Bismarck would be undone and the achievement of Napoleon would be restored and perpetuated. There is an old Welsh adage which says that it is easy to kindle a fire on an old hearthstone. This idea of a Rhineland under French domination is the old hearthstone of Charlemagne. Mazarin sought to relight its flames. Napoleon the First kindled on it a blaze that scorched Europe. Napoleon the Third had hopes of warming his chilling fortunes at the glow of its embers, and now the great victory of 1918 has set French ambitions once more reviving the fires on the old hearthstone of a Rhineland ruled by the Frank.

Altogether it is a bad look-out for Europe.[5]

America ought not to misunderstand the nature of the European plea for cancellation of all war-debts, including reparations. Europe is not suing America in forma pauperis. Britain certainly has never done so, and is not in the least disposed to do so now. She is in respect of war-debts more a creditor country than a debtor, with a substantial balance in her favour. But she has been and still is the largest international trader, and knows the folly and danger, from the standpoint of world business, of keeping alive these debts incurred for no value received. Her attitude is dictated by that common sense which knows when it is wise to be magnanimous.

America is the largest—but not so much the largest—war creditor. Has she not found out that she is not immune from the perils which have afflicted the trade of Britain, and that these perils are intensified if not created by combining an insistence on payment of debts with the exclusion at the same time of all the goods whereby alone they can be paid? Let America believe that when Europe pleads for cancellation, it is not the appeal of a shifty debtor who is whining for mercy. Europe has paid

    [5] From an article entitled "The Napoleonic Dream," first published in August 1923 and later in David Lloyd George, Is It Peace? (London, 1923), pp. 103–12. Reprinted by permission of Beaverbrook Newspapers Ltd.

until American banks are gorged with her gold, and Germany especially has made such efforts to pay that she is staggering at her bench from sheer exhaustion. France is putting forward no plea. She is quite content to let her debts be paid for her by her ancient enemy. Her theory is that it keeps the Germans out of mischief, and that anyhow they thoroughly deserve the trouble they are in because of the greater trouble they have wrought.

America holds the key of the gateway which leads to prosperity, for herself as well as for the world. Britain has already surrendered her keys. The Hoover moratorium was a forward step toward that gateway, but it stopped short of a final opening of the road. It delayed the threatened crash in Central Europe, but it has not averted it. No one knows what will happen when the moratorium lapses. The uncertainty paralyses enterprise. Industry and finance are afraid of moving forward lest they be overwhelmed by the crazy edifice, when its temporary props are withdrawn.

America had better make up her mind soon—as soon as the Presidential Election is over—to make the best of a bad job, bearing in mind the wise words that the Secretary to the American Treasury uttered years ago in his Debt Commission Report: The entire foreign debt is not worth as much to the American people in dollars and cents as a prosperous Europe as a customer. Europe cannot pay unless America takes her goods. If America cannot in her own interests take payment in goods— and she must be the sole judge of that—then Europe has no other means of paying, for her gold is already shared between America and France. If America follows the wise example of a country older in the ways of international commerce than herself, and agrees to cancellation, she will be cutting her loss to ensure a greater gain. She must know by now that she can no more keep out European bankruptcy from invading her fields and factories than she can keep the wind from sweeping across the Atlantic from the shores of Europe, over her highest barriers and through imperceptible crevices into her most carefully constructed shelters.

It is no use saying, "Let Europe go to perdition!" The last war proved that if Europe goes there, it will in the end drag America along. Twelve years of peace have furnished another illustration of the same inevitable truth. That is why no thoughtful American can say, "Ring down the fire-curtain, and let Europe burn to ashes!" Ashes cannot pay debts; neither can ashes buy cotton, wheat, or copper. But America knows now that sparks from a European conflagration can cross the ocean. Indeed, they have already crossed, and the fire is still blazing there. Wall Street is a spectacle of blackened beams, and many an industry farther west exhibits skeletons of twisted girders. That is due to the fire which started in Europe; and the cellared riches that poured in from the depleted stores of Europe have only added fuel to the flames.

There is no country in the world so given to generous impulses as
America. And any great impulse in America leads straight to great action. One can never forget how during the War men and women of all
classes living in a land of overflowing abundance imposed voluntary
restrictions not only on their luxuries but on their plain comforts in
order to provide a surplus for distribution amongst the needy population
of their Allies in Europe. If America hesitates today to crown her
honourable mood of sacrifice for humanity in the War by relieving the
panting millions of Europe of a burden they agreed in the hour of their
agony to carry for American lenders, it is not because the people of the
great Republic are greedy, or grasping or mean. It is because they are
suspicious of Europe and not without some reason. Is it not possible
somehow to remove those suspicions when they are legitimate, not by
smooth words but by tangible deeds?

International suspicion is the root, not of all evil, but of some of the
worst of evils. Nations like dogs are always convinced that the other
dog is out to steal their bone and they take elaborate precautions against
the fancied calamity, wasting time and energy which would be much
more profitably employed in procuring a fresh supply. Much of our
world trouble has arisen from national misunderstanding and suspicions,
and its perpetuation is due to the same cause. However much man has
progressed individually in his social attitude towards his fellowman, in-
ternationally he is still in the canine stage. The Founder of the Christian
Faith answered the question, "Who is my neighbour?" with the reply,
"He who has fallen amongst thieves." Modern Nationalism answering the
question, "Who are my neighbours?" would respond, "They who would
fall on my country like thieves." That is the explanation of these Chinese
Walls of Armaments and Tariffs. Can we do something to dispel these
suspicions which like a dense fog are hanging on frontiers and prevent-
ing one nation from seeing another as it really is? Until we do so all
nations must suffer alike from this blighting weather that keeps back
the spring. America may say to Europe: "While you pretend that you
are too poor to pay your debts, you are finding annually a sum of £520,
000,000 to maintain and strengthen your colossal armaments. These
expensive and destructive pests got you into a horrible mess a few years
ago, and you dragged us in. Now you are worse than ever; you are spending more each year on incendiary bombs. If we forgive your debts you
will spend still more. Cut down those threatening and dangerous machines for human slaughter! Then we will reconsider the situation."

That would be quite a reasonable attitude to take up; although it is
not quite the same thing, as I have pointed out, to spend money, even
foolishly, inside a country in its own currency as to transmit it to another
country in the currency which would be accepted there. All the same,
armaments are a menacing and hazardous expenditure, and it would be a
service to humanity if America made the fullest use of her dominant

financial position to enforce such a reduction as would render them harmless.[6]

HITLER: NO AGGRESSIVE INTENTIONS [7]

By 1936 Lloyd George had been out of office for fourteen years. He felt that Britain was being led by men lacking in vision and drive, and he turned momentarily and despairingly toward Adolf Hitler, in whom he thought he saw a man of vision.

He is a born leader of men. A magnetic, dynamic personality with a single-minded purpose. He is not merely in name, but in fact the natural leader. He has made them safe against potential enemies by whom they are surrounded. The old trust him. The young idolize him. . . .

The idea of a Germany intimidating Europe with a threat that its irresistible army might march across frontiers forms no part in the new vision. The Germans will resist to the death every invader of their own country, but they have no longer the desire themselves to invade any other land. The leaders of Modern Germany know too well that Europe is too formidable a proposition to be overrun and trampled down by any single nation, however powerful may be its armaments. They have learned that lesson in the war. Hitler fought in the ranks throughout the war, and knows from personal experience what war means. . . . The establishment of a German hegemony in Europe, which was the aim and dream of the old militarism, is not even on the horizon of Nazism.

It is now an avowed part of the Hitler policy to build up an army which will be strong enough to resist every invader from whatever quarter the attack may come. I believe he has already achieved that measure of immunity. No country, or combination of countries, could feel confident of overwhelming the Germany of today.

But it will take Germany at least ten years to build up an army strong enough to face the armies of Russia or France on any soil except her own.

Her conscript army is very young—there is a gap of years to fill up in the reserves, and particularly in officers. As an offensive army, it would take quite ten years to bring it up to the standard of the great army of 1914.

Everywhere I found a fierce, uncompromising hostility to Russian Bolshevism, coupled with a genuine admiration for the British people,

[6] From David Lloyd George, *The Truth About Reparations and War Debts* (London, 1932), pp. 128-32. Reprinted by permission of William Heinemann, Ltd. and Beaverbrook Newspapers Ltd.

[7] From an article published in the *Daily Express*, September 17, 1936. Reprinted by permission of Beaverbrook Newspapers Ltd. For the full text of Lloyd George's talks with Hitler, see Martin Gilbert, *The Roots of Appeasement* (New York, 1966). Appendix II, pp. 197–211.

with a profound desire for a better understanding with them. The Germans have definitely made up their minds never to quarrel with us again . . .

"LET US MAKE PEACE INEVITABLE INSTEAD OF WAR"[8]

It was the Spanish Civil War which alerted Lloyd George to a sense of the irremedial split between dictatorship and democracy. By 1937 it confirmed his belief in the need for democratic intervention and in the responsibility of the democracies to try to check totalitarian expansion. In 1938 and 1939 he was one of the few Englishmen who saw the need to try to bring Russia into any anti-Nazi or anti-Fascist alignment. Together with Churchill once more, he spoke in Parliament on the urgent need for rapid rearmament. He stressed the importance of an alliance of all Europe's threatened states, and the paramount urgency of seeking Russian support. But when, in March 1939, Neville Chamberlain, the Prime Minister, decided to enter into alliances with states threatened by Germany (in particular Poland and Rumania), he still refused to approach Russia seriously. Lloyd George reestablished his Parliamentary reputation in a series of anti-Government speeches.

There is a general tension and strain manifest in every country in the world, and more particularly in the countries that would be involved in the event of a failure to come to a peaceable adjustment of the difficulties. Everyone is apprehensive; I think I may say that everyone is anticipating another blow from the dictator powers. No one knows where it will come, but there is a general feeling of dread that it is coming somewhere.

The situation reminds me very much of the feeling that prevailed in the early spring of 1918. We knew there was a great attack coming from Germany, but no one quite knew where the blow would fall. I remember that the French thought it would fall on their front, while our Generals thought it would fall on ours. Even the French Generals were not agreed as to the part of their front on which the attack would fall, and our Generals were equally divided. All that we knew was that there was a tremendous onslaught coming somewhere, and the whole atmosphere was filled with, I will not say fear, but with uneasiness. We could see the tremendous activities behind the German lines, and we knew that they were preparing something. That is more or less what

[8] From *Hansard*, May 19, 1939. Reprinted by permission of the Controller of Her Majesty's Stationery Office. The Leader of the Labour Party, Clement Attlee, speaking immediately after Lloyd George in this debate, described his speech as an "extremely gloomy picture of the world situation, but I am afraid that it is a true picture."

seems to me to be the position to-day. We are all frightened—or perhaps frightened is hardly the word, but we are all very nervous; we are all very anxious; the whole world is under the impression that there is something preparing in the nature of another attack from the aggressors. Nobody quite knows where it will come. We can see that they are speeding up their armaments at a rate hitherto unprecedented, especially in weapons of the offensive—tanks, bombing aeroplanes, submarines. We know that they are occupying and fortifying fresh positions that will give them strategic advantages in a war with France and ourselves.

Any man who has ever made any study of war will see exactly what is going on. They are not preparing for defence. If you watch closely, you will see that the military chiefs of the higher ranks in Italy and Germany are travelling around Europe for long conversations. They are inspecting and surveying, from Libya to the North Sea, all sorts of situations that would be of vital importance in the event of war. There is a secrecy in the movements behind the lines which is very ominous . . . They are not preparing to defend themselves against attack from either France, Britain, or Russia. That has never been threatened. I have never heard, either privately or publicly, any hint or suggestion that we were contemplating an attack upon either Italy or Germany in any quarter—and they know it quite well. Therefore, all these preparations are not for defence. They are for some contemplated offensive scheme against someone or other in whom we are interested.

The country is interested in preparations for war, but it wants most of all to know how we are going to keep out of it. It wants our preparations to have a double purpose: to be not preparations for an inevitable war, but such preparations as to make peace inevitable. The way to do that is undoubtedly to assemble together such a force here, in France, in Turkey and in Russia, as will make the dictators, who are shrewd men, realise that they cannot run the risk of another act of aggression without facing the possibility of, perhaps not immediate, but ultimate disaster to themselves and to their countries. I hope that we shall look at the present position from that point of view. Let us make peace inevitable instead of war. There are two ways of ensuring peace. As well as making victory more certain, it is necessary to have the dictators know that we have behind us the kind of forces that will make our ultimate triumph secure, so that they will not challenge the issue. There are two ways. One is the strengthening of our own military forces to prepare for any emergency. We have been discussing that so often recently that I do not propose to take up any time in dealing with that proposition.

The second way is to secure the co-operation of as many independent nations as we can assemble in order to resist aggression. With regard to that proposition, we have procrastinated seriously and dangerously. I cannot imagine a government taking the risk which the present Government have taken in negotiations, not in coming to terms, but in failing to come to terms, with Powers whose assistance to us will not only be useful, but will, I think, be essential. I am speaking now from a purely military point of view. The Axis Powers have been very busy. They have been very relentless in gathering together all the support they can for a conflict which they knew in their hearts they could not challenge alone. Let us see what they have done in the last few months. They have captured three countries, which hold the most vital strategic positions in Europe. Czecho-Slovakia—we all remember what this meant, and undoubtedly it was a vast defeat for democracy. There is an old Welsh ode which says about our mountains that they are castles built by God to protect us. That is what the Bohemian mountains did. They have now been transferred from the realm of liberty to that of the oppressors, who have captured the fortifications, some of the most renowned arsenals in the world, and the whole of the armaments of the Czech Army, a fine army of 40 divisions. That has gone.

Russia is only asking for exactly the same terms. She will come in wholeheartedly, with the whole of her tremendous force, provided we say that France, ourselves and Russia shall be in on exactly the same terms. Let there be no distinction between one and the other—no insulting distinction. What is the good of this political snobbery that only wants to help a proletariat Government provided you do not rub shoulders with it? The issues are too tremendous for that. To say simply she must come in with a guarantee here and must send her troops there—that is not a full and whole-hearted alliance. Why do we not make up our mind, and make it up without any loss of time, that we shall come to the same terms with Russia as we do with France? If you do that, then I should say— though it is a dangerous thing to predict in a world like this—that the chances against war would go up. If they are fifty-fifty now, I should put it at ten to one against war, if the Government have got the courage to face criticism, whether it comes from their own side or elsewhere, and the French Government the same. I know what is happening. I know what happened in France when we were dealing with Czecho-Slovakia. The Government there hinted to their supporters "We could not have done this had it not been for Britain." We are getting the same thing here in the newspapers. It is being hinted "We would be prepared to do it, if it were not for France." Let us take a resolve, a clear one, and, above all, a prompt one, to deal with the situation.

"WHERE IS THE DARING? WHERE IS THE SKILL?" [9]

When war came in September 1939 Lloyd George was not asked to join Neville Chamberlain's Government. But he continued to

[9] From notes of remarks made privately by Lloyd George on September 27, 1939, to a small all-Party group of Members of Parliament. Quoted in Robert Boothby, *I Fight to Live* (London, 1947), pp. 195–96. Reprinted by permission of Lord Boothby.

speak both publicly and privately on what he considered to be the weaknesses of Chamberlain's policy. Shortly after the outbreak of war he spoke privately to a number of Members of Parliament. Robert Boothby took notes of Lloyd George's points:

(1) We should never have guaranteed Poland without Russia.

(2) Having guaranteed Poland, we should have secured Russia at once, and at any cost.

(3) We had allowed ourselves to be out-manoeuvred at every turn by men of incomparably superior political ability.

(4) We should have attacked the German munition factories and air bases in the West within twelve hours of the declaration of war, with the object of engaging the greater part of the German air fleet in battle over ground chosen by us. This was the only move by which we could hope to bring some relief to Poland. The only conceivable objection to such action was that we were not yet strong enough in the air, even in combination with the French; in which case we should not have declared war.

(5) As a result of our folly, we had now to abandon hope of establishing an eastern front.

(6) In these circumstances he thought that the power of the weapon of blockade could be greatly exaggerated. It took four years of incessant battering on two fronts during the last war to reduce the Germans to a condition in which our blockade became finally effective.

(7) From a psychological point of view the dropping of what he called "imbecile tracts" over Germany had been a great mistake. They could only have increased the morale of the German people.

(8) One thing was quite sure, and that was that the man who had landed us in this mess could not get us out of it.

(9) The present War Cabinet could never be made an effective instrument for conducting a world war. Only two of its members—Churchill and Hankey—knew anything about the direction of a war. And it was a physical impossibility for a man to be simultaneously a member of a War Cabinet and head of a fighting department.

(10) We were now confronted with a world struggle for power, in which war was merely one instrument of policy. We had unfortunately allowed ourselves to be forced into a most disadvantageous position, from which it was essential to extricate ourselves.

(11) No one could dogmatize about policy without being in possession of all the relevant facts. But in certain circumstances it might be wise, not only from a political but from a strategic point of view to open negotiations, if only for the purpose of gaining time.

(12) A War Cabinet of five or six men should now be sitting from eight in the morning till midnight daily, examining every aspect of the political, strategic, and economic situation with a view to deciding policy in the light of events. It was probable that, in the course of the next few weeks, we should be called upon to take decisions which would settle, one way or another, the fate of the British Empire. He saw no signs that adequate consideration was being given by the ablest minds in this country to the gigantic world issues involved.

At the conclusion of his observations he remarked that his advice had never been sought by the present Government. And he asked—what were our war aims now? Did they include the restoration of Danzig to a non-existent Poland, or of Colonel Beck's estates in Galicia? He said that, as he had anticipated, Churchill had done good work at the Admiralty. But that was only one aspect of the tremendous problem which confronted us; and he confessed that he viewed the future with the gravest anxiety.

The following day I lunched with Mr. Lloyd George alone. I never saw him so troubled and anxious. "We ought to be attacking now," he kept on repeating. "Why aren't we attacking? If it is because they haven't got the stuff, they should never have given the guarantee to Poland. In the meantime, Germany is producing far more arms than we. Delay only widens the gap. The situation gets worse not better." He reverted to the theme of a negotiated peace. "They would say it was defeatism, but it might be necessary to play for time. This is a struggle for world power, in which aeroplanes are one weapon and diplomacy is another. If you haven't got the aeroplanes, you may have to resort to other methods. The Treaty of Amiens did not prevent the ultimate overthrow of Napoleon. In any case," he added, with a flash of the old fire, " we must play this weak hand with daring. Then, with luck, we might win. For the Germans are bound to make mistakes. But where is the daring? Where is the skill?" He sighed deeply. "I wish I knew the facts," he said. "They tell me nothing." Perhaps it was as well he didn't know them, for they were even worse than he supposed. However, in the end, although only just in time, we got the daring, the skill, and the luck; and the Germans made the mistakes.

"NOBODY IS SATISFIED" [10]

On May 7, 1940, Chamberlain's Government was severely criticized in Parliament for what many Englishmen were convinced was its incompetent conduct of the war. On May 8 Lloyd George made a

[10] From *Hansard*, May 8, 1940. Reprinted by permission of the Controller of Her Majesty's Stationery Office. Lloyd George was encouraged to make this speech by a number of Labour Party leaders, who respected his judgment on foreign affairs, and may well have been willing to serve under him again, as Labour ministers had done during the First World War.

dramatic Parliamentary speech. In it he crystallized the general discontent and demanded Chamberlain's resignation. Lloyd George's speech, coming as it did from so experienced an elder statesman, who had himself obtained power at a critical moment in the First World War, helped to mobilize opinion against Chamberlain. It presented in a stark and dramatic form the demand that Chamberlain must go. Two days later Chamberlain resigned and Churchill became Prime Minister. Lloyd George had thus played a small but significant part in bringing his friend to power.

I intervene with more reluctance than usual in this Debate. All my hon. Friends know very well that I hesitated whether I should take part in it at all, because I thought it was more desirable that we should have a discussion in which Members not of front-bench rank should take a good deal of the time, but I think that it is my duty, having regard to the fact that I have some experience of these matters. . . . I feel that I ought to say something, from such experience as I have had in the past of the conduct of war in victory and in disaster, about what I think of the present situation and what really ought to be done. I have heard most of the speech of the right hon. Gentleman the Secretary of State for Air, and I should think that the facts which he gave us justify the criticism against the Government and are no defence of the Government. He said that we had practically no chance of making good in our Norwegian expedition unless we were able to have air bases there which would enable us to put our fighters into the air in order to counteract the very destructive effect of the German aeroplanes. But we knew there were no air bases available. We knew they were in the hands of the enemy.

The right hon. Gentleman admits that. He says that the Government knew beforehand that there were no air bases unless they were captured from the enemy. He even intimates that the object of the Trondheim expedition was to capture an air base. In that case we ought to have had picked men, and not a kind of a scratch team. We ought to have sent the very best men available, especially as we could not send the whole of our forces in the first instalment. The first instalment ought to have been picked men, because the Germans had picked men, as is generally accepted. We sent there, I think, a Territorial Brigade which had not had very much training. They were very young men, but they were the advance party of an expeditionary force which had to accomplish a task upon which the success of the whole force depended. We ought also to have had combined action between the Army and the Navy. We had neither. We gambled on the chance of getting air bases. We did not take any measures that would guarantee success. This vital expedition, which would have made a vast difference to this country's strategical position, and an infinite difference to her prestige in the world, was made dependent upon this half-prepared, half-baked expeditionary force, without any combination at all between the Army and the Navy. There could not have been a more serious condemnation of the whole action of the Government in respect of Norway. They knew perfectly well that the Germans were preparing for a raid on some adjoining country, probably in the Balkans, and it is a severe condemnation of them that they should have gambled in this way. The right hon. Gentleman spoke about the gallantry of our men, and we are all equally proud of them. It thrills us to read the stories. All the more shame that we should have made fools of them.

Now, the situation is a grave one—I agree with what was said about that by the Prime Minister—and it would be a fatal error on our part not to acknowledge it. In such experience as I have had of war direction I have never tried to minimise the extent of a disaster. I try to get the facts, because unless you really face the facts you cannot overcome the difficulties and restore the position. There is no case, in my judgment, for panic. I say that deliberately, after a good deal of reflection. But there is a grave case for pulling ourselves together. We cannot do that unless we tell the country the facts. They must realise the magnitude of our jeopardy. We have two immense Empires federated in the struggle for liberty, the two greatest Empires in the world, the British Empire and the French Empire, with almost inexhaustible resources but not easily mobilised, not easily roused, especially ours.

You are not going to rouse the British Empire—because you will have to do it not merely in Britain but throughout the world—to put forth the whole of its strength unless and until you tell it the facts and realities of the peril that confronts it. At the cost of unpleasantness, I am going to do that, not with a view to terrifying them or spreading dismay and consternation, but with a view to rousing real action and not sham action such as we have had. It is no use saying that the balance of advantage is in our favour, or adding up the numbers of ships sunk on either side. That kind of petty-cash balance-sheet is not the thing to look at. There are more serious realities than that.

First of all, we are strategically in a very much worse position than we were before. Notice those words, "strategically better," "strategically worse," because victory or defeat may depend upon the application of those two words. The greatest triumph of this extraordinary man Hitler has been that he has succeeded in putting his country into an infinitely better strategical position to wage war than his predecessors did in 1914, and by what he has done now he has increased his own advantages and he has put us into greater jeopardy. Let us face it like men of British blood. Graver perils than this have been fought through in the past. Let us face it; just look at it. Czecho-Slovakia, that spear-head, aimed at the heart of Germany, broken. A million of the finest troops in Europe of a very well-educated race of free men, all gone. Such advantage as there is in Czecho-Slovakia, with its great lines of fortifications and its Skoda works, which turned out the finest artillery in the 1914 war, are in the hands of Hitler. That is one strategic advantage which we have handed over to the enemy. . . .

With regard to our prestige, can you doubt that that has been impaired? You have only to read the friendly American papers to find out, highly friendly papers that were backing us up through thick and thin, in a country which was pro-Ally. I do not know whether hon. Members ever listen to the British Broadcasting Corporation's relay of the American commentator Mr. Raymond Gram Swing. He is very remarkable. He gave an account of the change in American opinion. He said that what has happened was a hammer blow to Americans. They were perfectly dazed. Before that, they were convinced that victory was going to be won by the Allies, and they had never any doubt about it. This is the first doubt that has entered their minds, and they said, "It will be up to us to defend Democracy."

Then there are the neutral countries. We promised Poland; we promised Czecho-Slovakia. We said: "We will defend your frontiers if you will revise them." There was a promise to Poland, to Norway, and to Finland. Our promissory notes are now rubbish on the market. [Hon. Members: "Shame."] Tell me one country at the present moment, one neutral country, that would be prepared to stand up and finance us on a mere promise from us? What is the use of not facing facts? . . .

We have to restore that prestige in the world if we are to win this war. There is also the fact that the state of our preparations is known to the world. We started these preparations five years ago, in 1935. In 1935 a promise of rearmament was made; in 1936 active proposals were submitted to this House and were passed without a Division. The Government said they would commit us to £1,500,000,000. If they had asked for more and had said that it was necessary, there was no party in this House which would have challenged it. [Interruption.] If any party had challenged it, you had your majority. What has been done? Is there anyone in this House who will say that he is satisfied with the speed and efficiency of the preparations in any respect for air, for Army, yea, for Navy? Everybody is disappointed. Everybody knows that whatever was done was done half-heartedly, ineffectively, without drive and unintelligently.

For three or four years I thought to myself that the facts with regard to Germany were exaggerated by the First Lord [Winston Churchill] because the then Prime Minister [Stanley Baldwin] said that they were not true. The First Lord was right about it. Then came the war. The tempo was hardly speeded up. There was the same leisureliness and inefficiency. Will anybody tell me that he is satisfied with what we have done about aeroplanes, tanks, guns, especially anti-aircraft guns? Is anyone here satisfied with the steps we took to train an Army to use them? Nobody is satisfied. The whole world knows that. And here we are in the worst strategic position in which this country has ever been placed.

Sir Patrick Hannon (Birmingham, Moseley): We have our sea power.

Mr. J. J. Davidson (Glasgow, Maryhill): And your dividends.

Mr. Lloyd George: I wish we had used it in some parts of Norway. I do not think that the First Lord was entirely responsible for all the things that happened there.

Mr. Churchill: I take complete responsibility for everything that has been done by the Admiralty, and I take my full share of the burden.

Mr. Lloyd George: The right hon. Gentleman must not allow himself to be converted into an air-raid shelter to keep the splinters from hitting his colleagues. But that is the position, and we must face it. I agree with the Prime Minister that we must face it as a people and not as a party, nor as a personal issue. The Prime Minister is not in a position to make his personality in this respect inseparable from the interests of the country.

The Prime Minister: What is the meaning of that observation? I have never represented that my personality—[Hon. Members: "You did!"] On the contrary, I took pains to say that personalities ought to have no place in these matters.

Mr. Lloyd George: I was not here when the right hon. Gentleman made the observation, but he definitely appealed on a question which is a great national, Imperial and world issue. He said, "I have got my friends." It is not a question of who are the Prime Minister's friends. It is a far bigger issue. The Prime Minister must remember that he has met this formidable foe of ours in peace and in war. He has always been worsted. He is not in a position to appeal on the ground of friendship. He has appealed for sacrifice. The nation is prepared for every sacrifice so long as it has leadership, so long as the Government show clearly what they are aiming at and so long as the nation is confident that those who are leading it are doing their best. I say solemnly that the Prime Minister should give an example of sacrifice, because there is nothing which can contribute more to victory in this war than that he should sacrifice the seals of office.

"LET US KNOW THE FACTS" [11]

After Churchill had been Prime Minister for a year, Lloyd George made his last important Parliamentary speech. It was a strong attack

[11] From *Hansard*, May 7, 1941. Reprinted by permission of the Controller of Her Majesty's Stationery Office.

on what he considered were major weaknesses in Churchill's war-time government. Churchill replied savagely that it was "the sort of speech with which, I imagine, the illustrious and venerable Marshal Pétain might have enlivened the closing days of M. Reynaud's Cabinet." But many of Lloyd George's strictures were sound ones.

There are parts of the war administration of the Government about which there is dissatisfaction and disappointment among their own supporters, and an anxious desire that there should be a drastic amendment. It is rather straining party loyalty to invite them to express confidence about something in regard to which, almost without exception, the Members supporting the Government in the country have noted very considerable dissatisfaction. I picked up at random two papers giving expression to that feeling. They are both supporters of the Government, each of them being at an extreme end of the political pole. One of them is the "Times"; the other is the "Daily Herald." They are so far apart in their extremes of opposition that, as sometimes happens in this globular universe, they have actually met, and they are joining in supporting the same Administration. Here is a passage:

> There is a widespread feeling, which it would be foolish to ignore, that we have fallen short in tackling problems of large-scale organisation.

That is from the "Times." There is more of it. It goes into details—very important details—of organisation. About the worst is the administration of the problem of food production. Here is the "Daily Herald":

> Of this we are sure, that British output is still far below its peak, and that in several branches of vital industry the skill and energy of the workers are being dissipated by feeble organisation, that many a sound management is fettered by red tape and lack of organisation in some of the Government Departments.

The "Daily Herald" has published illustrations of this feebleness. Those are fair samples of the kind of criticism which is rampant, and which is quite general.

What is the present situation? The issue of the war is certainly by no means decided. If our enemies make that assumption, I think that they are definitely wrong, and if we, by our organisation and by our future conduct of the war, pursue counsels of wisdom, I think they will be definitely disappointed. The issue is by no means decided on either side, but the war is passing through one of its most difficult and discouraging phases. I was a member of a Government when we had many phases of

that kind. Even at the time when I was Prime Minister we had one. But
we have had our third, our fourth great defeat and retreat. We have the
trouble now in Iraq and Libya. We have the German seizure of the
islands. We have the tremendous havoc among our shipping, not merely
in losses but in what has not been taken enough into account, in damage.

We have also had our very dazzling successes. The victory of September
was a very remarkable and a very thrilling one and, for the time being,
conclusive. I have already expressed an opinion in this House with regard to the campaign of General Wavell, and I repeat it. I regard that
campaign as one of the most brilliant series of successes won by any
British General in any long-continued war. But we have suffered severe
wounds, painful and serious wounds—none fatal, in my judgment, but
grave if neglected. The nation, before it can help—and it has to do a great
deal more than it has done up to the present moment—must know the
real facts. I took this line in the first year or two of the last war. I always
thought it a mistake to obscure or to gloss the facts. I said, "You will
never get the people of this country to do their best until you tell them
the real truth, and the moment you do that, they will respond to every
call which is made upon them." We are not an infantile nation, and it
is not necessary to withhold unpleasant facts from us, so as not to frighten
us. This is not a nation easily frightened. It has faced too many crises,
too many defeats, in the past to be frightened by anything that has happened, even up to the present moment. Therefore, I beg the Government
to let us know the facts.

I agree that it is not our business to spread gloom. I do not discourage
statements which are optimistic, but they must be based on facts, otherwise
they will not be believed. A road which is founded on the quicksands of
illusion never yet led to victory. Certainly that is true of a people like
ours, fearless and steadfast, not a panicky people, a people who have in
their own hearts faith and confidence which have come from centuries of
success, and of overcoming difficulties. The real danger, if anything, is
that we should not grasp realities even when we are told about them. If
there is a wound inflicted, diagnose it honestly—probe it. I am all for
cleansing it of foreign matter put in by propaganda. Let us clean the
wound and then cure it. . . .

Are we making the best use of our man-power? All I know is that on
the land the men have been taken away at a time when food is vital for
the life of the country. Are the factories fully equipped? Is the best use
being made of your vigorous young men in the factories? That is not the
impression. I have talked to a great many people who are in contact
with them, and there is a general sense of dissatisfaction and doubt. I
do not know whether we have had a discussion upon man-power, but I
think we ought to have one. I think the Prime Minister ought to reconsider the whole distribution of man-power, especially in reference to the
American policy that is developing. . . .

You have first of all to see that, whatever happens, the people will not be short of food. If they are, you may produce the conditions which resulted in the defeat of Germany in the last war. You could really double the output. I am speaking from some knowledge and experience. I am speaking from consulting men who know better than I do scientifically. You could double the output of food if you gave agriculturists plenty of machinery, which they have not got—they are short of it—plenty of fertilisers, which they have not got, and plenty of men to cultivate the land. You have millions of acres which are producing practically nothing.

The second thing I should like to say is this: You have to do more for the shelter and protection of the people against air raids. I do not believe that that problem has been considered on a sufficiently large scale. I remember very well how the old soldiers disdained trenches. They said, "You will destroy the morale of the soldiers. It is far better that they should face all these perils." But there is a limit to the morale of human nature to which you ought never to put it to the strain. I am certain that if you considered the problem of shelters on a great scale for your population and for some of your most essential factories, it could be done, and we could defy all these raids for the year or two when we may not have supremacy.

That brings me to my last point. The Prime Minister must have a real War Council. He has not got it. He is a man with a very brilliant mind, one of the most remarkable men who have graced this House with their presence. There is no doubt about his brilliant qualities, but for that very reason, if he will allow me to say so, he wants a few more ordinary persons. He wants men against whom he can check his ideas, who are independent, who will stand up to him and tell him exactly what they think, but it is no use their doing so if they know nothing about it. I am not disparaging the men, at least some of the men, whom he has in his Cabinet. I have seen one or two of them at work. No man who has a big war job has time for anything else in the way of reading papers and studying questions of strategy. He is a man who has to produce weapons of war in a hurry and every moment of his time is taken up with people who go to consult him. How can he go on studying questions of Iraq and Libya and Dakar and the mountains of Albania? How can Ministers deal with all the questions arising in regard to the Atlantic? They go to the Cabinet and their opinion is asked. They know that the Prime Minister has thought it out and they have not. They have not had time to think it out.

There ought to be men there who have nothing to do except to study these problems and give the Prime Minister their advice after the study. There are men of different types of mind and they very often discover objections which are not obvious to the most brilliant intellect. There is the Minister of Labour, for instance. He has a gigantic task. He has almost two departments. How can he devote his mind, his common sense, to problems of this kind? He would be a valuable counsellor but I say that he is no good coming after a day spent in thrashing out every kind of detail that comes up.

I remember that when I was made Minister of Munitions I found it impossible to attend the Cabinet for some time. Mr. Balfour once said "By the way, where is the Minister of Munitions? We have not seen him for a long time." I could not attend the Cabinet. The Prime Minister has had a prejudice against this suggestion, but he has now started by taking Lord Beaverbrook from the task of making machines and he is now to devote the whole of his time to war problems. That is not enough. The Prime Minister ought to have three or four absolutely independent men, men of experience, but, above all, men of commonsense, who will read through all the papers and, what is more, examine the differences between the Departments. Where the Government are failing is in regard to those differences. I know that departmental war, and if the Prime Minister had three or four men inside the Cabinet who were quite independent he could depute to them the examination of these differences. We have a very terrible task in front of us. No one man, however able he is, can pull us through. I invite the Prime Minister to see that he has a small War Council who will help him—help in counsel, help him in advice, and help him in action.

PART TWO

THE WORLD LOOKS
AT LLOYD GEORGE

Who shall paint the chameleon?
Who can tether a broomstick?

—J. M. KEYNES ON LLOYD GEORGE

Lloyd George mesmerized many of those who met him. Others seemed equally easily repelled or bewildered by his unusual personality. He was a source of frequent and often bitter controversy during his lifetime. Almost every contemporary writer on historical or political matters tried to portray him. Many pamphlets, speeches, and books were written, both against him and in his defense, for almost the whole course of his long and busy life, and particularly between 1916 and 1922. In this section I have chosen extracts which will enable the reader to gauge some of the controversy and the unusual range of disagreement and anger which he provoked. From these extracts it should be possible to sense the strong impact which he made upon his contemporaries, and to begin to understand something of the many facets of the man himself.

DAILY MAIL: "AN IRRESISTIBLE PUSHFULNESS"[1]

Lloyd George's opposition to the Boer War transformed him from a Welsh firebrand to a national figure. His frequent clashes with Joseph Chamberlain marked him as a bold and outspoken figure. The Parliamentary Sketch-Writer of the Daily Mail *compared the new radical with his distinguished adversary, himself once equally outspoken.*

The man of now, like the man of then, has an indomitable, unquestioning, self-confidence, an irresistible pushfulness. Sprung from no exalted parentage, he has forced his way forward by the same dogged

[1] Quoted in Frank Owen, *Tempestuous Journey* (London, 1954), p. 112. Reprinted by permission of Associated Newspapers, Ltd.

91

tenacity. . . . Look to him in debate, leaning forward, eager, keen, alert, hand-to-ear, ready to spring on his prey and rend him to pieces—the very reflection of what his great adversary once was.

The moment he opens his mouth to speak, the same similarity is so striking as to make the listener start involuntarily. Listen! The same clear, low-pitched, cruel voice; the same keen, incisive phrases; the same mordant bitterness; the same caustic sneer; the same sardonic humour; the same personal enmity. It is the very reincarnation of the present Colonial Secretary in his younger days—a spectre of his dead self arisen to haunt him.

Will Time, that has had so mellowing an influence on that great Imperialist, work a similar change in the virulent Little Englander? Will he a score of years hence be the tower of strength of the Imperialist or the Parochial Party?

THE TIMES: UNWORTHY TACTICS [2]

In 1902 the Conservatives introduced an Education Bill in Parliament which proposed to place all local education under the control of local County Councils. A local tax was to be levied to pay for all schools. This outraged the Welsh nonconformists, who saw themselves helping to subsidize Anglican schools. Many Liberals, led by R. B. Haldane, were glad to see education put under a single authority; they believed the Bill would lead to better education, and enable Britain to compete educationally with Germany. But Lloyd George sided with, and led, the nonconformist discontent. He opposed the Bill at every stage in the House of Commons, and bitterly attacked its supporters. In Wales, he urged open rebellion against it. The Times *newspaper issued a rebuke.*

Five or six years ago, in his callow youth, these schemes might have been regarded as promising methods of self-advertisement adopted by a young politician who must at any cost attract attention. But that time is long gone by. Mr. Lloyd George should no longer use tactics worthy of his own distant past, and of Mr. Winston Churchill's present. He has become a serious politician, and a serious claimant for high office.

[2] Quoted in Frank Owen, *Tempestuous Journey* (London, 1954), p. 130. Reprinted by permission of the editor of *The Times*.

HAROLD NICOLSON: "UNUSUAL DEMAGOGIC POWERS" [3]

The contrast between Lloyd George and his Liberal colleagues during the Liberal Government of 1906 to 1915 was described by the diplomat and historian Harold Nicolson in 1952.

Mr. Lloyd George, in April 1908, had succeeded Mr. Asquith as Chancellor of the Exchequer. Imaginative, resourceful, impetuous, endowed with unusual demagogic powers and compelling personal charm, Mr. Lloyd George was not encumbered by the vestigial affections which his colleagues still cherished for the ancient monuments of English tradition. Nor did he possess the tastes, intellectual or other, which British statesmen in the past had striven either to enjoy or to simulate. In their rare hours of relaxation Mr. Asquith would study Epictetus or Mr. P. G. Wodehouse, Mr. Haldane the *Kritik der reinen Vernunft,* Lord Morley *Le neveu de Rameau;* Sir Edward Grey would murmur Wordsworth to himself while observing the habits of the birds and fishes and Mr. Birrell would compose another volume of his *Obiter Dicta.* The relaxation of Mr. Lloyd George was to sing wild hymns to a harmonium. The very fact that he was closer to the people than were his classic colleagues enabled him to realise more clearly than they that the old Gladstonian formulas were losing their glamour and their potency; and that if Liberalism were not to become outmoded or overwhelmed by the rising tide of socialism, some more stimulating doctrine must be devised. He determined to preach Social Democracy and lead the attack on privilege —a cause and a battle which were to him supremely congenial.

F. E. SMITH: EXCESSIVE BURDENS [4]

F. E. Smith, a distinguished lawyer, who had entered Parliament in 1906 as a Conservative, spoke strongly against Lloyd George's proposed increases in taxation which would reduce a rich man's income of £40,000 a year to £20,000.

[3] From Harold Nicolson, *King George the Fifth* (London, 1952), p. 102. Reprinted by permission of Sir Harold Nicolson.

[4] From a speech delivered at Liverpool, August 29, 1909. Quoted in F. E. Smith, *Speeches Delivered in the House of Commons and Elsewhere* (Liverpool, 1910), p. 327. Reprinted by permission of the Second Earl of Birkenhead. F. E. Smith, later Lord Birkenhead, became a close personal and political friend of Lloyd George. Their relationship is described in Lord Birkenhead, *Frederick Edwin Earl of Birkenhead,* 2 vols. (London, 1933). There is an essay on Lloyd George by Lord Birkenhead in *Contemporary Personalities* (London, 1924).

For myself, I think that these burdens are excessive. But I do not ask your pity for the individual. He can no doubt live adequately upon the £20,000 a year, as indeed he could upon £5000, possibly even upon £500. I am asking you one question, and one only—What is the effect of such proposals upon your interests? Is such a man likely to invest his money here and employ you, or in the Colonies, the Argentine, or the United States, and employ others? And in answering this question, never lose sight of two indisputable facts. First, as I have told you, that more English capital went abroad in a recent year than ever previously; and, secondly, that in the same year here in England unemployment and pauperism were eating into the vitals of our people.

We see, therefore, the danger of loose Socialistic proposals, and how, like a boomerang, they strike, with injurious rebound, the nation which invokes their specious aid. So far we find no justification for the title the "People's Budget," unless, indeed, it is so called just as a certain powder is termed "insect" powder not because it nourishes insects, but because it destroys them.

BEATRICE WEBB: A HOSTILE VIEW [5]

Beatrice Webb was never an admirer of Lloyd George's social reform policy. She and her husband, who dominated the Fabian movement, disliked the giving of benefits which were not made dependent upon the good behavior of the recipient.

The splendid reception by all parties of Lloyd George's scheme of sickness insurance is a curious testimony to the heroic demagogy of the man. He has taken every item that could be popular with anyone, mixed them together and produced a Bill which takes some twenty millions from the propertied class to be handed over to the wage-earners, *sans phrase,* to be spent by them, as they think fit, in times of sickness or unemployment. If you add to this gigantic transfer of property from the haves to the have-nots the fact that the tax is to be collected in the most costly and extravagant fashion, and that the whole administration of the fund is to be put into the hands of the beneficiaries who are contributing only one-third, there is enough to make the moderate and constitutional Socialist aghast.

[5] From Beatrice Webb, *Our Partnership,* eds. Barbara Drake and Margaret Cole (London, 1948), pp. 473–75. Diary entry dated May 13, 1911. Reprinted by permission of the Passfield Trustees. An important volume of memoirs on the evolution of National Insurance is Sir H. Bunbury, ed., *Lloyd George's Ambulance Wagon* (London, 1957). For a full discussion of Lloyd George's role in the National Insurance Legislation, see Bentley B. Gilbert, *The Evolution of National Insurance in Great Britain* (London, 1966).

The first asset he started with was the word insurance. To the governing class insurance has always meant the voluntary contributions of the persons benefited—a method of raising revenue which has saved the pockets of all other persons. During the controversy about old-age pensions, insurance gradually acquired a compulsory element, and the Conservative Party became pledged to raising money from wage-earners, employers, and the general taxpayer, as an alternative to non-contributory pensions. Hence, by using this word Lloyd George secured the approval of the Conservative section of the community. Then there were the friendly societies who stood in the way. So he puts them into possession of the whole machinery of distribution: a fund that is mainly contributed by non-beneficiaries is to be wholly administered by the beneficiaries. This scheme has the adherence of the friendly society world and of the larger part of the working class.

Now the question is: Can he hustle it through this session? If he does not, the scheme won't survive the criticism of all the interests imperilled by it. He has extraordinary luck. The Coronation shortens the time, distracts the attention, and makes everyone inclined to a sentimental gift to the working-class. The Parliament Bill paralyses the opposition— they dare not oppose any popular scheme. The Labour and Irish parties stand to gain—the Liberals are naturally averse to even criticising their leader's magnificent demagogy. If the Cabinet backs him up, the scheme will go through. The only way of stopping it would be for all the outraged interests to make the ordinary M.P. feel that he would lose votes heavily. But they have precious little time to organise this pressure.

Sidney, on the whole, wishes the Bill to go through. I am not sure that I do. He believes that the big and difficult matter is to get the money voted, and that the inanities of both the method of raising the revenue, and the character of the provision given, could and will be altered by subsequent legislation. I fear the growth of malingering and the right to money independently of the obligation to good conduct. I cannot dismiss my rooted prejudice to relief instead of treatment. . . .

L. S. AMERY: "BRAZEN DEFIANCE" [6]

The Conservative politician and tariff reformer L. S. Amery was outraged, during the Marconi scandal, when Lloyd George defended his actions in a speech at the National Liberal Club in July 1912. Lloyd George, deciding on this occasion that attack was the best form of defense, denounced his critics as "hungry humbugs steeped

[6] From L. S. Amery, *My Political Life* (London, 1953), I, 424. Reprinted by permission of the Rt. Hon. Julian Amery and David Higham Associates, Ltd. In 1917 Amery became Assistant Secretary to Lloyd George's War Cabinet, and the two men became close colleagues, Amery being given political appointments in both the Colonial Office and at the Admiralty 1919–22.

*in smugness and self-righteousness" and claimed that he was being
persecuted by the Conservatives because he was trying to "lift the
poor out of the mire and the needy out of the dunghill." Amery
challenged Lloyd George and his colleagues:*

Now that the truth—or at any rate a substantial portion of it—
has come out, Ministers are attempting to bluff the country into believing that while they have done nothing that is not wholly admirable
and worthy of imitation, they have been the victims of a cruel campaign
of slander invented by the sheer devilish malignity of their political
opponents. Really that won't wash. The cruel campaign is largely a fig-
ment of their own imagination. No serious journal or responsible person
has ever charged them, or charges them now, with corruption. The fact
remains that they did speculate improperly, and that they did for
months mislead the House of Commons and the public. Most men, I
think, in such circumstances would realize that they had made a serious
mistake and would keep quiet. Lord Murray wisely chose the seclusion
of Bogota. Mr. Lloyd George prefers to crow brazen defiance to the
public conscience from his own dunghill at the National Liberal Club.
We can afford to leave him there.

LORD BEAVERBOOK: HESITATIONS IN 1914 [7]

*Lloyd George's reluctance to accept war against Germany in
1914 has led to conflicting charges against him. Some argue that
he nimbly abandoned his pacifist principles when he saw that, in
a patriotic war, they would quickly become a political liability.
Lord Beaverbrook, who watched Lloyd George in action and subsequently brooded deeply upon the crisis moments of his career,
wrote in retrospect:*

Those who insist on regarding Mr. Lloyd George as the inveterate
Jingo of the war from start to finish are wrong in their facts and mistake
their man. The then Chancellor of the Exchequer approached the prospect of intervention with the greatest reluctance, and suffered far-reaching incertitudes of mind.

[7] From Lord Beaverbrook, *Politicians and the War 1914–1916* (London, 1966),
pp. 28–30. Reprinted by permission of the Trustees of the Beaverbrook Foundations.
Other important accounts of the Cabinet crisis before the outbreak of war are in
John Viscount Morley, *Memorandum on Resignation* (London, 1928) and Winston
S. Churchill, *The World Crisis* (London, 1923), Vol. I.

He consulted with those of his colleagues who had pacifist leanings—or at least they consulted with him. He brought forward a theory, held by the existing French General Staff, that if the Germans violated Belgian neutrality they would pass only through the furthest southern corner, leaving Brussels and the plains of Flanders north of and untouched by their armies.

In the course of these conversations Mr. Lloyd George demonstrated to his friends with a map how small an infraction of neutrality such a military move would imply. He marked on the map with his finger the direction he thought the German march through Belgium would take. "You see," he would say, "it is only a little bit, and the Germans will pay for any damage they do."

At the eleventh hour he came down on the right side. When the Germans invaded Belgium he was influenced in favour of the decision. With this decision there vanished the last hopes of the pacifists and any prospect of that kind of anti-patriotic opposition which supported France and Napoleon against the Ministries of Pitt and his successors. Mr. Lloyd George alone had the genius to play Charles James Fox, and he declined the role.

It appears to me that both Mr. Lloyd George's hesitation and his final decision do him equal credit. He was reluctant to abandon the schemes of social amelioration he had devised and to plunge into war. He did not wish to put the future happiness and prosperity of all the people of the Empire on the hazard of a throw. But when he realised that his country was up against a Power which knew no moral scruples and was dangerous both to the Empire and humanity he took his decision firmly.

Once Mr. Lloyd George was in the war the very power of imagination which had given him pause gradually wrought him up to the fiercest activity in the struggle.

F. S. OLIVER: "A HOPELESS HASH" [8]

F. S. Oliver, an intelligent and outspoken Conservative, reflected in 1915 the growing Conservative attraction toward Lloyd George.

Things are not too satisfactory, either in the field or in the Cabinet. On the other hand I think they are all moving in the right direction. Lloyd George, a combination of energy, emotion, ignorance of and total incapacity for business of any kind, has made a sensation as

[8] From Stephen Gwynn, ed., *The Anvil of War: Letters Between F. S. Oliver and His Brother 1914–1918* (London, 1936), pp. 105–106. Letter dated June 10, 1915. Reprinted by permission of Macmillan & Co., Ltd.

Minister of Munitions, and for the moment a hopeless hash. He is an intelligent creature, however, and no doubt will shortly adapt himself to the circumstances of the new post and will confine himself to what I believe in your country is called "uplift." At this he is better than any other man living.

A. G. GARDINER: "THE MAN OF THE PEOPLE IN THE SEAT OF POWER" [9]

While Lloyd George was Minister of Munitions the perceptive journalist, A. G. Gardiner, sought to analyze his methods and intentions.

He has little use for shelters on mountain sides or elsewhere. He has the fever of motion in the blood, and is always at the gallop. "Rest!" said a famous Frenchman, "shall I not have all eternity to rest in?" And Mr. George, too, is determined to reserve his rest till the great silence falls. He has never learned the gentle art of loafing, never sat on the beach in the sunshine all the morning and flung pebbles at nothing in particular, never felt that intoxicating peace which falls on one when there is literally nothing to do and all the day to do it in. A holiday is splendid for a day, tolerable for two days—the third day you discover that he has flown. He has poetry in him; but it is not the poetry of "wise passiveness." You will never hear him mention Wordsworth. It is the poetry of life and action that moves him—the poetry of sudden and swift emotions, of old romance, with the clash of swords and the hint of battles long ago. He delights to picture those descents from their fastnesses in the mountains of the wild Welshmen upon the towns on the Welsh marches. You may almost catch the thunder of the hoofs and see the flames of the burning towns that they leave in their wake. And at the head of the raiders there rides a slight man with a large head, a gay laugh and a dancing eye. I think I know him.

For the fundamental fact about Mr. George is that he is a fighter, and since it is no longer possible to lay waste the towns on the Welsh marches with fire and sword, he is out with other weapons to lay waste English Toryism. He leaps to battle as joyfully as Lord Herbert of Cherbury. "The first words I heard," says that fiery Welshman in his autobiography, "were 'Darest thou come down, Welshman?' which I no sooner heard, but, taking a sword in one hand and a target in the other, I did in my shirt run down the stairs, open the door suddenly, and charged ten or twelve of them with that fury that they ran away."

[9] From A. G. Gardiner, *Pillars of Society* (London, 1916), pp. 296–97, 299–301, 301–303. Reprinted by permission of J. M. Dent & Sons, Ltd.

That is Mr. George's way to the life. A challenge is music in his ears. He is down the stairs and at 'em, and if there are ten or twelve, why, so much the happier. He pinks them all with flashing impartiality, wipes his sword, and goes back to bed. . . .

It may be said that the great uprising in 1906 made Mr. Lloyd George. It certainly gave him his opportunity. It foreshadowed vast changes in the State; but it was formless—a vague revolt against existing conditions. It was for the Government to give direction and shape to that revolt. If it could not do so, then Liberalism had failed and Protection would be the mould into which the future would run. For three years it seemed that the opportunity had been lost. It is true that great things were accomplished. United South Africa was founded and Old Age Pensions were granted. But we had opened up no new horizons. We were still in the old prison, and the Lords held the key of the gate. The country was turning against the Liberal party in weariness. Men were beginning to calculate when the election would come, and by how much the Liberals would lose. Mr. Chamberlain had made his bid. For the moment he had failed, but if his bid remained without challenge, if Liberalism could offer no alternative policy, then his victory was assured. It was the moment for a great adventure. If the Liberal Party was to save its life it must be ready to lose it, and with the instinct of the great strategist Mr. Lloyd George seized on the vulnerable point in the enemy's defences and staked everything on the throw. He attacked the land monopoly. It was a bold stroke. It brought him into conflict with powerful interests in his own party. A formidable cave of Liberal landed magnates threatened him. Journalistic fainthearts appealed to him to withdraw the land clauses of his Budget. Even in the Cabinet I fancy there were hints that the Budget would be better without them—that, in fact, Hamlet would be a better play without the Prince of Denmark. "If they go I go," was Mr. George's attitude. "This is a flag worth going into the wilderness with for ten years," he said. But the Prime Minister stood by him immovably, and the triumph was complete. The Liberal cause was rehabilitated, the land monopoly received its first check, and out of the struggle came the defeat of the House of Lords, with all that that defeat implied.

Now in this case personality certainly controlled events. The country was at the parting of the ways; but its direction was doubtful. Already it seemed to be turning, not confidently, but in despair of Liberalism, to Protection, and but for that dramatic stroke of the Budget of 1909 there is small doubt that today we should be discussing tariffs instead of social reform. The opportunity was there; but it was personality that seized it and moulded events in this way rather than in that.

It is his union of courage, imagination and sympathy that makes Mr. George the most formidable figure that has appeared in politics since Gladstone. He has vision touched with a certain humanity, and when he has seen his course he never hesitates or thinks of consequences. He is always out to "win or lose it all." . . .

No man ever rose to such power with so light an obligation to the past, by so free an action of his own powers of flight, with such an entire reliance upon the immediate teaching of life. All his lessons, like his talk, come straight from the mint of experience. Thus, speaking of the perils of the poor from insolvent friendly societies, he will tell you how, when he was a boy, he used to take his uncle's shilling a week to the friendly society. "And when he fell ill the society had failed." Out of that memory largely came the Insurance Act. The result is that he is the least doctrinaire of men. You will never hear him talk about a theory, and his speeches are brilliant improvisations upon a theme rather than elaborately constructed arguments. They have the quality of vision and swift intuition rather than of the slow processes of thought He is motived by quick sympathies, not by cold reason, and he is more at home in attacking a visible wrong than in defending an abstract right. His defence of Free Trade, for example, has never been one of his conspicuous achievements. Indeed, he is not happy in defending anything. He prefers to hear the cry, "Wilt thou come down, Welshman?" and he holds, with the German War Minister, that "the best parry is the lunge." From this reliance upon intuition and impulse comes not merely his strength but his weakness—that light hold of principles, that indifference to doctrine, which he shares with Mr. Chamberlain and which keeps you always a little uneasy. Where will his pragmatism lead him? You rejoice in this splendid breadth of sail that takes the wind so gaily; but you wish you were a little more sure about the sufficiency of the ballast in the hold. And then perhaps your doubts are resolved by remembering how loaded down the ship is with the ballast of old wrongs and present interests, how crushing is the *vis inertiae* of society and how priceless and rare is the dynamic energy which Mr. Lloyd George has brought into politics.

And, with all his likeness to Mr. Chamberlain, he has a saving quality that Mr. Chamberlain had not. It is that nearness to the heart of the poor which is, I think, ultimately the motive-power of his life. He came from the people and his heart remains with the people. That, in the absence of a political philosophy, is the compass that may keep his course true—that and the touch of imagination and poetry that gives wings to his purposes and range to his vision. His peril is that his attachment to democracy is sentimental rather than the product of ideas. He has as little contact with organised labour as he has with the theories of Socialism or philosophic Radicalism, and democratic sympathies alone, unfortified by democratic thought, may in time of stress, be strangely perverted. He is the portent of the new time—the man of the people in the seat of power. He has no precedent in our political annals. Our politics have been governed by men who have studied the life of the people as others have studied the life of ants and bees, objectively, remotely. Even Bright, Cobden, Chamberlain, were not of the people. They were of the middle-class, and knew the poor as the instruments of the great employer. Mr. George comes out of the great hive itself. In him democracy has found its voice and to him it will be loyal as long as he remembers.

E. S. MONTAGU: "HIS BRAIN IS THE MOST FERTILE WE POSSESS" [10]

Edwin Montagu had succeeded Lloyd George as Minister of Munitions. He was a close personal friend of Asquith, and owed his political advance to Asquith's patronage. In December 1916 he was at the center of the crisis which led to Asquith's fall and Lloyd George's premiership. He wrote two letters to Asquith during the crisis, expressing the Liberal dilemma.

. . . He [Lloyd George] says that you as Prime Minister, with the House of Commons on your shoulders, with appointments to attend to and with the thousand and one duties of the Prime Minister, should be relieved of the day to day work of the War Committee, but should maintain the supreme control of the War, seeing the Chairman of the War Committee every morning before it met, receiving their reports and conferring with them when you thought fit. He says that your duties prevent sufficiently frequent sittings and that by this means quicker decisions would be arrived at. He does not for one moment regard it as possible for the War Committee without the Prime Minister to challenge the Prime Minister's supreme control of the War, but he regards it as essential that the small War Committee should sit so frequently and act with such rapidity that the Prime Minister, whoever he were, ought not to have a place upon it, but he is loud in his assertions that you are the right Prime Minister in the right place. He will not budge from this position and I cannot do anything more.

I remain of opinion, unshakeable and based not only on affection, but on conviction, that there is no conceivable Prime Minister but you. I remain of opinion that Lloyd George is an invaluable asset to any War Government. His brain is the most fertile we possess. The speeches that he will make [if he resigns] will, in my opinion, not only make it impossible for the Government to carry on, but will plunge this

[10] From a letter of E. S. Montagu to H. H. Asquith, December 2, 1916 and letter dated December 4, 1916. Quoted in S. D. Waley, *Edwin Montagu* (Bombay, 1964), pp. 104–106, 107–110. Reprinted by permission of Asia Publishing House. The emergence of Lloyd George as Prime Minister is described by Cameron Hazlehurst on p. 148 of this volume.

country into recrimination and public debate in the face of the enemy which will hearten them up and shake to its foundations the Alliance. Added to this, I think it would be quite impossible, if Lloyd George and Lord Derby go,—and they are going together,—for Bonar Law to remain.

You may entertain your own opinion. I have expressed mine of the vital mistake that Lloyd George is making in plunging the country into this condition, but it is for you as Prime Minister, I assume, to try and prevent this. I cannot believe that this can be done by the mere publication of two formal letters, and I think it ought to be attempted by prolonged conversations rather than risk the events which I foresee.

It is all a nightmare to me. So far as I can discover, in matters of policy you and Lloyd George are in complete agreement. In matters of mutual confidence there is not much which I desire.

*   *   *

I do not want you to cease to be Prime Minister because I am certain that any other Prime Minister cannot succeed. At the same time,—you may think that I am mistaken, foolish, under the charm, or anything you like,—but I cannot think of a Government conducting the war without Lloyd George. Whatever office he has held, despite his obvious defects, during the war he has rendered services to the country which cannot be minimised. My friends who know that I urged you to send him to the War Office taunt me with what is described as his failure there because of his quarrels with the soldiers. But they are with him now, and he has achieved at least one thing in the War Office, which if the war goes on next year will save our armies from destruction; I mean his belated success in getting the army to attend to the railway communications and thus to avert the consequences of a breakdown of French transport. He is most valuable on the War Committee and his ever-active brain has suggested to you policies and measures in which you have been in agreement with him. His uncontrolled conduct of the war is unthinkable, but a combination of you and him is what every thinking man in the country requires.

I have had some experience of the same sort of thing here, if I may compare small things with great. I found lack of co-ordination when I came here and after considering all sorts of alternatives, such as Boards of Directors, Committees over which I should preside, I formed a Committee which is really my general staff.

I was warned that it would upset my authority, that I must be Chairman myself. I refused all this advice, I reserve the power of veto and of initiative, the Committee works from day to day and is speedy in the despatch of business. I have the confidence, I think, of the whole office, and I am certain that Lloyd George's authority in it was not greater than mine today.

I should never have consented to advise you to accept this proposal if I had felt that it would undermine your authority, and therefore it is no use elaborating this point. What has broken down the arrangement? What has caused your withdrawal of your own proposals? I see three causes:

(1) Northcliffe's article in *The Times*. It is lamentable to think that you should let him achieve the victory that he has long sought. He wanted to drive you out; he alone is fool enough not to believe in you. His efforts were resisted by Lloyd George, by Bonar Law, by Lord Derby, by Carson, by Robertson. Using information that he had no right to obtain, he sees a chance of success, takes it and is successful. He published that article in order to wreck the arrangement and you have let him do it. I do not say that this was avoidable, but I say that his personal victory in this matter is a matter of the deepest possible chagrin to me.

(2) The advice given you by McKenna, Runciman and Grey. That advice could have been foreseen. It came in my opinion rather late, when you had already made your offer to Lloyd George. Grey always wants to resign when there are complications. It is his pretty little way of assisting matters. Runciman is merely a reflection of McKenna, and McKenna's loyalty to you is above suspicion but always unwise, because he hates Lloyd George, whom you deliberately chose as your colleague and kept as your colleague, as much, if not more than he likes you. He can only see one object to be achieved, to drive Lloyd George out of the Government, and he takes no view but that. Far be it from me to underrate McKenna's abilities or the importance of his position, but he has irritated the Allies and the City and quarrelled with his best advisers, and if you had to choose between Lloyd George and McKenna, there is little doubt as to whom you could best do without, whichever is the best character.

(3) The question of personnel. Lloyd George wanted Carson in. I think his main object was Loyalty to Bonar Law, who had been working with him and who feels acutely the position in which his Party is being split by Carson's rival leadership. Carson is leader of the Opposition, and at a time when you are reconstructing your Government, surely to make a new Coalition in order to help Bonar Law and the Parliamentary situation, it is not a very unknown thing to take in the most conspicuous Opposition leader. But Lloyd George, I know now, would have been more accommodating than I imagined on personnel and would have given way certainly about Balfour.

However all this is over, and I am confronted with a position in which I see no help for it but your resignation and a Government which must split the country in the face of the enemy from top to bottom. Both these facts are horrible to contemplate. A Government which you do not lead means disaster. A split country means victory for the enemy.

I therefore feel it my duty to tell you, because I want to do nothing
behind your back, what I have done. Lloyd George sent for me this
afternoon and I spent some time with him. I found him in almost as
great a condition of misery and unhappiness as I am myself. Believe me
or not as you will, he wanted to work with you. He did not want a
victory for Northcliffe. He was completely satisfied with the arrangements
you had come to and meant to work them loyally. He does not want,
I am confident, to be Prime Minister . . .

I then saw Lord Derby, who is also miserable and who was on his
way to see you. We had a long talk. He also believes implicitly that
you and Lloyd George must work together. I told him that I thought
he could do something which I could not do. I told him that he was
a man of unchallenged integrity and above suspicion of intrigue. He
also enjoyed the King's personal friendship. I urged him to tell the
King that in his opinion it was disastrous to the country that you and
Lloyd George should be separated, that the King should not try and
find an alternative Prime Minister, but that he should send for you
and George together and he himself endeavour to arrange an accommodation between you. I know that George would be willing because he
is not so foolish as to want to try the impossible. That is all that I
can do. I ask your forgiveness for my part in all this. I may have given
you advice which you think to have been wrong now or in the past. I
am sorry that I have failed, but looking back throughout the whole
history of your Government, I can charge myself with never having
taken any action which I did not from the bottom of my heart think
was in your interests.

W. H. PAGE: "HE WILL BE FRANK" [11]

*When Lloyd George became Prime Minister the American Am-
bassador in London, Walter Hines Page, reported to Washington:*

So far as any outsider can say, they have made an exceedingly good
start. Of course, Lloyd George's enemies predict that he will not last
six months. But they are his enemies. His friends and the public in
general expect him to finish the war successfully, and (many think)
pretty quickly. To me, the new Government seems to promise well—
very well. There's a snap about it that the old Government lacked.
Lloyd George is not a spent force, but one of the most energetic projec-

[11] From Burton J. Hendrick, *The Life and Letters of Walter H. Page* (London,
1925), III, 309–10, 312. Reprinted by permission of Ives Hendrick, Co-Executor of
the Burton J. Hendrick Estate.

tiles that I've ever watched or come in contact with. He said more in half an hour yesterday than Asquith ever told me in his life . . .

What I sat down to write you was my belief that Lloyd George will keep the programme that he sketched to me as far as you are willing he should. He will be frank. He is most friendly. He has often expressed his admiration for you—long before he could have known that he would become Prime Minister—and during the year he has shown and expressed to his intimates his confidence in me. He wishes confidentially to use me as a medium to reach you and for you to reach him whenever either of you have need or even an impulse. He is very direct. He does not use circumlocution. He doesn't "intimate": he says things straight out. "Call me on the telephone any time you like," was his parting word. This from the present ruler of the British Empire; for the Prime Minister is of course not only the Chief Executive but the chief and leader also of the House of Commons. I am sure he is quite sincere. Much may come of it, or little may come of it, as you or he will.

This change of government is quite as complete as a change of administration at Washington—when one party goes out and the other comes in. All that I can yet say about it is that it promises well for us.

NEW EUROPE: "FAITH AND FIRE" [12]

A British view was expressed by the New Europe:

We have longed for a man who should be utterly a Man of War, because war is unhappily now our supreme business—not necessarily a soldier, still less a politician, but a man whose mind should be entirely given to the work in hand, caring for nothing else, thinking of nothing else, and staking his whole being on the achievement of his task. Have we found such a man? We do not yet know. We only know that Mr. Lloyd George has made mistakes in the past, that he has not always spoken or acted wisely, that he has seemed at times to be demagogue rather than statesman, but that there has nevertheless been in him, throughout the phases of his career up to the beginning of the war, a certain sweep and range of vision, a squareness of mind, a power of

---

[12] Quoted in Henry Wickham Steed, *Through Thirty Years* (London, 1924), p. 132. Steed, who was probably the author of the above quotation, was foreign editor of *The Times* throughout the First World War, and editor 1919–21. His book contains many interesting references to Lloyd George, and is very critical of his postwar policies.

rising to occasions, a readiness to face awkward facts, that distinguished him from and placed him *potentially* above his contemporaries. . . . Above all he has faith and fire. Faith goes to faith. The country has had from the outset greater faith in itself and in the Allied cause than many of its responsible leaders have shown; and it has certainly not had many opportunities of indulging its faith in leadership. It has responded to Mr. Lloyd George because, almost for the first time during the war, its ear was caught by an appeal corresponding to its own intensity of feeling.

WINSTON CHURCHILL: "INEXHAUSTIBLE MENTAL AGILITY" [18]

Ten years after Lloyd George had become Prime Minister, Winston Churchill, who had served under him as Minister of Munitions in 1917 and 1918, tried to summarize his achievements as wartime Prime Minister.

It was in facing with unquailing eye these awful contingencies during the opening months of his prime responsibility, that Mr. Lloyd George's greatest service to his countrymen will, I believe, be found by history to reside. Not only undaunted in the face of peril, but roused by each deepening manifestation to fresh energy, he drove the engine of State forward at increasing speed. The War Cabinet shared his burdens. If sometimes this loyal and capable group of men hampered him when he was right, they also furnished him with that environment of sound opinion and solid argument without which his own remarkable qualities of initiative could never have attained full power. They invested him also with a collective authority which rose high and dominating above the fierce pressures of the time.

The new Prime Minister possessed two characteristics which were in harmony with this period of convulsion. First, a power of living in the present, without taking short views. Every day for him was filled with the hope and the impulse of a fresh beginning. He surveyed the problems of each morning with an eye unobstructed by preconceived opinions, past utterances, or previous disappointments and defeats. In times of peace such a mood is not always admirable, nor often successful for long. But in the intense crisis when the world was a kaleidoscope, when every month all the values and relations were changed by some

[18] From Winston S. Churchill, *The World Crisis 1916–1918* (London: Odhams Press, Ltd., 1927), Part One, pp. 256–57. Copyright © 1927 by Charles Scribner's Sons; renewal copyright © 1955 by Winston Churchill. Reprinted by permission of Charles Scribner's Sons and the Hamlyn Publishing Group Ltd.

prodigious event and its measureless reactions, this inexhaustible mental agility, guided by the main purpose of Victory, was a rare advantage. His intuition fitted the crisis better than the logical reasoning of more rigid minds.

The quality of living in the present and starting afresh each day led directly to a second and invaluable aptitude. Mr. Lloyd George in this period seemed to have a peculiar power of drawing from misfortune itself the means of future success. From the U-boat depredations he obtained the convoy system: out of the disaster of Caporetto he extracted the Supreme War Council: from the catastrophe of the 21st of March he drew the Unified Command and the immense American reinforcement.

His ascendancy in the high circles of British Government and in the councils of the Allies grew in the teeth of calamities. He did not sit waiting upon events to give a wiseacre judgment. He grappled with the giant events and strove to compel them, undismayed by mistakes and their consequences. Tradition and convention troubled him little. He never sought to erect some military or naval figure into a fetish behind whose reputation he could take refuge. The military and naval hierarchies were roughly handled and forced to adjust themselves to the imperious need. Men of vigour and capacity from outside the Parliamentary sphere became the ministerial heads of great departments. He neglected nothing that he perceived. All parts of the task of Government claimed his attention and interest. He lived solely for his work and was never oppressed by it. He gave every decision when it was required. He scarcely ever seemed to bend under the burden. To his native adroitness in managing men and committees he now added a high sense of proportion in war policy and a power of delving to the root of unfamiliar things. Under his Administration both the Island and the Empire were effectually organized for war. He formed the Imperial War Cabinet which centred in a single executive the world-spread resources of the British Monarchy. The convoy system, which broke the U-boat attack at sea; the forward impulsion in Palestine, which overwhelmed the Turks, and the unified command which inaugurated the victories in France, belonged in their main stress and resolve as acts of policy to no one so much as to the First Minister of the Crown.

After the war, at the Paris Peace Conference, Lloyd George, together with Georges Clemenceau and Woodrow Wilson, tried to draw up the blueprint for a peaceful Europe. Few conferences have been concerned with such a wide range of vexatious problems and contradictory intentions. The following three extracts give some idea of the controversy Lloyd George aroused during the Peace Conference.

The first is from the Conservative writer and politician, F. S.

Oliver, the second from the journalist Sir Valentine Chirol, and the third from the economist J. M. Keynes.

F. S. OLIVER: FAULTS AND VIRTUES [14]

The greatest is my old enemy the Prime Minister. Clemenceau is swell in his way, but he does not approach Lloyd George in vision and initiative. Clemenceau might have been trusted to go on every year saying that the French would never give in, and perhaps making the French fight rear-guard actions back to the Bay of Biscay, but Lloyd George had imagination and enthusiasm combined with tremendous courage.

As you know, I have seen him in very intimate circumstances at all the really worst crises since he became Prime Minister. I have seen him well in health and ill, but I have never seen in him a quaver of fear or suffering from a failure of the imagination.

People talk a great deal about his faults. Well, he has probably bigger faults—than any other prominent politician; but you must expect a man's faults to be on a scale with his virtues. They always are.

VALENTINE CHIROL: "PALPABLE IGNORANCE" [15]

There was no Castlereagh in Paris. Discretion is not one of Mr. Lloyd George's virtues, and the conversations that passed at his little breakfast parties were not always kept "strictly private and confidential." Amongst the large staff permanently attached to the Delegation, professional diplomatists were relatively fewer than usual in numbers, and, as soon became apparent, less frequently consulted or listened to, though foremost amongst them was Sir Eyre Crowe, for many years a pillar of strength at the Foreign Office. As an old journalist I was much interested in attending—but merely as "an observer"—the crowded meetings of British newspaper correspondents summoned from time to time to the Majestic when Mr. Lloyd George, with his friend Lord Riddell, the proprietor of that refined Sunday paper, *The News of the World,* at his elbow, dispensed to them as much information as he thought good for them, and often, especially in answering questions put to him, skated with great skill over extremely thin ice. But even his adroitness

---

[14] From Stephen Gwynn, ed., *The Anvil of War: Letters Between F. S. Oliver and His Brother 1914–1918* (London, 1936), pp. 341–42. Letter dated November 14, 1918. Reprinted by permission of Macmillan & Co., Ltd.

[15] From Sir Valentine Chirol, *Fifty Years in a Changing World* (London, 1927), pp. 229–30. Reprinted by permission of the Executors of Sir Valentine Chirol's Estate and Jonathan Cape, Ltd. For Lloyd George's role at Versailles, see also Harold Nicolson, *Peacemaking 1919* (London, 1933, 1964).

could not always disguise his palpable ignorance of foreign affairs, and, worse still sometimes, his relapses into the fustian of the platform orator which he had discarded during the War.

J. M. KEYNES: "THIS GOAT-FOOTED BARD" [16]

Mr. Lloyd George's devotion to duty at the Paris Conference was an example to all servants of the public. He took no relaxation, enjoyed no pleasures, had no life and no occupation save that of Prime Minister and England's spokesman. His labours were immense and he spent his vast stores of spirit and of energy without stint on the formidable task he had put his hand to. His advocacy of the League of Nations was sincere; his support of a fair application of the principle of Self-Determination to Germany's eastern frontiers was disinterested. He had no wish to impose a Carthaginian Peace; the crushing of Germany was no part of his purpose. His hatred of war is real, and the strain of pacifism and radical idealism, which governed him during the Boer War, is a genuine part of his composition. He would have defended a Good Peace before the House of Commons with more heart than he did that which he actually brought back to them.

But in such a test of character and method as Paris provided, the Prime Minister's naturally good instincts, his industry, his inexhaustible nervous vitality were not serviceable. In that furnace other qualities were called for—a policy deeply grounded in permanent principle, tenacity, fierce indignation, honesty, loyal leadership. If Mr. Lloyd George had no good qualities, no charms, no fascinations, he would not be dangerous. If he were not a syren, we need not fear the whirlpools.

But it is not appropriate to apply to him the ordinary standards. How can I convey to the reader, who does not know him, any just impression of this extraordinary figure of our time, this syren, this goat-footed bard, this half-human visitor to our age from the hag-ridden magic and enchanted woods of Celtic antiquity? One catches in his company that flavour of final purposelessness, inner irresponsibility, existence outside or away from our Saxon good and evil mixed with cunning, remorselessness, love of power, that lend fascination, enthralment, and terror to the fair-seeming magicians of North European folklore. Prince Wilson sailing out from the West in his barque *George Washington* sets foot in the enchanted castle of Paris to free from chains and oppression and an ancient curse the maid Europe, of eternal youth and beauty, his mother and his bride in one. There in the castle is the King with yellow parchment face, a million years old, and with him an enchantress with a harp singing the Prince's own words to a magical

[16] From J. M. Keynes, *Essays in Biography*, ed. Sir Geoffrey Keynes (London, 1961, pp. 32–39. Reprinted by permission of Sir Geoffrey Keynes, Rupert Hart-Davis Limited, and the American publisher, Horizon Press.

tune. If only the Prince could cast off the paralysis which creeps on him and, crying to heaven, could make the Sign of the Cross, with a sound of thunder and crashing glass the castle would dissolve, the magicians vanish, and Europe leap to his arms. But in this fairy-tale the forces of the half-world win and the soul of Man is subordinated to the spirits of the earth.

Lloyd George is rooted in nothing; he is void and without content; he lives and feeds on his immediate surroundings; he is an instrument and a player at the same time which plays on the company and is played on by them too; he is a prism, as I have heard him described, which collects light and distorts it and is most brilliant if the light comes from many quarters at once; a vampire and a medium in one.

When the Treaty of Versailles had been signed Lloyd George returned to England. His interest in foreign affairs had been aroused. He sought reconciliation with Germany and at a series of conferences in Europe did his utmost to allay French suspicions and fears. He became fascinated by the problems of foreign policy, and felt that he could be their master. This meant frequent quarrels with his Foreign Secretary, Lord Curzon. The following two extracts discuss the relationship between Lloyd George and Lord Curzon. The first is by the diplomat and historian Harold Nicolson, the second by Winston Churchill.

HAROLD NICOLSON: "AN AROMA OF SECRET POLICY" [17]

Mr. Lloyd George does not possess the Anglo-Saxon temperament. His Celtic mysticism and imagination have, at moments of crisis, been of vast value to the British Empire. As manifested in the conduct of Foreign Affairs they have proved less efficacious. It has already been suggested that the influence of Great Britain, both in relation to foreign countries and to the component parts of the Empire, is based on credit or "prestige." That credit, in its turn, has been defined as resting upon "reliability." This essential element was lacking in the diplomacy of Mr. Lloyd George. The implication is not that the Prime Minister's methods were ever consciously evasive or misleading; the implication is that they were personal, forensic, intuitive, imprecise, variable, conceited and far too private.

It was above all this privacy which undermined confidence. It was not only a privacy of method, it was a privacy of aim. Had Mr. Lloyd George's policy been as open as it was persistent, less uneasiness would

[17] From Harold Nicolson, *Curzon: The Last Phase 1919–1925* (London, 1934), pp. 56–58. Reprinted by permission of the late Sir Harold Nicolson.

have been caused by the opaque and volatile methods by which he endeavoured to carry it out. His policy, in important respects, was not open; it was impenetrably closed. Two of his main objectives (friendship with Russia, hostility to Turkey) were anathema both to the French Government and to his own Tory supporters in the Coalition Cabinet. He refrained, therefore, from openly admitting these objectives, and at moments he would openly deny them. But they persisted. He would return to them again and again. Gradually, the impression was created that the Prime Minister, in certain vital directions, was pursuing a personal policy which he was unwilling either to avow or to abandon. An atmosphere of suspicion, an aroma of secret policy, hung about the white corridors of No. 10 Downing Street, and crept like poison gas among the garden huts which housed his secretariat.

Mr. Lloyd George has also been accused of taking upon himself too large a share of responsibility for Foreign Affairs. Here again the criticism applied not so much to principle as to method. The later stages of war had necessitated unity of command, not in the field only, but also in the council room. Mr. Lloyd George was abundantly justified in assuming during those years certain powers of direction and intervention which would not, in normal times, have been claimed by any Prime Minister. Even after the Armistice it was found that the main threads of diplomacy stretched back into the period of the Supreme War Council. There was no single moment at which their continuity could be abruptly severed and the resultant loose ends entrusted to other hands.

WINSTON CHURCHILL: "A PRICELESS GIFT" [18]

You could hardly imagine two men so diverse as Curzon and Lloyd George. Temperament, prejudices, environment, upbringing, mental processes were utterly different and markedly antagonistic. There never of course was any comparison in weight and force between the two. The offspring of the Welsh village whose whole youth had been rebellion against the aristocracy, who had skipped indignant out of the path of the local Tory magnate driving his four-in-hand, and revenged himself at night upon that magnate's rabbits, had a priceless gift. It was the very gift which the product of Eton and Balliol had always lacked—the one blessing denied him by his fairy godmothers, the one without which all other gifts are so frightfully cheapened. He had the "seeing eye." He had that deep original instinct which peers through the surface of words

[18] From Winston S. Churchill, *Great Contemporaries* (London, 1937), pp. 279–80. Reprinted by permission of Odhams Press Limited, publishers and proprietors of the copyright. The relationship between Curzon and Lloyd George is discussed and documented in volume three of Lord Ronaldshay, *The Life of Lord Curzon* (London, 1928).

and things—the vision which sees dimly but surely the other side of the
brick wall or which follows the hunt two fields before the throng. Against
this, industry, learning, scholarship, eloquence, social influence, wealth,
reputation, an ordered mind, plenty of pluck, counted for less than nothing. Put the two men together in any circumstances of equality and the
one would eat the other.

LORD BEAVERBOOK: "HE CLUNG TO THE WHEEL"

*Lloyd George was a busy peacetime Prime Minister, particularly
in his newly discovered field of foreign affairs. But his political
position, based as it was upon the alliance of Liberal and Conservative leaders, was not a secure one. His policies toward Ireland, Turkey, and Russia seemed too contradictory to inspire universal trust.*

On the first day of January 1921 few people stopped to think on
the amazing and unprecedented position of Lloyd George. Certainly his
own colleagues, Bonar Law, Chamberlain, Birkenhead, even Churchill,
showed no sign of consciousness of the extraordinary political situation.

Lloyd George was a Prime Minister without a Party.

Of his own group of followers, made up mostly of Office-holders, many
were ashamed of their association with the Tories, and longing to return
to their old tried and trusted leader, H. H. Asquith, who was still in the
running for Downing Street.

The back-bench Members of the Coalition Liberal Party were "uncertain, coy and hard to please." They could not be counted. They would
not stand up. It is right to say that some waited eagerly and impatiently
for honours and places from Lloyd George's bountiful hand. They were
loyal. The rest, almost without exception, hoped for reunion with Asquith.

But the weakness of Lloyd George's following was counter-balanced in
the minds of men by the Prime Minister himself. His name made up the
balance of his strength.

Then again many Tory Members had been persuaded to believe that
their own seats depended upon the Liberal votes in their constituencies
which had been delivered to them at the last election by the almighty
hand of the Prime Minister.

He was in the eyes of men supreme and indispensable.

Then 1921 ushered in two cruel years which were to rip away all the
gold brocade and the tinsel too. The illusions were being shattered and a
great tragedy was being enacted for all to see.

The Greeks told us of a man in high position, self-confident, so
successful as to be overpowering to all others. Then his virtues turned to

failings. He committed the crime of arrogance. His structure of self-confidence and success came tumbling down. He struggled against fate, but he was doomed. So it was with Lloyd George in the year 1921 and into 1922. Then all was over. His plans good and bad came to nothing. He fell and never rose again.

The brilliant schemes and stratagems which he resorted to in war, outwitting Generals and Politicians, Peers, Prelates and the King and all to save Britain, he now applied with daring and skill to save himself from defeat by the Members of the House of Commons. He was confident that what he had once done, he could do again. To keep the seat of power, the place of patronage, he was prepared to stand out as the leader of Empire-minded men—or appear as the Liberal Apostle of Free Trade: as the Man of Peace in Europe—or the Man of War against Turkey and France: as the hammer of the Russian Bolsheviks—or their noble conciliator: as the Tribune of the British working classes—or the Champion of the Tory Landlords against Labour: stern enemy of the Irish—or their tender friend spreading his covering wings about another Celtic race ground under the heel of the oppressor. He took up each position in turn during those tragic years of 1921 and 1922.

Sometimes and simultaneously he took up contradictory standings. His daring was wonderful to look upon. But to those who never forgot his greatness in his great days, the spectacle wore thin and ere long became pathetic . . . "God hath made man upright; but they have sought out many inventions."

What a world of power and dignity and authority he might have lived in had he taken a different turn. Spurning all paths of pleasantness, he might have walked out into the desert of Opposition. There he could have reunited his disparate Liberals, attracting to himself the youth of Britain. His return to power would have been a certainty.

Yet he could not. The driver's seat was as he believed his rightful place. He clung to the wheel guiding the vehicle of state until he was rudely flung forth—the fate of every politicians who stays too long.[19]

Of Lloyd George a year later, in March 1922, Beaverbrook wrote:

Here was a man who had done battle with the most dreadful foe his country had ever faced. Great fleets and grand armies had moved at his command. The utmost perils had left him undaunted. He was ever fertile in inspiration and resource. He subdued not only the enemy

[19] From Lord Beaverbrook, *The Decline and Fall of Lloyd George* (London, 1963), pp. 9–11. Reprinted by permission of the Trustees of the Beaverbrook Foundations.

without, but also the enemy within. He had to contend with recalcitrant colleagues, stubborn Admirals, treacherous Generals, who were quite ready to conspire behind his back, and even to involve the King himself in their intrigues. He looked on tempests and he was not shaken.

Now the same man showed himself as a faltering temporizer. The genius was still there, and so was the mental and physical vigour. But the will had gone. The great war leader who was capable of ordering armies and navies to advance into battle was incapable of ordering a dissolution of Parliament. Trying desperately to shore up a crumbling Coalition, he suffered humiliation. If he had had the power of decision, he could have forced there and then an immediate dissolution in the face of all opposition. For the sake of a few more months of power he pledged the future, a pledge that was never redeemed. He had taken the second step on the way to destruction.

Before the year was out he was ejected from the Cabinet Room and Downing Street he loved so much, never to return. Lloyd George in the days of his greatness commanded friend and foe and fate itself. Now he was himself the sport of fate.[20]

SIR GEOFFREY SHAKESPEARE: THE ULTIMATUM TO IRELAND [21]

Toward Ireland Lloyd George acted with characteristic bluntness, yet obtained the result which had eluded English politicians for over a century. The negotiations for the Irish Treaty were long and complex. In the final discussions Lloyd George presented the Irish delegates with an ultimatum, threatening war "within three days" if they did not sign the Treaty whereby they were to obtain their independence. One of Lloyd George's Private Secretaries observed this move with a certain apprehension, particularly as it was he who was to travel to Ireland with the ultimatum. In his memoirs he reflected upon the crisis.

I have sometimes wondered since whether Lloyd George was right in presenting that ultimatum. I am convinced on mature reflection that but for the ultimatum we might have had no treaty. Supposing

[20] From Lord Beaverbrook, *The Decline and Fall of Lloyd George* (London, 1963), pp. 141–42. Reprinted by permission of the Trustees of the Beaverbrook Foundations. The dinner about which this comment was written was held at Lord Beaverbrook's house near London, the Vineyard, on March 27, 1922. Beaverbrook recalled that Lloyd George was "wooly in outlook and confused in argument."
[21] From Sir Geoffrey Shakespeare, *Let the Candles Be Brought In* (London, 1949), pp. 87–88. Reprinted by permission of Sir Geoffrey Shakespeare, Bt.

the Irish delegation had not signed that night; that the negotiations had terminated inconclusively; that the final decision was left over to the Republican atmosphere in Dublin, which had a few days previously rejected Dominion status. Would the treaty have emerged intact? I doubt it. As it was, here were the five Irish delegates committed before the world by their signatures to the approval of the treaty and going before the Irish Cabinet and the Dail to recommend its acceptance. Even so, the treaty survived only by the narrow margin of seven votes in the Dail, with 121 members voting.

If, then, Lloyd George was right in attaching the utmost importance to the *fait accompli* and to the Irish signing that night, he was entitled to use the most potent weapon in his armoury. The delegates to whom the ultimatum was delivered had been in prison, had been hunted, had seen their comrades executed or shot, their homesteads razed to the ground. Savage guerilla warfare had ravaged their homeland. The ultimatum conjured up before their eyes further years of bloodshed and reprisals on a vaster scale.

I have, however, never understood why the Irish accepted the ultimatum at its face value. Why did they not call the bluff? Lloyd George stated over and over again that he had promised to let Sir James Craig know next day (Tuesday, December 6) one way or the other. Supposing Arthur Griffith had said: "What is sacrosanct about Tuesday? We have waited hundreds of years for a settlement. Ask Craig to wait one week. If you feel you must inform him tomorrow, telephone to Dublin Castle or direct to Belfast and explain the delay. Are you really going to break the truce and plunge Ireland again into war without giving the Irish Cabinet the chance even of discussing your latest proposals?" How could Lloyd George have persisted with the ultimatum if Arthur Griffith had argued like this?

But the Irish delegation did not counter the ultimatum with logic. They bowed to it and signed.

I am nevertheless puzzled to find the reason. Was it that Arthur Griffith, having won the substance of Irish independence, signed because he, too, thought it would be more difficult for the Dail to repudiate it?

Perhaps, as so often is the case, the simplest explanation is the true one. In the debate in the Dail on the treaty Barton said: "The English Prime Minister, with all the solemnity and the power of conviction he alone of all men I have ever met can impart by word and gesture, declared that unless the delegation signed war would follow immediately." Lloyd George had reached the limit of his patience. He threatened war, he looked war, and he intended war, unless they signed. No one could doubt his sincerity when his words "imparted conviction," his eyes flashed lightning. How dare they question the ultimatum? They were awed and they signed.

A. FENNER BROCKWAY: "CRIMINAL NEGLIGENCE OF DUTY" [22]

Mounting public discontent against Lloyd George in 1922 sprang from the widespread belief that he was obtaining money for political purposes by selling knighthoods and peerages. The granting of "honours" is an essential part of the British system. Titles are the expected reward for many years of public service or political prominence. It was abhorrent to a public bred on tradition that Lloyd George should twist this system to his personal advantage. A young Socialist, Fenner Brockway, attacked the "honours' scandal" in an Independent Labour Party pamphlet. Like Thomas Paine over a century before, Brockway saw no reason to preserve titles at all, if they were to be awarded irresponsibly.

An inevitable result of immoral methods of bestowing titles is that grossly unworthy men are recommended to the King for honours. There is the notorious case of Sir Joseph Benjamin Robinson, the gold and diamond magnate, of Wynberg, who was announced among the new peers in June, 1922, in recognition of "national and imperial services" —a case so outrageous that Sir Joseph Robinson himself felt compelled, after the discussion in the House of Lords, to ask the Prime Minister to relieve him of the peerage.

In 1921 this great benefactor of the Empire was ordered by the Supreme Court of South Africa to pay a sum of over £500,000 for having defrauded the Randfontein Estates Company, of which he was chairman. It had been his duty to acquire certain mining properties for the company. "His method of performing this duty" (I quote from the speech of Lord Harris, House of Lords, June 22, 1922), "was to purchase the freehold for himself, and then to resell it to the company at an enormously higher price. He concealed from the shareholders the fact that he had made this illicit profit by means of a certain company promotion which the Court described as a 'device to camouflage the transaction.' " How much has Sir Joseph Robinson subscribed to the Coalition funds? What other service has he rendered the nation or the Empire?

During the debates in the Lords and Commons, in addition to the case of Lord Waring (which is still being contested), it was asserted without contradiction that within the last four years men have been given titles who have been found guilty of the following offences:

1. Understating his income in respect of an alimony for his divorced wife. The Judge said that he could consider himself fortunate in not being prosecuted for perjury.

[22] From A. Fenner Brockway, *Lloyd George and the Traffic in Honour* (London, 1922), pp. 12–13, 16. Reprinted by permission of Lord Brockway.

2. Rendering false accounts in relation to advertising contracts.
3. Food hoarding during the war.

Mr. Lloyd George admitted in the House of Commons on July 17, 1922, that some "mistakes" had been made. *Mistakes!* Would "criminal negligence of duty" on the part of the Prime Minister and his advisers be too strong a phrase? . . .

Mr. Lloyd George and his colleagues assert that rewards for party contributions do not necessarily involve the sale or purchase of honours. But does anyone who is aware of the ways of political life believe that the one is possible without the other, or that the purchase and sale of honours has not in fact occurred?

It is freely stated that Mr. Lloyd George has amassed a Party Fund of between two and three millions with which to fight the next election, and, in view of his profligate bestowal of honours, this statement is quite credible. But the voice of the People can defeat the Prime Minister despite all his ill-gotten millions.

Let the people press for the abolition of all titles. America gets on without them, and so can we. Where they have no power attached to them titles are silly, childish things, about which no dignified human being should care a halfpenny. Where titles carry legislative power, it is outrageous that they should be presented in this manner. We are supposed to be a democratic country politically, and it is time that we denied anyone the right to legislate for us without authority derived by popular election.

If conservative public opinion, clinging to tradition, insists that titles of some kind are to remain, they should be bestowed not by the head of one party in recognition of party services, but by a National Commission representative of all parties, and in recognition of public services, in the broadest sense of that term, only.

Mr. Lloyd George says that this would mean the end of the Party system. It need not: let the other parties finance themselves by small subscriptions from their membership, as the I.L.P. and the Labour Party do.

But, even if it did, the destruction of the Party system would be an untold blessing compared with the besmirched public life resulting from the foul and corrupt methods by which the old Parties are financed.

STANLEY BALDWIN: "A DYNAMIC FORCE IS A VERY TERRIBLE THING" [23]

Lloyd George's Coalition was destroyed in 1922 when the Con-servatives, upon whose support he relied, decided to withdraw from

---

[23] Quoted in G. M. Young, *Stanley Baldwin* (London, 1952), pp. 41–42. Reprinted by permission of Lord Baldwin.

*it, and reestablish their political independence. A junior Cabinet
Minister, Stanley Baldwin, was instrumental in persuading the
backbench Conservative Members of Parliament to turn against
the Coalition. He did so in a speech at the Carlton Club on October
19, 1922. When Lloyd George learned of Baldwin's intended rebellion he asked derisively, "Does little Baldwin think he can turn
us out?" Within a month of Baldwin's challenge the Coalition was
over, Lloyd George was relegated to a political wilderness from
which he never escaped, and Baldwin was Chancellor of the Exchequer. Baldwin told the Carlton Club meeting:*

. . . the essence of coalition is voluntary association, and you cannot compel people to coalesce in any particular form; and it seems to
me that a fatal mistake was made in agreeing to go to an election without
consulting the party as to whether they were willing or not to continue
the arrangement which they entered into in 1918.

As I am only going to speak for a very short time, I will not beat
about the bush, but will come right to the root of the whole difficulty,
which is the position of the Prime Minister. The Prime Minister was
described this morning in *The Times,* in the words of a distinguished
aristocrat, as a live wire. He was described to me, and to others, in more
stately language, by the Lord Chancellor [Lord Birkenhead], as a dynamic force, and I accept those words. He is a dynamic force, and it is
from that very fact that our troubles, in our opinion, arise. A dynamic
force is a very terrible thing; it may crush you, but it is not necessarily
right.

It is owing to that dynamic force, and that remarkable personality,
that the Liberal Party, to which he formerly belonged, has been smashed
to pieces; and it is my firm conviction that, in time, the same thing
will happen to our party. . . . I do not propose to elaborate, in an
assembly like this, the dangers and the perils of that happening. We
have already seen, during our association with him in the last four
years, a section of our party hopelessly alienated.

I think that if the present association is continued, and if this meeting
agrees that it should be continued, you will see some more breaking
up, and I believe the process must go on inevitably until the old Conservative Party is smashed to atoms and lost in ruins.

LORD BEAVERBROOK: "HE HAD ALWAYS SOUGHT THE HEIGHTS"[24]

*Bonar Law, Leader of the Conservative Party since 1911, had
served under Lloyd George in 1917 and continued to do so after*

[24] From Lord Beaverbrook, *The Decline and Fall of Lloyd George* (London,
1963), pp. 233–34. Reprinted by permission of the Trustees of the Beaverbrook

the war, until forced to retire from politics in 1921 by ill health.
He had thus worked closely and loyally with Lloyd George for four
years. But in 1922, when the Conservatives rejected Lloyd George's
leadership and broke up his coalition, Bonar Law led the malcon-
tents and returned to politics as Conservative Prime Minister.
Within a year he was forced to retire on account of severe ill health.
Lord Beaverbrook arranged a dinner for the two former Prime
Ministers.

Here were two men who had served in the highest office of state
and each had come to an end. Bonar Law had come to the end of his
life and the shadows of his death were already gathering round him.
Lloyd George had many years to live but the shadows of decline were
gathering round him. There were to be flashes of revived activity, moments of brilliance and an occasional false hope of further greatness
still to be achieved. But these manifestations meant nothing. The path
led inexorably downwards. The heights were behind and the valley was
ever deepening before. Lloyd George was never again to hold any public
office.

Those two men of the shadows were as different as any two men could
well be. Bonar Law was modest and self-effacing. He and Lloyd George
had first come together in 1916. Then it was that Bonar Law, called upon
to from a Government, relinquished the honour to Lloyd George. Bonar
Law was content that all the public glory and the triumph should go
to his colleague, whom he served with unswerving loyalty. He had never
sought the first place for himself. When confronted with necessity he
accepted it with reluctance and laid it down with relief. Ambition was
a word in a dictionary he had never opened.

By contrast, Lloyd George was alive with ambition. He had always
sought the heights—and when he grasped the last glittering prize he
could not bear to let it go. In the end it was violently snatched from
him. He was brilliant where Bonar Law was quiet. He was circuitous
where Bonar Law was simple and direct. Gratitude meant little more to
him than ambition meant to Bonar Law.

Yet here were these two different men, plainly attached to each other,
talking intimately together over long-forgotten incidents and events,
mostly unimportant; quarrels and disputes of 1922, altogether forgotten.
They were men who had done the country the greatest service, each in
his own way. In spite of their contrasting characters they respected each

---

Foundations. This dinner took place on September 12, 1923. Bonar Law died in
November of the same year. There is important material on the relationship between the two men in Robert Blake, *The Unknown Prime Minister* (London,
1955).

other and with affectionate phrases they addressed each other. They had tasted the fruits of power and felt its penalties. Now they had come to the last meeting in the eventide of understanding. They parted in an atmosphere of companionship. They were two friends destined never to meet again.

After 1922 Lloyd George was a politician without a powerful political party behind him. He tried to reestablish himself by a series of proposals to conquer unemployment, and to revive Liberalism on the basis of radical social reform. But social reform was now the Labour M.P.s' province. Their political strength was based upon their radical intentions. They formed their first Government in 1924 and their second in 1929. Lloyd George might have the same ideas, but they had political power. The first extract of three critical pamphlets at this time is from a Labour Party pamphlet. The second is from a speech by the Conservative leader Stanley Baldwin, who had been Prime Minister from 1924 to 1929 and was to return as Prime Minister from 1935 to 1937. He too controlled a political party to which Lloyd George was no threat. The third extract is from a Liberal who rejected Lloyd George's leadership of the Liberal Party, and sought to warn his fellow Liberals of the dangers if Lloyd George were ever to be their leader again.

THE LABOUR PARTY: "THE GAMBLER'S LAST THROW" [25]

Since 1906, when a Liberal Government came to office, Mr. Lloyd George has enjoyed a far greater share of responsibilities of power than any other British statesman. He was in office during the trade depression of 1908 when unemployment reached a level of 9.5 per cent. He was in office in 1921, at the head of a Tory-Liberal Coalition, when the great post-war trade depression first reached its height. And, above all, he was in office during the war and the years which immediately followed its close, when there was a matchless opportunity for preparing in advance for a depression whose coming all sensible people clearly foresaw.

What use did this new knight-errant of the workless make of all these opportunities? Not once, but a dozen times, he had the chance of taking effective measures to prevent the sinister spread of unemployment. He brushed aside almost every opportunity and every suggestion, from whatever source it came. He did next to nothing to provide work; and, because he did next to nothing then, the problem that the country has to

[25] From the Labour Party pamphlet, *How to Conquer Unemployment* (London, 1929), with a preface by J. Ramsay MacDonald. Reprinted by permission of the Labour Party.

face to-day is far harder than it need have been if the right measures had been taken at the right time.

Mr. Lloyd George has not the excuse that, in those days, the remedies for unemployment were unknown. Every one of the proposals which he now produces, with an air worthy of Maskelyne and Devant, was put forward, and urged upon him and his colleagues, by the Labour Party fully a dozen years ago. For, even while Mr. Lloyd George was still engaged in "hanging the Kaiser" and "making Germany pay," the Labour Party was already pressing upon those in authority the need to prepare, while times were favourable, for the bad times that were certainly coming when Mr. Lloyd George had muddled the peace. Later, when the insane provisions of the Peace Treaties had caused depression to spread throughout Europe, and this country, heavily dependent on overseas trade, was paying the price of Mr. Lloyd George's ignorance of economics, once more the Labour Party urged upon him the necessity of taking steps to counteract his errors, both by emergency measures for the provision of employment and by permanent steps for the reorganisation of the British industrial system. Mr. Lloyd George would have none of Labour's proposals. *The very plans which, caricatured and distorted, he is putting forward to-day he has again and again rejected when they were urged upon him by the spokesman of Labour. . . .*

He has pledged himself, *if his party is returned to power,* to "reduce the terrible figures of the workless in the course of a single year to normal proportions," and to "enrich the nation and equip it for competing successfully with all its rivals in the business of the world." These sound brave words; but Mr. Lloyd George, of course, knows full well that there is not a chance in a hundred million that he will be called upon to redeem his pledge. *The Liberal Party will not be returned to power at the forthcoming election; and, if it is not, what is the pledge worth?* Mr. Lloyd George has pledged himself and his party to nothing. His much advertised pledge is no more than a variant of the old saying that "Pigs might fly—if they had wings."

Mr. Lloyd George may talk about reducing unemployment to normal proportions—whatever that may mean. *But why did he not think of doing this before?* He has had his chance—chance after chance has been his, and he has missed them all. His latest "stunt"—for that is what the famous pledge is—can only be regarded as the gambler's last throw. Mr. Lloyd George is discredited in the eyes of the nation—even in the eyes of many among his own party. He is trying to manage a dramatic "come-back." Having rigged himself out at some political costumier's in a pair of theatrical corduroy breeches, he is posturing before the public as the champion of the workers. But his borrowed trousers are a sad misfit: they cannot cover the naked ineptitude of his past handling of the unemployment problem.

Mr. Lloyd George was the man who let the rich make huge fortunes out of the War, because he preferred borrowing and financial inflation to making the rich pay a larger part of the cost in taxation. *The country is still staggering under the burden of debt which he piled up in those fateful years.* And now Mr. Lloyd George is at his old games again. For him, as for the spend-thrift who squanders his inheritance in advance, borrowed money costs nothing. But the public is well aware that, if it does not pay to-day, it will have to pay to-morrow, and to pay more for the privilege of not paying to-day. The colossal sums that have to be paid in interest on the existing debt have taught the public that, even if they have not taught Mr. Lloyd George. He is ready to mortgage the future as gaily as ever; but to the electorate the style of his promises is too suggestive of the tone of a moneylender's advertisement. Wise men shove such things into the waste-paper basket without more ado. . . .

STANLEY BALDWIN: "HIS FEET ARE NO LONGER ON THE GROUND" [26]

Socialism at present is making very little running. They have issued a book containing some 60, 70, or more items of a programme which they hope to carry out some day or another. But we still are in ignorance of what they will attempt to do in the next Parliament if returned to power. They are waiting. They are trusting to win less on their programme than by lulling us to sleep on our apathy.

And while they have been waiting, the bold spirit of Mr. Lloyd George has jumped in, and has outbid every card in their hands. I wish to-night to direct myself for a time to the policy which he has put forward. Mr. Lloyd George is a very remarkable man, and I can hardly trust myself to find words in which to describe his characteristics. I have to go to a far greater man than myself to find any description apt for him. I remember that Thomas Carlyle in describing another great man who was the wonder of his generation used these words which might have been written of the leader of the Liberal Party: "He spent his whole life in plastering together the true and the false, and therefrom manufacturing the plausible."

His feet are no longer on the ground. He has gone up into the ethereal blue in an aeroplane, and he has flung across the sky in smoke, "We can conquer unemployment." That is not the first pledge he has made, nor will it be the last, and just as the appetite grows by what it feeds on, so the promises of 9d. for 4d., made in his comparative youth, are scrapped and scattered to the winds for this greater promise of 9d. for nothing. . . .

It is exciting politics. It affords good stunts for the newspapers.

[26] From a speech by Stanley Baldwin at Leicester on March 21, 1929. Quoted in the Conservative Party pamphlet, *Liberal Unemployment Plans Exposed* (London, 1929), pp. 2, 13. Reprinted by permission of Lord Baldwin and the Conservative Party Central Office.

Columns can be written about it, but for the country it will mean nothing but the piling up of debt and taxation. It is, as Mr. Lloyd George says, as sound as the Welsh mountains. The Welsh mountains are celebrated for their wild scenery, and would probably afford pasturage for a few goats.

CHARLES MALLET: A LIBERAL CRITIC [27]

Since Mr. Lloyd George succeeded in securing control of the Party organisation he has not ceased to press his claims to leadership with all the resources he commands. His energy and eloquence are very great. His physical vitality is still remarkable. His speeches are as full of liveliness as ever. One especially, in January 1927, where he took as his text a subject on which his authority cannot be disputed—"waste everywhere, everyhow, and all the time"—showed characteristic freshness in drawing attention to social and political problems which Liberalism might set itself to solve. His hold on the Liberal Press has increased. By his personal influence with newspaper proprietors he has been able to reduce to docility or silence almost all independent criticism there. His influence in the selection of Liberal candidates has been pushed as far as possible. It is the old story of the paymaster calling the tune. . . .

Liberals as a whole are not aware of the devices which, to secure his own ascendency, Mr. Lloyd George encourages and employs. I have before me at this moment a group of pamphlets published in his interest, all unsolicited gifts from his friends. One is a bitter attack on certain independent Liberals. Another is an ill-natured biography of Mr. Baldwin. A third is a dithyrambic panegyric, beginning with a portrait of Mr. Lloyd George at his astutest, and ending with the quotation"I have made thee a little lower than the angels and crowned thee with glory and honour." A fourth is an appeal from a Liberal candidate to be allowed to launch upon me a hundred copies of a work to illustrate the "outstanding public services" of his leader. It may well be that Mr. Lloyd George knows nothing of these particular pamphlets. It may even be that the famous fund does not in all cases pay the bills. But Mr. Lloyd George and his agents are unquestionably the chief promoters of this whole system of personal advertisement. And it will be a melancholy thing for the independence and the character of Liberalism if it allows its leaders to be foisted on it in this way. . . .

It is a mistake, said Mr. Bonar Law once with cruel candour, to "over-deify" Mr. Lloyd George as an electioneering force. Character and consistency still count with British voters; and for the lack of them no cleverness in programme-spinning can atone.

Mr. Lloyd George's remarkable qualities no one will deny. The

[27] From Charles Mallet, *Mr. Lloyd George: A Study* (London, 1930), pp. 290–92, 302–13. Reprinted by permission of Ernest Benn, Ltd.

romantic story of the young Welshman, humbly born and bravely
nurtured, fighting his way to influence and power, revealing early his
industry, his intrepidity, his large ambition, his genius for handling a
popular audience, his strong sympathy with the democracy from which
he sprang; passing into Parliament, and rapidly acquiring there, by
his nimble wits and his persuasive speeches, a reputation hardly second
to the reputation he had won at home; passing on to Ministerial office,
and showing there again the same genial and resourceful shrewdness,
the same quick eye for a bargain, the same fearlessness in fighting, if
fighting seemed likely to bring advantage or renown—that story is long
since familiar to the world. Often in those early days he won admiration
both from friends and from opponents. Once he rose to a high level,
when in the Boer War he imperilled his popularity and future for the
sake of a great public cause. But more than once it seemed to his
friends that he was capable of sinking to a lower level also, and was
a little too anxious, when opportunity offered, to push his own fortunes,
to play for his own hand. As time went on, observers noted a growing facility in political manœuvre, in compromise, in "gammon," in
intrigue. All humour, no doubt, has in it possibilities of humbug, and
all finesse possibilities of fraud. As power came to him, his natural self-
assertiveness increased. His restless ambition grew with it, his scheming
became more determined and persistent. He meant well by his friends.
But he never perhaps felt much compunction in pushing aside any
who stood between him and his objects. In 1916 he probably comforted
himself with the illusion that his supremacy was essential for his
country's good. And his success was rendered easier by the fact that the
colleagues whom he then threw over—men of far finer quality and
temper—did not, as it happened, care to push themselves.

The Great War brought to Mr. Lloyd George a great personal
triumph. Whatever his merits, he reaped also a full harvest from the
labours of other men. But success did not strengthen his character. It
brought into prominence its weaker sides—the passion for self-assertion
and intrigue, the headstrong, dominating temper, the easy indifference
to principle, the conviction that a gift for managing men and manipu-
lating opinion, the control of the Press and the control of money, were
the things that really counted for leadership in public life. The simplicity, which had once been his charm, became more and more over-
laid with assurance, genial assurance when not thwarted, but less
agreeable when it did not get its way. The purer aims of youth
perhaps had vanished. But much of its vitality and restlessness remained. And even the restlessness was to some extent a sign of force. The
Liberal Party must always be a party of movement, and in all parties
there is a natural temptation to identify movement with programmes.
Mr. Lloyd George has utilised this instinct to the full; and his large
resources have enabled him to create a factory of everfresh proposals,

which have undoubtedly interested, occupied, propitiated—dare I add, bamboozled?—a large number of able Liberals who liked neither his record nor his ways. Some of these proposals are of real value, and admirable work has been done in thrashing them out. Some are more open to criticism. Some are too obviously mere electioneering. But they all have served their purpose in drawing adherents to Mr. Lloyd George's standard, and in diverting to new issues, or at least to new discussions, the thoughts and doubts of candidates whom Mr. Lloyd George desired to have under his control. . . .

Suppose that Mr. Lloyd George succeeded one day in securing a majority in Parliament, or effected a combination which put him into office, what kind of leadership might Liberals expect? Is the past no clue to future actions? Could we altogether close our eyes to our experience in order to give him a fresh trial, a clean sheet? In Foreign Affairs alone his accession to power might prove embarrassing. No British Minister of modern times has made himself so generally distrusted: and the distrust is not personal rancour; it is based on a vivid recollection of his ways. The politician who was as much responsible as any man for the Treaty of Versailles, but who, before the ink was dry upon the paper, began his schemes to alter and upset it, who was so deep in the intrigues which followed that our Allies in France, in Italy, in Greece, and even in America, became hardly less suspicious of him than our enemies elsewhere, and whose passion for abortive conferences made our Foreign Office helpless and our diplomacy absurd, may have had some excuses for his bewildering vacillations, but his troubles arose too often from his curious reluctance to avow the truth. In the end he lost the esteem of every country, and his return to power might shake the confidence of all. The politician who in the dangerous Turkish crisis of 1922 was ready to plunge us back into war, and who rejected with contempt proposals to resort to the "wheezy harmonium" of the League of Nations, is not the man to inspire respect for ideals of arbitration, if he takes up the cause of disarmament again. No Foreign Office in the world would wish to see Mr. Lloyd George's methods of bluff and manœuvre substituted for the safer and more honourable influences which since his day have worked for European peace.

KEYNES AND HENDERSON: "WE NEED THE BREATH OF LIFE" [28]

Lloyd George's former critic, J. M. Keynes, was one of the few people who considered his economic program to be realistic. Together with another economist, Hubert Henderson, he wrote

[28] From J. M. Keynes and H. D. Henderson, *Can Lloyd George Do It? An Examination of the Liberal Pledges* (London, 1929), pp. 43–44. Reprinted by permission of Sir Geoffrey Keynes and Mrs. Hubert Henderson.

a defense of Lloyd George's plans to conquer unemployment by a
policy of increased economic activity.

It is not an accident that the Conservative Government have
landed us in the mess where we find ourselves. It is the natural outcome of their philosophy:—

"You must not press on with telephones or electricity, because this
will raise the rate of interest."

"You must not hasten with roads or housing, because this will use
up opportunities for employment which we may need in later years."

"You must not try to employ everyone, because this will cause
inflation."

"You must not invest, because how can you know that it will pay?"

"You must not do anything, because this will only mean that you
can't do something else."

"Safety First! The policy of maintaining a million unemployed
has now been pursued for eight years without disaster. Why risk a
change?"

"We will not promise more than we can perform. We, therefore,
promise nothing."

This is what we are being fed with.

They are slogans of depression and decay—the timidities and ob-
structions and stupidities of a sinking administrative vitality.

Negation, Restriction, Inactivity—these are the Government's watch-
words. Under their leadership we have been forced to button up our
waistcoats and compress our lungs. Fears and doubts and hypochondriac
precautions are keeping us muffled up indoors. But we are not tottering
to our graves. We are healthy children. We need the breath of life.
There is nothing to be afraid of. On the contrary. The future holds
in store for us far more wealth and economic freedom and possibilities
of personal life than the past has ever offered.

There is no reason why we should not feel ourselves free to be
bold, to be open, to experiment, to take action, to try the possibilities
of things. And over against us, standing in the path, there is nothing
but a few old gentlemen tightly buttoned-up in their frock coats, who
only need to be treated with a little friendly disrespect and bowled over
like ninepins.

Quite likely they will enjoy it themselves, when once they have got
over the shock.

Lloyd George had few supporters after 1929. He was growing
old. He appeared garrulous and uncertain to many who met him.
The newspapers portrayed him as a historical figure to be admired

for what he had done in the past, but of no concern to the present. There were however those who still visited him, looking for a leader, and hoping to find in him the answer to the economic lethargy and diplomatic ineptitude of contemporary politics. Harold Nicolson had retired from diplomacy, and was a National Labour Member of Parliament seeking a bridge between what he regarded as the two extremes of impotent Socialism and arrogant Conservatism.

HAROLD NICOLSON: LLOYD GEORGE REMINISCES [29]

In the hotel I found Lloyd George. He had been making a speech in the Drill Hall, and was flushed with pleasure and excitement at the plaudits of the mob. It is almost inconceivable that he should be the same man that I lunched with four years ago at Churt before his operation. He was absolutely bursting with vitality, roguishness, wit and reminiscences. He began by attacking Baldwin for his cowardice and lack of leadership, stating that Austen Chamberlain had told him that when he was Foreign Secretary, he could never get a decision out of Stanley Baldwin who, in fact, never even listened to his arguments. Ll.G. said that this showed his difference from Asquith. The latter always listened, always gave a decision, and never let one down. He was the ideal peacetime Prime Minister, and about the worst War Minister there could be, "since" (and at this Ll.G. popped a shrewd little eye sideways at me) "he hated war."

This led him on to a discussion of Cabinets in general and to a eulogy of his own War Cabinet in the great days. "Never," he said, "have I had such great minds around me—Smuts, Balfour, Bonar Law (the public have never realised the creative common-sense of Bonar Law—he was the most constructive objector that I have ever known), and Curzon. Curzon was not perhaps a great man, but he was a supreme Civil Servant. Compared to these men, the front benches of today are pigmies." He then proceeded, much to my surprise, to give imitations of Curzon, Arthur Balfour, and, strangely enough, Attlee. I had never imagined that Ll.G. was a mimic, but he managed in some curious fashion to recall to me the physical presence of Balfour and Curzon, and to render Attlee with a vividness that was unsurpassed.

At last I insisted on leaving and said something about his being the same man as he was in 1917. "Yes," he flashed at me, "Gladstone went on till he was 85, and so shall I."

[29] From Harold Nicolson, *Diaries and Letters 1930–1939*, ed. Nigel Nicolson (London, 1966), pp. 268–69. Diary entry dated July 6, 1936. Reprinted by permission of the late Sir Harold Nicolson.

*After Lloyd George's death many of his contemporaries set
down what they thought to be his main achievements and weaknesses. These assessments are an essential adjunct to the historical
perceptives which are to follow. Indeed, the mature reflections
of a contemporary are as important in seeking to understand a great
man as the remoter judgments of historians. The following extracts should be studied carefully, for in them one can find
almost every view upon which future historical judgments will
have to be based. Churchill's speech was his longest piece of writing
about Lloyd George. Lord Hankey was Secretary to Lloyd George's
War Cabinet. Sir Geoffrey Shakespeare worked in Lloyd George's
Secretariat after the First World War. Colin Coote was a Liberal
Member of Parliament who subsequently turned to journalism
and rose to be Editor of the Conservative newspaper,* The Daily
Telegraph. *L. S. Amery was a leading Conservative politician
who had watched Lloyd George in action at close quarters during
the war. Robert Boothby was a Conservative Member of Parliament
with an outspoken tongue and a critical, constructive, and com-
passionate mind.*

WINSTON CHURCHILL: "WITHOUT A RIVAL" [30]

*When Lloyd George died, Churchill, then Prime Minister,
spoke of him in the House of Commons.*

Shortly after David Lloyd George first took Cabinet office as
President of the Board of Trade, the Liberals, who had been in eclipse
for twenty years, obtained in January, 1906, an overwhelming majority
over all other parties. They were independent of the Irish; the Labour
Party was in its infancy; the Conservatives were reduced to little more
than 100. But this moment of political triumph occurred in a period
when the aspirations of 19th century Liberalism had been largely
achieved. Most of the great movements and principles of Liberalism
had become the common property of enlightened men all over the
civilized world. The chains had been struck from the slave; a free
career was open to talent; the extension of the franchise was moving

[30] From *Hansard*, March 28, 1945. Reprinted by permission of the Controller of
Her Majesty's Stationery Office. This speech was reprinted in Winston S. Churchill,
Victory (London, 1946), pp. 87–90. The reader should also consult Lord Beaverbrook's speech in the House of Lords on the same day, reprinted as Appendix 7,
pp. 416–18 of Lord Beaverbrook, *Men and Power* (London, 1956).

irresistibly forward; the advance in education was rapid and continuous, not only in this Island but in many lands. Thus at the moment when the Liberal Party became supreme, the great and beneficent impulses which had urged them forward were largely assuaged by success. Some new and potent conception had to be found by those who were called into power.

It was Lloyd George who launched the Liberal Radical forces of this country effectively into the broad stream of social betterment and social security along which all modern parties now steer. There was no man so gifted, so eloquent, so forceful, who knew the life of the people so well. His warm heart was stirred by the many perils which beset the cottage homes: the health of the bread-winner, the fate of his widow, the nourishment and upbringing of his children, the meagre and haphazard provision of medical treatment and sanatoria, and the lack of any organized accessible medical service of a kind worthy of the age, from which the mass of the wage earners and the poor suffered. All this excited his wrath. Pity and compassion lent their powerful wings. He knew the terror with which old age threatened the toiler— that after a life of exertion he could be no more than a burden at the fireside and in the family of a struggling son. When I first became Lloyd George's friend and active associate, now more than forty years ago, this deep love of the people, the profound knowledge of their lives and of the undue and needless pressures under which they lived, impressed itself indelibly upon my mind.

Then there was his dauntless courage, his untiring energy, his oratory, persuasive, provocative, now grave, now gay. His swift, penetrating, comprehensive mind was always grasping at the root, or what he thought to be the root, of every question. His eye ranged ahead of the obvious. He was always hunting in the field beyond. I have often heard people come to him with a plan, and he would say "That is all right, but what happens when we get over the bridge? What do we do then?"

In his prime, his power, his influence, his initiative, were unequalled in the land. He was the champion of the weak and the poor. Those were great days. Nearly two generations have passed. Most people are unconscious of how much their lives have been shaped by the laws for which Lloyd George was responsible. Health Insurance and Old Age Pensions were the first large-scale State-conscious efforts to set a balustrade along the crowded causeway of the people's life, and, without pulling down the structures of society, to fasten a lid over the abyss into which vast numbers used to fall, generation after generation, un-cared-for and indeed unnoticed. Now we move forward confidently into larger and more far-reaching applications of these ideas. I was his lieutenant in those bygone days, and shared in a minor way in the work. I have lived to see long strides taken, and being taken, and going to be taken, on this path of insurance by which the vultures of

utter ruin are driven from the dwellings of the nation. The stamps
we lick, the roads we travel, the system of progressive taxation, the
principal remedies that have so far been used against unemployment—
all these to a very great extent were part not only of the mission but
of the actual achievement of Lloyd George; and I am sure that as time
passes his name will not only live but shine on account of the great,
laborious, constructive work he did for the social and domestic life of
our country.

When the calm, complacent, self-satisfied tranquillities of the Victorian
era had exploded into the world convulsions and wars of the terrible
Twentieth Century, Lloyd George had another part to play on which
his fame will stand with equal or even greater firmness. Although
unacquainted with the military arts, although by public repute a
pugnacious pacifist, when the life of our country was in peril he rallied
to the war effort and cast aside all other thoughts and aims. He was
the first to discern the fearful shortages of ammunition and artillery
and all the other appliances of war which would so soon affect, and in
the case of Imperial Russia mortally affect, the warring nations on
both sides. He saw it before anyone. Here I must say that my hon.
and gallant Friend the Member for Wycombe [Sir A. Knox] was a
truthful and vigilant prophet and guide in all that information which
we received. He was our military representative in Russia. But it
was Mr. Lloyd George who fixed on these papers, brought them forth
before the eyes of the Cabinet, and induced action to be taken with the
utmost vigour possible at that late hour.

Lloyd George left the Exchequer, when the Coalition Government
was formed, for the Ministry of Munitions. Here he hurled himself
into the mobilization of British industry. In 1915 he was building
great war factories that could not come into operation for two years.
There was the usual talk about the war being over in a few months,
but he did not hesitate to plan on a vast scale for two years ahead. It
was my fortune to inherit the output of those factories in 1917—the
vast, overflowing output which came from them. Presently Lloyd
George seized the main power in the State and the leadership of the
Government. [HON. MEMBERS: "Seized?"] Seized. I think it was Carlyle
who said of Oliver Cromwell: "He coveted the place; perhaps the place
was his." He imparted immediately a new surge of strength, of impulse,
far stronger than anything that had been known up to that time, and
extending over the whole field of war-time Government, every part of
which was of equal interest to him.

I have already written about him at this time, when I watched him
so closely and enjoyed his confidence and admired him so much, and
I have recorded two characteristics of his which seemed to me invaluable in those days: first, his power to live in the present yet
without taking short views; and secondly, his power of drawing from

misfortune itself the means of future success. All this was illustrated by the successful development of the war; by the adoption of the convoy system, which he enforced upon the Admiralty and by which the U-boats were defeated; by the unified command on the Western Front which gave Marshal Foch the power to lead us all to victory; and in many other matters which form a part of the story of those sombre and tremendous years, the memory of which for ever abides with me, and to which I have often recurred in thought during our present second heavy struggle against German aggression, now drawing towards its victorious close.

Thus the statesman and guide whose gentle passing in the fullness of his years we mourn to-day served our country, our Island and our age, both faithfully and well in peace and in war. His long life was, from almost the beginning to almost the end, spent in political strife and controversy. He aroused intense and sometimes needless antagonisms. He had fierce and bitter quarrels at various times with all the parties. He faced undismayed the storms of criticism and hostility. In spite of all obstacles, including those he raised himself, he achieved his main purposes. As a man of action, resource and creative energy he stood, when at his zenith, without a rival. His name is a household word throughout our Commonwealth of Nations. He was the greatest Welshman which that unconquerable race has produced since the age of the Tudors. Much of his work abides, some of it will grow greatly in the future, and those who come after us will find the pillars of his life's toil upstanding, massive and indestructible; and we ourselves, gathered here to-day, may indeed be thankful that he voyaged with us through storm and tumult with so much help and guidance to bestow.

LORD HANKEY: LLOYD GEORGE AS WAR LEADER [31]

Before 1914 Lloyd George had displayed no conspicuous interest in the science of war. He had not been a very active member of the Committee of Imperial Defence. When war broke out, he had to find his feet in a world that was new to him, and he did this characteristically by visits to the theatre of war and by frequent conversations with all and sundry, whatever might be their rank or station in life, who were in daily contact with the hard realities of the situation. His independence of judgment is shown in his unceasing condemnation, in opposition to the views of all our leading generals, of the policy of concentrating on the Western Front.

[31] From Lord Hankey, *The Supreme Command* (London, 1961), II, 575–77, 867–70. Reprinted by permission of George Allen & Unwin Ltd. For Hankey's assessment of Lloyd George at the Paris Peace Conference in 1919, see Lord Hankey, *The Supreme Control at the Paris Peace Conference* (London, 1963).

In stature Lloyd George was rather small, but he possessed the stocky solid frame of many of his fellow-countrymen, and his healthy complexion gave evidence of a sound constitution. His head was square and large, with a wealth of black hair gradually turned grey by the cares of office. The dominating feature of his face was his eyes, ever changing, now tender with emotion, now sparkling with fun, now flashing with anger; eyes astute, unfathomable. And from the man there emanated an extraordinary sense of power and strength, such as I have never encountered in any other. Hundreds of times I have watched him listening quietly while some seemingly insoluble problem was debated. One view after another would be expressed; one solution after another proposed and rejected. When all had spoken, Lloyd George would often intervene with some novel and ingenious proposal, which his fertile mind had thrown up, and which he would urge with such logic, conviction and conscious power that opposition would cease and his decision would be accepted in silence or with a few muttered words of assent.

It was believed at the time that Lloyd George read nothing, and he seemed almost to encourage that idea at times. In fact he was an omnivorous reader. He usually woke early. His official papers were placed by his bedside overnight, and at an early hour he would apply himself to them. If one wanted to ensure that he read a particular paper, this could be put beyond doubt by persuading his private secretary to place it high up among the documents on his bed table. By breakfast time the Prime Minister had mastered the contents of a mass of official and unofficial documents, and had skimmed through the whole of the London Press as well as a good many provincial newspapers, especially the Welsh ones, and was ready to begin—what was really his main fount of knowledge—sucking the brains of the best men he could get on every subject. This was a continuous process. At breakfast, lunch, dinner and between meals, whenever opportunity offered, Lloyd George was engaged in picking up knowledge from every sort and kind of person, in fact, from anyone who had knowledge to impart—and especially knowledge bearing directly or indirectly on the war. Not that he did not enjoy his moments of relaxation, which he often mixed up with his business in the oddest way. A social evening would convert itself unexpectedly into a conference of the most serious kind, and conversely a serious discussion would develop on unconventional lines. Great organizer and administrator though he was, he was not enamoured with official routine. This made him rather a difficult man to serve in an official capacity. He required constant studying and humouring. One had to be ready for anything at the shortest notice. Frequently, almost daily indeed, I used to be invited to breakfast, lunch or dinner, or sometimes all three, for Lloyd George, like Asquith, was extraordinarily hospitable. The conversation would take a serious turn. One person after another would be sent for until the meal had become a conference of the most important kind requiring a formal record. To feed oneself with one hand, and to take notes with the other is neither agreeable nor good for the digestion!

One saving point, however, from the point of view of his staff was that Lloyd George rarely held official meetings late at night, which wears most people out quicker than anything else. During the whole period of the War Cabinet, including the Imperial War Cabinet and Supreme War Council and other directing bodies, I have only been able to trace four formal postprandial meetings, and they rarely if ever lasted until midnight.

On Sundays, even when there was no particularly serious crisis on hand, one had to be prepared to proceed at a moment's notice to Walton Heath, and, like the family doctor, I have sometimes been called out of church for this purpose. But that was the way the genius of the man worked, and so great was his hold on the imagination, so unsparing was he of himself, so disarming his cordiality and friendship, so inspiring his unfailing courage, that neither his colleagues nor his officials complained at his erratic methods, nor gave anything short of their best. Others have written of the charming simplicity of his life at that time, of his devotion to his family and to the things of the country, especially mountain scenery and walks through woods and heaths. He was also fond of good music of a simple kind, especially his beloved Welsh hymns. He was a keen Nonconformist, but not a bigot. He had one further trait—the gift of humour. His joyous mind, finding vent in remarkable outbursts of fun and wit, often helped the Prime Minister himself as well as his colleagues in the War Cabinet and at international conferences to bear their staggering burden and to tide over a difficulty. "A merry heart maketh a cheerful countenance," and that counts for something in time of war. . . .

Co-ordination was accomplished in one great field of war effort after another, first, in that of home administration by the creation of the War Cabinet and its Secretariat; then in that of the Empire by calling into existence the Imperial War Cabinet; and finally in the vast arena of inter-Allied war effort by the establishment of the Supreme War Council. In neither case did he act on a mere impulse of "brainwave." In all these matters he had matured his plans long before. Day and night, month in, month out he was looking ahead and planning his schemes of organization. But when the psychological moment came he invariably acted with lightning rapidity. The War Cabinet was in operation all day on December 9, 1916, although he had only begun to form his new Government on the night of the 7th. The Imperial War Cabinet was summoned within a week or two of his coming into office, before the new machinery of Government had had time to settle down. The opportunity of the Italian disaster was seized upon for the visit to Rapallo and for the decision, which he insisted on in the teeth of opposition from his own principal military adviser, to establish the Supreme War Council in accordance with long matured and carefully considered plans. So it was with the unified command. Undeterred by the Nivelle failure he never abandoned his intention to bring about this great reform.

I have a vivid recollection of being summoned out of the Cabinet room at Downing Street, where an international conference was in progress, to interpret for Lloyd George and Foch over a cup of tea. After comparing notes with the French General over the desirability of a unified command, and after establishing complete agreement, the Prime Minister concluded by affirming his intention to bring it about when the opportunity offered and added "and I know the man for the job," looking hard at Foch. It fell to Milner, whose mind ran with his chief's on the subject, to seize the psychological moment at Doullens, but Lloyd George followed up the original step by the work of extension and consolidation at Beauvais and Abbeville.

A noteworthy feature of many of his greatest innovations was the way in which he would seize the opportunity of some terrible disaster to bring his plans to fruition. This was true of the three cases mentioned. It was true of the foundation of the Ministry of Munitions, when he flung himself into the breach at the moment of crisis, and equally true of the adoption of the convoy system. In the latter case he took advantage of the moment when shipping losses had reached their maximum to put the Admiralty into a position where they were forced themselves to propose a reform which up to that time they had opposed. His political courage had always been tremendous and inspired by the public interest.

Of course no man could have accomplished all that Lloyd George did single-handed. Part of his genius lay in his choice of men. He determined from the first that his Government should be a true National Government, not a coalition like that from which Asquith had suffered before him. Of course it contained a political element—Bonar Law, Balfour, Curzon, Robert Cecil, Walter Long, Austen Chamberlain, Arthur Henderson and George Barnes, to mention only a few. But several of his key men were without any political following to speak of and some of them were at the time of their appointment almost unknown to the country as a whole—the brothers Geddes, Joseph Maclay, H. A. L. Fisher and Robert Horne. Moreover, he did not by any means limit his consultations to the official circle. Every moment of the day that was not devoted to the War Cabinet, the Imperial War Cabinet, some international negotiation or some other of the multifarious duties of a Prime Minister, including, of course, his Parliamentary duties and speeches in the country, was occupied by interviews with men and women of high or low degree, who, he thought, could give him useful information, or stimulate his mind. Breakfast, lunch, tea and dinner were almost entirely given up to this process of increasing his stock of knowledge and ideas.

When he left London for the country, whether at his home at Walton Heath or during his rare visits to his beloved Criccieth, there was a constant stream of motor cars or of travellers by train and an endless succession of more or less informal conferences. Whenever I had the good fortune to accompany him on these excursions, which was usually the case, my time was as fully occupied with taking and writing up notes as though I had been in the office of the War Cabinet at 2 Whitehall Gardens—with the difference that I lacked the facilities of a Government office and I must often have failed but for my indefatigable stenographer, Sylvester, whose energy was inexhaustible. And it was just the same—only more so—when we visited Paris, Versailles, or Rome, or St. Jean de Maurienne, or Rapallo, or Calais, or Beauvais, or Abbeville, or Boulogne or any other foreign place for purposes of inter-Allied business. There was a constant stream of callers, an endless succession of conferences and visits, most of which required some kind of official or semi-official record. Here also the visitors were by no means confined to the official circle but would include politicians in Opposition, well-informed journalists of many nationalities and anyone whose information or ideas might be useful.

The fact that he was never content to rely entirely on the ideas of his own fertile mind and of his immediate entourage adds lustre to Lloyd George's extraordinary achievements.

SIR GEOFFREY SHAKESPEARE: "AT HEART, A PEASANT" [32]

His voice had a unique quality. It was soft, rich and musical, and flexible in its range. If he had been a singer he would have been a tenor.

He enjoyed rude health. His energy and vitality, physical and mental, were unbounded. I am convinced that one reason for his success in public life was his robust constitution. He was capable of immense and continuous application, and never seemed to be bowed down by the strain of work or the press of events. The more desperate the situation, the more buoyant and resilient he became. However fierce the tempest, he seemed to have the power of detaching himself from his environment and calmly surveying the scene.

He could sleep at will, and when possible he snatched a short sleep after lunch. He went to bed early, usually at ten, threw off the problems

[32] From Sir Geoffrey Shakespeare, *Let Candles Be Brought In* (London, 1949), pp. 39–43, 64–68. Shakespeare was Private Secretary to Lloyd George 1921–23. He held political office at the Admiralty under Churchill, 1939–40. Reprinted by permission of Sir Geoffrey Shakespeare, Bt.

of the day and read himself to sleep with a wild-west adventure story—his favourite relaxation—sometimes leaving the light burning all night. He woke early, soon after six, and read the pile of papers and memoranda which his secretaries had laid by his bedside.

No one except Winston Churchill ever took so much trouble in preparing his speeches. For days beforehand he soaked himself in the subject by reading and talking about it and by picking the brains of experts. Then he started to make pencil notes and headlines. I have saved from the waste-paper basket several of these scraps of paper and two of them are reproduced in these pages. Then he would dictate a verbatim draft of what he intended to say. Finally the typist made a copy of the headlines of this in their proper sequence. For days before his speech Lloyd George was unapproachable. He was so immersed in his subject that it was difficult to get him to switch his mind to another problem. When the day of the debate came he delivered his speech. Imagine my consternation when sometimes it bore no relation to the speech he had prepared. The debate had taken an unexpected turn. But he was equal to it. From the mine of his research and study he produced spontaneously argument, analysis and facts even more compelling than those in the carefully prepared draft. When the speech was over he was as happy as a sandboy, and so were we until the next ordeal was due. All great speakers suffer from nerves before a big speech. When Sir John Simon was waiting to wind up for the Government at the end of a debate I asked him whether he felt nervous. He replied: "I feel just like a man sentenced to death, who is to be hanged shortly."

Lloyd George marshalled his arguments with great skill. He was a consummate advocate. At one time he was nearly persuaded to become a barrister and to practise in the English courts. But he hesitated to take the plunge. If he had done so I believe he would have become one of our greatest advocates. He knew instinctively how to concentrate on his strong points and how to gloss over his weak ones.

He was impatient of official opposition. Once, I remember, when Hearst, the powerful American newspaper magnate, was visiting England, Lloyd George wanted to entertain him. Tongues in Whitehall started to wag. "Meet this implacable enemy of Britain?—very unwise and impolitic," was the advice from one quarter. "But that is why I want to meet him," countered Lloyd George; "he may become more friendly." So he was invited to lunch at No. 10 Downing Street, and he came. Nothing but good for this country flowed from that meeting.

Lloyd George was no respecter of persons. It was not merely officials who taxed his patience. Famous economists who challenged his conclusions or who weakened them by qualifications or reservations sometimes came in for his wrath. At one conference at the Liberal Summer School at Cambridge on the land question Lloyd George wanted to link together in one dramatic phrase the problem of the land and the problem of unemployment. "One million idle men and one million idle acres." I have forgotten whether it was Maynard Keynes, Walter Layton or Hubert Henderson who objected to this over-simplification of the problem. Lloyd George was furious at this lack of comprehension. Both sides were in essence right. The economists wanted to insert several links in the chain of reasoning, while Lloyd George, as always, jumped straight to the vital conclusion. . . .

During the course of his career he made enemies, not only because of his reiteration of unpopular views, but because of the methods he employed to propagate them. He had been brought up in a school of bitter controversies in North Wales, and when he criticised anyone in a speech he hit as hard as he knew how. His favourite method was to kill by ridicule, and, as nobody likes being ridiculed in public, he left behind him in his path a trail of angry resentment. The objects of his attacks seldom forgave him. Often on reading the draft of a forth-coming speech his secretaries tactfully suggested a softening of the sting in his criticism of an opponent. Lloyd George would seldom listen to such advice. "What!" he cried. "That is the part of my speech I like best. Why do you always ask me to cut out my purple patches and to deliver a dull and tepid speech?"

Sir Geoffrey Shakespeare then contrasted Lloyd George with Churchill:

I have never come in contact with any other two men so richly endowed with natural genius or with a greater capacity for sustained concentration. When there was any task to be tackled, neither of them had any other interest till it was accomplished. The devotion to it of sixteen, eighteen, twenty hours a day was not uncommon with either. A man can accomplish much if he is a genius, even if he is lazy; a man who is no genius can accomplish much if he is industrious; but when a genius is industrious and capable of intense application there is no limit to his achievement. No one who has not been intimately associated with a Prime Minister in peace and war can imagine the terrible burden of responsibility imposed upon him. No one in that position can survive the vicissitudes and disappointments, unless he has the hide of a rhinoceros, a will of steel, or a supreme confidence in his own mission. Both Lloyd George and Winston Churchill faced their responsibilities without flinching. . . .

In tackling a problem, both were unencumbered by convention or tradition. Both were empirical in their approach, i.e. they were not afraid to make experiments; each resembled the other in infinite resource, inventiveness and alertness of mind. Each refused to be daunted by misfortune, or baffled by disappointment or obstacles. Both expected a wish or an idea to be translated into action with the minimum of delay. Each, in fact, almost conceived that what he wanted done had already been done.

Like Churchill, Lloyd George was a fascinating talker, but he was the better listener. He was always the listener. He loved hearing the views of other people, particularly of young people, on any current problem. Churchill is not a listener. He is inclined to be impatient. He forms his own view and adheres to it. Besides, his talk is so vivid and colourful that few people want to talk when he is present.

Lloyd George took a radical view in searching for any solution to a problem. As I have explained in another chapter, he was, at heart, a peasant and always came down on the side of the under-privileged. Churchill also takes the broad radical view, in spite of his aristocratic tradition and upbringing. But it is not the same instinctive reaction that Lloyd George's was. I attribute it, in part, to the American blood in his veins.

Of the two men, Churchill has been, in my opinion, more loyal to his colleagues than Lloyd George was. I do not wish to infer that Lloyd George was not delighted to see old friends, but he spent a great deal of time trying to conciliate opponents or to win the confidence of critics, often to the neglect of his friends. Winston Churchill never forgets a service rendered to him and delights in rewarding his friends for their loyalty, sometimes even to his own disadvantage.

SIR COLIN COOTE: "NO PRINCIPLES AT ALL" [33]

I got into trouble not long ago for having written that L.G. was in every way inferior to Asquith, save as an actor. This was too harsh and summary a judgement. We soldiers returned from the war with something very like hero worship for him. His courage had shone in the darkest hours. He had got us the tools to finish the job. His charm in private was mesmeric and exercised over both sexes. He could speak with the tongues of men and of angels. The fertility of his mind was immense. But I must speak of him as I found him, and though a Liberal, I could well understand why the Tories threw off his leadership at the Carlton Club meeting in 1922. He had really no principles at all, only emotions. He excited admiration, but not respect. His own party, after the break-up of the Coalition, could never stomach him for long, however sound his ideas and however large his fund. He could take the hypocrisy out of any situation—for example, when Neville Chamberlain rushed joyfully off to Munich, he said, "In my time,

[33] From Colin R. Coote, *Editorial* (London, 1965), pp. 96–97. Reprinted by permission of the author.

they came to see me." But he omitted to recall that no British statesman had been more fulsome in his praise of Hitler than David Lloyd
George. It was he who administered the death thrust to the Chamberlain Government in the Norway debate; but a few weeks earlier he
had been explaining to a large audience in a committee room upstairs
that we had no chance of winning; that we should make peace at once,
spend five years collecting our strength, and then go bald-headed for
Hitler. Clearly the lamp of his genius had come to burn too unevenly.
It stank rather than illumined. Is it too unkind to say that he was
the greatest man who has ever been a great cad, or the greatest cad
who has ever been a great man? Perhaps it is, but it is certainly too
kind to say, as some have done, that he was the most creative force
in British political history.

L. S. AMERY: A "ROGUE ELEPHANT" [34]

For a few years after the close of the First World War Lloyd George
was not only the dominant personality in our parliamentary life, but
the greatest figure in Europe. In 1922 he was not yet sixty, at the
height of his mental and physical powers, with a dynamic energy
that was to show no signs of flagging for at least another fifteen years.
That he fell, like Lucifer, "never to hope again," was not the least
significant aspect of the story of the inter-war years; significant alike
of his own personality and of the working of our political system. For
six years he had been the head of a government resting on a Conservative majority which not only admired him, but would have been
increasingly prepared to trust him, if only he had not too often shaken
their confidence or shocked their susceptibilities. Even after they rejected him he might have won them back on the Imperial policy with
which his tour in the United States and Canada inspired him, and
which would have only been a natural development of the Imperial
outlook which he had displayed in the war years. The temptation to
"knife Baldwin" was too strong for him.

There remained no other immediate alternative but to creep back
into the Liberal fold where he was ill at ease and profoundly distrusted,
a distrust which he only increased by his reluctance to surrender the
large fund which he had collected in his Coalition days. Alone of leading politicians during the next few years he faced the supreme issue
of unemployment which Baldwin had challenged and then shirked.
But his amazing campaign on that issue, for all its masterly documenta-

[34] From L. S. Amery, *My Political Life* (London, 1955), III, 395–96. Reprinted
by permission of the Hutchinson Publishing Group, Ltd. and David Higham
Associates, Ltd. Also of interest is Amery's comparison of Lloyd George and
Churchill, reprinted in Martin Gilbert, *Churchill* (Englewood Cliffs, N.J., 1967),
pp. 154–56.

tion and for all his vast expenditure, did far less when it came to the election of 1929 to help the Liberal Party than to damage the Conservatives. For the next two years he oscillated between alliance with Conservatives or with Socialists, to neither of whom he was in a position to deliver the goods in the shape of a coherent Liberal vote. There remained one last chance. When all the other party leaders yielded to panic in the economic crisis of 1931 he alone had both the understanding of its real nature and the demagogic power which might have rallied the demoralized Socialist rank and file in a whirlwind campaign against the "money barons," and have made him the real leader of the Socialist Party. But at that moment he lay helpless in the surgeon's hands, and the crisis was left to be handled by Samuel who could only see the opportunity which coalition offered of bringing the Liberal Party back into the political picture.

The root of the trouble lay not so much in his personal untrustworthiness which was often exaggerated. It lay rather in the fact that he had no central core of political principle or conviction, but only reacted with swift decision and immense energy to the immediate external situation. A pacifist, once he had accepted the war, he could not rest till it was won. Once out of the harness of the war effort and faced with all the complexities, domestic and international, of the aftermath he began to go to pieces. And at that moment he lacked the steadying and sustaining influence of party loyalty behind him. That influence he was never to regain in his old Party whose inevitable disintegration he had done so much to hasten. For the rest of his days he was doomed to be a parliamentary "rogue elephant" shouldered aside by the disciplined herds on either side, and made all the more an incalculable "rogue" by his enforced sojourn in the jungle. In the more open game of French parliamentary politics he could hardly have failed to upset governments and find himself in short-lived power from time to time. The rigid team play of Westminster could afford to disregard his eloquence and dispense with the contribution which his dynamic energy might still have made to our affairs.

ROBERT BOOTHBY: "TOTALLY WITHOUT VANITY" [35]

It was the fashion in 1922 to disparage the Prime Minister and all his works. As undergraduates, we were assured by our elders and betters that Mr. Lloyd George lacked principle, that he sold honours, that he had promised homes for heroes and failed to deliver them. We knew, of course, that he had been the principal architect of victory; but even the frequent scintillating appearances of Lord Chancellor Birkenhead

[35] From Robert Boothby, *I Fight to Live* (London, 1947), pp. 26–33. Reprinted by permission of Lord Boothby.

in our midst failed to restore our faith in his waning star. At the beginning of the Autumn term, Sir Austen Chamberlain came down to a joint dinner of the Canning and Chatham Clubs, and took the occasion to make an earnest public appeal for the preservation of the Coalition Government. A fortnight later Mr. Baldwin advised a meeting of the Tory Party at the Carlton Club that they should break with Mr. Lloyd George; and his advice was accepted by a substantial majority. Mr. Baldwin was at this time President of the Board of Trade; and it is significant that he did not see fit either to resign or to give the Prime Minister any warning before he struck. The reason for this was no doubt a perfectly genuine one. Not for the last time, he underestimated his own power. He did not think he could possibly succeed, and confessed afterwards that he had prepared himself to retire from public life. Nevertheless, the timing of the blow and the suddenness with which it was delivered were the main causes of a personal triumph which made him the dominating figure in British politics for the next fifteen years.

When Mr. Lloyd George tendered his resignation, King George V said: "He will be Prime Minister again." So it seemed to everyone at the time. The combination of himself at the summit of affairs with Balfour, Austen Chamberlain, Horne, Birkenhead, and Churchill constituted a formidable instrument of government. They all went into the political wilderness together. Bonar Law, the only statesman of comparable experience and authority, was a sick man. For a brief period he succeeded in riding the political storm, and holding what Lord Birkenhead described as a Government of second-rate brains in power, sustained by the driving force of Lord Beaverbrook. But if, during this interlude, a centre party had been formed out of the galaxy of unemployed political talent available, it is almost certain they would have been recalled to office at his death; and the course of history would have been altered. The event was different. Lloyd George turned to the left, and began the long and fruitless task of attempting to reconcile the disputes between the splintered fragments of the Liberal Party, which ended only when his political support was confined to the members of his own family. Baldwin, emerging as one of the ablest politicians of our time, outmanœuvred him at every turn, as he was later to outmanœuvre both Lord Beaverbrook and Lord Rothermere; and gradually brought the recalcitrant members of the Conservative Party, plus Churchill, under his wing. . . .

In order to justify his action in October, 1922, Mr. Baldwin persuaded himself that we were heading for war with Turkey. This was not the case. The crisis was over. Despite the fact that we had been abandoned at a critical moment by the French and by the Italians, Lloyd George, with the support of Churchill and two or three other members of the Cabinet, had challenged the armed might and the genius of Kemal with a few battalions—and won. *It was the last occasion on which Great Britain stood up to a potential aggressor before the outbreak of the second World War.*

*   *   *

Mr. Lloyd George was ever indulgent to youth, and I came to know him very well between the years 1926 and 1940. He was often accused by my own party of lack of principle; and it is a fact that he was never wedded to any of the quack nostrums which so often do service in purely party politics. He had a penchant for *ad hoc* solutions, provided they would work; and compromise was never distasteful to him. He even had his doubts about the efficacy of free trade in the modern world. But he seemed to me to be governed by two fundamental and unchanging instincts, which gave an underlying unity to his life and work. The first was a patriotism which attained white heat during the first World War. The second, a genuine hatred of oppression in any form. This accounts alike for the opposition to the Boer War, and his passionate, albeit mistaken, support of the Greeks in 1921 and 1922. It also accounts for his motives and objectives when he was laying the foundations of our social system in the years before 1914. They were simply and even naïvely expressed in an interview he gave as Chancellor of the Exchequer, when he said: "I want things done. I want dreams, but dreams which are realizable. I want aspiration and discontent leading to a real paradise and a real earth in which man can live here and now, and fulfil the destiny of the human race. I want to make life better and kinder and safer—now at this moment. Suffering is too close to me. Misery is too near and insistent. Injustice is too obvious and glaring. Danger is too present."

It is almost impossible for us to realize the mingled indignation, consternation, and hatred with which he was regarded by the landed aristocracy at that time. The notorious Limehouse speech looks very mild stuff to-day; and his attacks on the dukes—"A fully equipped duke costs as much to keep up as two *Dreadnoughts*; and dukes are just as great a terror, and they last longer"—only make us laugh. But he supplied the motive force which destroyed the power of the House of Lords, and paved the way for the political emancipation of the working class. Lord d'Abernon said that the essential cause of Lloyd George's mutability in regard to persons was his obstinate immutability in respect to things. "His conduct when tiger-shooting would depend entirely on the classification he gave to the tiger. If it appeared to him that the animal was of aristocratic type, no one could be more keen and eager, none more ardent and bold. If, on the other hand, Celtic imagination could endow the object of pursuit with some remote affinity with the underdog, it would be prudent for his companion not to expect meticulous fidelity."

I never saw him as a "mover of men and events," in which capacity Mr. Churchill has paid such striking tribute to his powers. But I once asked John Buchan, who was by no means his blind admirer, what he felt about Mr. Lloyd George as a War Minister. "I put him in the class of Cromwell and Chatham," came the unhesitating reply. I remember also an occasion in 1926 or 1927, when I was staying at a country house in a party which included several distinguished statesmen. One evening after dinner the conversation turned to the ever-absorbing topic of Lloyd George, and someone asked the rhetorical question: "Well, can you point to one concrete or permanent piece of work he has ever accomplished?" Lord Balfour, who had appeared to be asleep in the corner, stirred in his armchair, gazed meditatively at the ceiling, and remarked, "He won the greatest war in history. That really was something of an achievement." Pressed for an explanation, Lord Balfour went on to say that, in his considered opinion, we should never have inflicted the defeat that we did upon Germany in 1918 without Lloyd George. "That," he added, "can be said of no other man."

We were apt, in those days, to criticize with severity the Peace Conference of 1919 and the Treaty of Versailles; but they compare pretty favourably to-day with the Potsdam Agreement of 1945, and the subsequent performances of the "Big Four." We forgot too soon how hard and how skilfully Lloyd George had fought for Britain in council, how every fundamental objective of British policy had been attained as a result of his superb advocacy and iron determination, and how vital to our security and well-being these objectives were. The surrender of the High Seas Fleet, the limitations on its future size, the absolute prohibition—for all time—of German submarines and German military aircraft, the permanent demilitarization of the Rhineland, the mandates over the former German colonies, the right of the Dominions to full and separate representation at the Peace Conference itself and in the League of Nations—all were essential British interests, and all achieved. No wonder the King went hat in hand to receive his Prime Minister at Victoria Station when he returned from his triumphant labours.

In two respects, and two only, can it be said that Lloyd George failed at Paris. He did not realize in time the desperate need of France for a guaranteed security. Had he done so, he might have carried all before him, including the just settlement of the Silesian frontier problem between Germany and Poland, for which he strove in vain. At Genoa, in 1922, he made heroic efforts to undo the damage caused by the increasing French sense of insecurity. But it was then too late. Poincaré sabotaged the Genoa Conference, and Lloyd George never forgave him. I remember him saying in 1926 that the life-blood of France had been drained at Verdun, and that she had become a second-rate Power. All the more reason for giving her the guarantees she sought. She was no less indispensable to our own security then than she is now.

Mr. Lloyd George also failed to realize the importance of economics to the future of Europe. The Supreme Economic Council was mistakenly abolished. Frontiers were drawn without regard to economic realities; and no attempt was thereafter made to impose any kind of economic integration upon a politically disintegrated continent. The reparation clauses were also the subject of much legitimate criticism at the time. But here Lloyd George left many doors ajar; and it is only fair to say that he would never have agreed to a settlement of our debt to America unless it had formed part of a general settlement of the problem of international indebtedness, in accordance with the terms of the famous Balfour Note. The fact remains that, had the provisions of the Treaty of Versailles been upheld and enforced, the second World War could not have occurred.

A frequent ground of complaint against Mr. Lloyd George was that, after he had been relieved of responsibility, his speeches were mischievous. When a great man sees the main achievement of his life in increasing jeopardy he is apt to be bitter. For ten years, during which he was never consulted by any government on any subject, it was Lloyd George's fate to watch the fruits of the victory he did so much to win being cast away by lesser men. He derived consolation from the conversion of a piece of waste land in Surrey into one of the finest orchards in the country—a task into which he threw all his passionate energy. . . .

But Mr. Lloyd George could never keep off, or out of, politics for long. One Friday afternoon in the late 'twenties, when an unimportant private Bill was being debated, I came across him behind the Speaker's chair, and asked him what on earth he was doing in the House. The reply was unexpected. "To anyone with politics in his blood, this place is like a pub to a drunkard. The craving comes over you, and you can't keep away."

I cannot leave this subject without paying a humble tribute to the almost overwhelming personal charm which, more than anything else, frightened Mr. Baldwin. Lloyd George was totally without vanity of any kind. He did not know the meaning of the words envy, jealousy, or snobbery; and he was not only a great talker, but a great listener. A rare combination.

PART THREE

LLOYD GEORGE IN HISTORY

Historians have been somewhat daunted by Lloyd George's career. Only one, Professor Bentley B. Gilbert, has as yet examined in any detail the archives for the period of Lloyd George's most vigorous social reform measures. The vast bulk of official material on most aspects of Lloyd George's career has not yet been examined very thoroughly. In the historical section I have chosen a number of historians who, while approaching Lloyd George from different angles or writing books on different subjects, have found themselves drawn to the need for a description of Lloyd George himself. They were, of course, writing without access to the vast bulk of Lloyd George's private collection of personal and political papers, which only became fully available to scholars in 1967. It will take some years for historians to scrutinize and digest this material, and for a definitive biography to be produced.

Nevertheless, despite this problem of sources, enough is known about Lloyd George's career for us to look at it through the historian's eye. His Parliamentary and political speeches alone provide a major source, which, though often ignored, can lead the historian far along the road to understanding Lloyd George. We have seen also the varied and outspoken opinions of contemporaries, and from these too the historian can draw many lessons.

Our first extract, from Malcolm Thomson, shows the importance to Lloyd George of his entry upon administrative office, and describes its effects upon him.

The second, on the crisis of December 1916, has been specially written for this volume by Cameron Hazlehurst of Nuffield College, Oxford, one of the historians currently working on the Lloyd George archives, who has been assembling historical material from a wide range of sources in preparation for his work on Lloyd George's rise to power.

The third is by Professor Alfred Gollin in which he analyzes Lloyd George's character at the moment of his becoming Prime Minister.

The fourth, by Robert Blake, contrasts Lloyd George with General Sir Douglas Haig, the Commander-in-Chief against whom he so often pitted himself.

The fifth is by the politician and historian Roy Jenkins, describ-

*ing the relationship between Asquith and Lloyd George after
1924, and the reasons for their failure to come together again in
order to reestablish some form of Liberal unity.*

*The sixth is from Kenneth O. Morgan's study of the Welsh
influences on Lloyd George, and on his political career.*

*The final extract is from A. J. P. Taylor's lecture on Lloyd
George's rise and fall, in which he brilliantly analyzes Lloyd
George's last years as Prime Minister.*

Malcolm Thomson: "He Had to Curb His Restless Independence"[1]

Entry upon administrative office in the Liberal Cabinet
was a turning-point in Lloyd George's career. In two important respects
he had to re-orient his political attitude and activities.

The first and perhaps the most difficult of the new demands made
on him was the necessity of acting henceforward as a member of a
team. He had had no past training in this role and little natural taste
for it. He had missed the drilling in the team spirit which his colleagues
had acquired on the football and cricket fields of their public schools.
His mother had forbidden him "bandy," the local hockey game, after
he had sustained an injury whilst playing it. She was always afraid
that her children might hurt themselves playing rough games, and
discouraged them from joining in them. Lloyd George afterwards greatly
regretted this. Since boyhood he had never had time or opportunity
for games until after becoming an MP., when he took up golf; and
in his schooldays at Llanystumdwy he had been a ringleader of his
fellows; never one of the pack. In politics he had been a free-lance,
taking his own line and propounding programmes rather than accepting them. Though a member of the Liberal Party, he had when he
thought fit been ready to defy and oppose its great leader Gladstone.
He had renounced Rosebery's leadership; and had even, on occasion,
insulted Campbell-Bannerman. His bold stand against the Boer War,
while it demonstrated his supreme courage and sincerity, showed him
also as one who would take his own line, regardless of Party policy.

Now he had to curb his restless independence and learn to adapt
himself to the theory of joint Cabinet responsibility. He was ever

[1] From Malcolm Thomson, *David Lloyd George* (London, 1949), pp. 161–62. Reprinted by permission of the author.

a quick learner, and on the whole he mastered this lesson reasonably well, though it was never entirely congenial. In his early years as a Minister he was aided by the fact that his colleagues were theoretically in sympathy with the policies which he was bent on carrying out. It is not so hard to be one of a team if the others approve your course and follow your lead. Later on a time would come when this ceased to be the case. Then he found himself chafing at the bond until it broke.

A second important change imposed on him was that from being a critic of the Government to becoming a constructive legislator and administrator. That he would be capable of drafting legislation might well have been surmised from his admitted brilliance in the framing of valuable amendments and new clauses to Bills under discussion in Committee. But many of his friends and most of his opponents doubted his capacity to harness down his restless energy and combative spirit to the humdrum responsibilities of a department. How, in particular, could this fiery guerilla, this "below-the-gangway gamin," be expected to handle with discretion, the nation's commercial interests? It had been widely assumed that the Prime Minister would assign him one of the posts without portfolio in which he could act as the Government's orator and debater—tasks for which his supreme ability was undoubted.

These doubts and hesitations, however, were quickly proved to be unwarranted. If Lloyd George had not learned in his youth to play, he had certainly learned to work, and his zeal for work was unquenchable. He might in some of his personal habits be rather slipshod and unbusinesslike. He was notorious for failing to deal with correspondence, and before he took office his locker used to be stuffed with unanswered letters. But that was a matter which could be and was quickly rectified, once he had risen to the dignity of having his own private secretary. Lapses such as neglect of correspondence were due not to idleness but to preoccupation with other matters in an extremely active and crowded life. As a private member Lloyd George, in addition to maintaining his solicitor's practice, had been far busier politically than the leaders of the Party, but without financial resources such as those leaders possessed with which to pay for secretarial assistance. Now, as President of the Board of Trade, with the skilled support of the Civil Service at his disposal, he was able to give his whole time to front-ranking matters without having also to be his own clerk.

Cameron Hazlehurst: The Conspiracy Myth[2]

The most succinct statement of the conspiracy theory of Asquith's overthrow is that by Mr. David Thomson. (*England in the Twentieth Century*, Penguin Books. Harmondsworth, 1965, pp. 47–48.):

> At the end of 1916 Asquith was ousted from power by a complex intrigue, conducted by Lloyd George with ruthless skill. . . . Lloyd George, in effect, detached the Unionists under Bonar Law from Asquith and compelled them to support himself.

There are four propositions in this account which need to be closely scrutinised.

First, that Asquith was *ousted* from power.

Second, that Asquith was ousted by a *complex intrigue.*

Third, that this intrigue was *conducted*, with ruthless skill, by *Lloyd George*; and

Fourth, that Lloyd George *compelled* the Tories to support himself.

*　*　*

Was there a complex intrigue aimed at the overthrow of Asquith? And was this intrigue conducted by Lloyd George?

There are two initial difficulties about the intrigue argument. There is, first, a problem of definition. We all know what we mean by an intrigue or a conspiracy. And we all know that conspiracies are "bad things." But if we are not precise in our selection of criteria we run the risk of condemning more than we intended to do.

In developing the intrigue argument, Thomson resorts to a phrase used by Winston Churchill. The overthrow of Asquith was, says Thomson, one of those "secret, obscure, internal processes of which the public only now know the main story." The trouble about this is that when Churchill spoke of "secret, obscure, internal processes" he was referring not only to December 1916, but to the fall of the Liberal government in May 1915, and to the fall of the Lloyd George government in 1922.

All three episodes, according to Churchill, were of essentially the

[2] These extracts are taken from a hitherto unpublished lecture delivered by Cameron Hazlehurst at Nuffield College, Oxford, in January 1967. Printed by permission of the author.

same kind. If by intrigue one means secret negotiations, a private deal settled by a few politicians behind the backs of their colleagues, or the smashing of a government by its own leaders without consultation with the cabinet—if it means any or all of these things—then the making of the 1915 coalition was just as much an intrigue as that of December 1916.

When Asquith, Bonar Law, and Lloyd George agreed to form a coalition government in May 1915, Asquith had consulted no Liberal colleague other than Lloyd George. As far as the rest of the cabinet and the Liberal Parliamentary Party was concerned the whole operation was as secret and as obscure as any deal that could be conceived. The decision was made at a hastily arranged meeting after only fifteen minutes' discussion.

The second difficulty about the intrigue argument is that even if one can prove the existence of an intrigue to overthrow Asquith, and that it was the intention of most of the intriguers to replace Asquith by Lloyd George, one has still to prove that this intrigue was *conducted* by Lloyd George. One may be able to demonstrate the existence of all sorts of conspiratorial activity, but one is not entitled to assume, because Lloyd George was the principal beneficiary of this activity, that he *must* have been its instigator.

Thomson's third proposition was that, with ruthless skill, Lloyd George "conducted" an intrigue against his chief. Thomson offers no evidence in support of this charge. So we must turn to a more detailed indictment, Dr. Trevor Wilson's *The Downfall of the Liberal Party* (Collins, London, 1966).

Throughout Dr. Wilson's book, the most damning interpretations are produced for Lloyd George's actions or his failures to act. Dr. Wilson's description of Lloyd George in the period 1914 to 1918 is consistently and unjustifiably hostile. Consider, for example, page 29. There, in a footnote, is the statement—unsupported by any argument or evidence—that by December 1916 Lloyd George's affiliations with the Liberal Party were "uncertain." On page 41, we are told, again without justification, that among Lloyd George's qualities were "blatant disloyalty to his colleagues" and "open intriguing for office." On page 45 we find him "blatantly craving for power." A page further on it is "ingratitude and lack of scruple . . . overweening ambition, instability of attachment to party and colleagues."

Now I am not suggesting either that Lloyd George is innocent of *all* these charges or that Wilson does not give us *any* evidence in support of a dark portrait of Lloyd George. Nor am I arguing that this view of Lloyd George is simply an invention of modern historians like Wilson and Thomson. Many of his contemporaries believed that Lloyd George was unscrupulous and ambitious. But it is not enough to cite contemporary gossip and opinions—especially the opinions of those least likely to be objective—as evidence of a man's character. Nor is it permissible to pronounce with confidence about Lloyd George's behaviour and motivation in any particular event until a full investigation of that event has been made . . .

The fourth proposition which I extracted from Thomson's account was that Lloyd George achieved his alleged aim of toppling Asquith by splitting the coalition and "compelling" the Tories to desert Asquith.

The notion that Lloyd George *compelled* men like Bonar Law, Curzon, Austen Chamberlain or Walter Long to do *anything* is fantastic. It is true that the Tory ministers withdrew their support from the Asquith government, as it was constituted at the beginning of December 1916. But we need a more convincing explanation of this decision than the mysterious demonic power of Lloyd George.

*　　*　　*

In October 1915, *Sir Edward Carson* resigned from the government, and quickly began to criticise the organisation and policy of his former colleagues. He was joined in opposition by an ever-growing band of Tories—the Unionist War Committee—who numbered, by the middle of 1916, an estimated 150. Carson and his followers were anxious about the way in which the war was being conducted. They were in the forefront of the movements for compulsory military service and direction of labour. They pressed for harsher treatment of enemy aliens, pacifists, and conscientious objectors. And they conducted campaigns for more state control of food distribution, coal, and shipping. Throughout 1916, Carson and his rebel Tories—supported by Lord Milner in the House of Lords, and a violent section of the press—became more and more convinced that Asquith's methods of controlling the war effort were leading to disaster. And they blamed Bonar Law as much as Asquith. As the leading Tory in the cabinet, he shared a large measure of responsibility for the state of affairs.

The showdown came in the House of Commons on 8 November 1916. The incident: the famous Nigeria Debate—a debate and division on the subject of how to dispose of captured enemy property in Nigeria. Bonar Law, as Colonial Secretary, defended the government's intention to have a sale open to any buyers except known citizens of enemy countries. Carson, with the backing of the Unionist Business Committee (another independent Conservative group), argued on protectionist and patriotic lines that the property should only be sold to British subjects. It was a bitter debate. And Bonar Law insisted that an adverse vote would be interpreted as a motion of want of confidence in the government. Bonar Law was, in fact, throwing down a challenge which fulfilled exactly the conditions of a pledge which he had made the previous year to resign if the vote of his own party went against him.

When the votes were counted, the government had an ample majority; but a closer analysis revealed that, of the Tories who voted, 65 supported Carson and only 71 went into the government lobby with Bonar Law. If four more of those Tories present had voted with Carson, then, under the terms of the pledge which he had given in 1915, Bonar Law would have been obliged to resign and thereby bring down the government.

It was reported by Asquith, who seemed to derive some peculiarly misplaced amusement from the situation, that Bonar Law emerged from the debate with his teeth chattering. Certainly the vote gave Bonar Law only a precarious majority; and even that was much less satisfactory than the figures at first glance indicated. One reason for Bonar Law's discomfort was that those who voted against him included several men whom he had previously considered as his friends, and who had backed him for the leadership of the Tory Party in 1911. But much worse, and something which might have set his teeth on edge, was that 30 of the Tories who voted with him that night were actually members of Carson's personal ginger group, the Unionist War Committee. The support of these 30 could not be relied upon for the future.

In fact, when Bonar Law surveyed the opposition which emerged on 8 November 1916, there were several other disquieting elements about it. He could see, for example, that Carson, the champion of Ulster, was joined by a large body of his old enemies, the Irish Nationalists— a strange and disturbing combination. The Irish Nationalists had been disaffected since the middle of the year when a Home Rule settlement negotiated after the Easter Rebellion was sabotaged by unyielding Unionists in the cabinet. The Nationalists were now ready to combine, even with Carson, to bring discomfort to Bonar Law and perhaps to dislodge the government. And the final warning sign was the presence of a restless Winston Churchill and ten other Liberals voting alongside Carson.

The Nigeria Debate convinced Bonar Law that, unless urgent action was taken, there was a danger that the Tory party would be split and the government would fall. It was to prevent both these calamities that Bonar Law agreed to meet with Carson and Lloyd George to try to devise a scheme of reconstruction. Dr. Wilson has argued (page 91) that: "It is hard to doubt that . . . the unexpressed and perhaps unacknowledged, object for which Lloyd George and Bonar Law were working" was the substitution of Lloyd George for Asquith as Prime Minister.

I am convinced that this was not the object either of Law or of Lloyd George. It is clear from a memorandum which Law himself drew up late in December 1916 that Law entered into negotiations with Carson on the subject of how best to reorganise the higher direction of the war only after it had been agreed that the basis of all their plans was

the retention of Asquith as Prime Minister. Referring to the beginning
of his discussions with Carson, Law wrote:

> I then said to him that if we started on that basis—Mr. Asquith to
> continue as Prime Minister—then I was prepared to take any measures and
> to exercise any pressure that it was in my power to exercise, in order to
> improve the existing state of things.

In explaining the actions of the rest of the Conservative ministers,
we must begin with the fact that they did desert Asquith. What their
motives were must in some cases remain conjectural. What we can say,
however, is that in choosing to follow Bonar Law and serve under
Lloyd George they may have been deserting their Prime Minister but
they were remaining loyal to their party. Most of the Tory ministers
were probably not enthusiastic to serve under Lloyd George. They shared
much of the distrust and dislike of him which characterised his principal
Liberal enemies: McKenna, Harcourt, and Runciman. But if they stood
out of a government in which Bonar Law participated, it would be
tantamount to the repudiation of his leadership, and would cause a
damaging breach in the Tory ranks.

One desertion hurt Asquith more than any of the others. It was
Balfour, the former Conservative Prime Minister, who had replaced
Churchill at the Admiralty in 1915. In the days immediately before
Asquith resigned, Balfour's removal from the Admiralty had been one
of the points at issue between Lloyd George and Asquith. Lloyd George
insisted that Balfour had to go, and Asquith refused to consider dis-
missing him. Yet, when Lloyd George was entrusted with the task of
forming a ministry, he realised (with some prompting from Bonar
Law) how useful it would be to secure Balfour's services. Balfour could
be used in a post where he could not impede the running of the war,
but where what was left of his prestige would glow both at home and
overseas. Thus Balfour was offered, and he accepted, the office of
Foreign Secretary.

There was, in Balfour's conversion, in Bonar Law's adherence to Lloyd
George, in the acceptance of places in the new ministry by Austen
Chamberlain, Robert Cecil and Walter Long, there was in none of
these compulsion by Lloyd George. They were the actions of men convinced that their course was dictated by the national interest. Only in
the sense that he precipitated a situation in which their personal prefer-
ences were forced to take second place to the overmastering demand of
duty could it be said that Lloyd George compelled the Tories to serve
himself.

It was this same patriotic conviction which was the primary impetus
behind the formation of the so-called triumvirate of Lloyd George,
Bonar Law, and Carson. The three feared that unless some drastic

reorganisation and reinvigoration of the war effort took place Britain might lose the war. Carson and Bonar Law were, it is true, also impelled by a desire to stave off the disruption of their own party. Were they all conspirators? Their conspiracy consisted simply of this: they met together several times over a period of three weeks. Despite considerable distrust of each other they forged agreement about the arrangement which they wanted Asquith to adopt. From the moment that their proposals crystallised into a definite plan, they put their cards on the table.

The crux of the triumvirate's plan was that Asquith himself, while remaining Prime Minister, should cease personally to supervise the day to day conduct of the war. A small council of three or four, led by Lloyd George, should be responsible. The final proposals, drafted by Asquith, and accepted by Bonar Law and Lloyd George, were:

> The Prime Minister to have supreme and effective control of war policy. The agenda of the War Committee will be submitted to him; its chairman will report to him daily; he can direct it to consider particular topics or proposals; and all its conclusions will be subject to his approval or veto. He can, of course, at his own discretion attend meetings of the Committee.

This arrangement has been depicted by some historians, and was described by some contemporaries, as being wholly incompatible with traditional notions of the scope of prime ministerial authority. According to Dr. Wilson (page 91) the scheme to which Asquith was asked to assent:

> was so humiliating and unworkable that at best it made his departure from office only a matter of time. Lloyd George was to become head of the small war cabinet which would direct war policy, and neither Asquith nor any of his supporters was to belong to it. Indeed, the only control which the nominal premier and cabinet might exercise over this body was a veto they would hardly dare to use for fear of bringing on themselves the collective resignation of the war cabinet.

If what Dr. Wilson says is true then Thomson was justified in saying that Lloyd George intrigued for the purpose, and with the result, of ousting Asquith. But is it true? No one has presented the case against this view more cogently than Winston Churchill. Churchill first pointed to the important fact that Asquith did not summarily dismiss the proposals which were made. If the arrangement were studied with attention he said:

> it will appear to have contained many features of great advantage to him [Asquith]. Viewing the issue from a detached standpoint, I reached the conclusion, as did Sir Edward Carson, that the position of the Secretary

of State for War [Lloyd George] under it would become one both of difficulty and weakness. On him would fall all the brunt of battling with the naval and military Chiefs . . . The appeal in all cases would have been to the Prime Minister who, free from the friction of the discussions of the War Committee, yet fully informed on every point, would have been able to decide with final authority. On the other hand, Mr. Lloyd George, publicly appointed to preside over the Committee actually directing the conduct of the war, would have been held responsible for every misfortune that occurred and there were bound to be many. I warned the Secretary of State for War, when he told me what was passing, of these obvious dangers, but he was determined to persist in his course.

It is clear that to Asquith, in the circumstances which existed late in 1916, these arrangements were the best for which he could hope. The obvious dangers to which Churchill referred were obvious opportunities to a Prime Minister as skilled in the political arts as Asquith. By the late afternoon of Sunday, 3 December 1916, a compromise agreement was reached.

After a friendly and constructive conversation with the Prime Minister, Lloyd George and Bonar Law left Downing Street convinced that the crisis was over. It is, however, Dr. Wilson's opinion that *no* final agreement was ever reached. According to Dr. Wilson, the scheme which was presented to Asquith was deliberately designed to be so unacceptable that he would reject it. And the proof that the scheme was never intended to be accepted is alleged to be the firm suggestion by Lloyd George that Carson should re-enter the ministry as a member of the supreme ruling body. Dr. Wilson argues that Carson's inclusion among the members of the proposed war committee ensured that the negotiations would not succeed. "Of all the men in England," he says, (page 95) "whom Lloyd George might, without flippancy, have nominated, Carson was the most difficult for Asquith to accept. Carson's contempt for the Prime Minister, and determination to drive him from office, had been proclaimed throughout the land."

No one would deny that ideally Asquith would have preferred not to have Carson as a colleague. But Dr. Wilson overstates his case. Asquith had, after all, made no difficulties about receiving Carson into the ministry in May 1915 even though it was well known that Carson had less than a year before been engaged in encouraging preparations for civil war in Ireland. When it came to admitting critics into the government's ranks, Asquith could hardly be regarded as resolute. No one, not even Carson, entertained a more vicious loathing for Asquithianism or intrigued more vigorously against the Prime Minister than Lord Milner. Yet at the same time as he was making difficulties about Carson, Asquith was trying to buy off Milner by dangling the jobs of Coal Dictator and Food Dictator before him.

But there is something far more damaging to the theory about Carson's unacceptability than this. On the Saturday afternoon immediately before his resignation and in the middle of the negotiations which he was conducting with Lloyd George and Bonar Law, Asquith drove into the country ostensibly to get some sunshine and peace. The desire for peace and sunshine are understandable, though on a bitterly cold winter afternoon the chance of finding warmth even in Kent was remote. However, the real reason for making this journey was not a search for contentment and sun, but the hope that not far away from his own destination Asquith would find Carson. Carson could not be found. It is strange enough that a Prime Minister, with all his retinue of secretaries and intermediaries, should be unable to locate the leading figure on the opposition benches. Indeed, the evidence would suggest that Asquith made no attempt to set a search in motion. To have done so would doubtless have aroused the natural inquiry: what was the purpose of the proposed meeting? The question is still worth asking. The two men were not in the habit of exchanging social calls. It must at least come from within the bounds of possibility that Asquith wanted to explore the prospects of a separate deal with Carson, probably at the expense of Lloyd George. Driven into a corner, as he was in December, Asquith was prepared to consider any way out. If it meant including men like Milner and Carson in his team then he was, at least until December 4, quite ready to swallow his pride.

There is no doubt that at no stage in their discussions did Asquith, Lloyd George and Bonar Law reach a final decision about the *membership* of the new war committee. But the problem of personnel, though delicate, was secondary. The proof of this must surely be that all three men, Asquith, Lloyd George and Bonar Law, thought and acted as though the crisis was over when they had reached agreement about the size and functions of the new war committee. It is also of great significance that, before the subject of the membership of the committee was resolved, Asquith issued an official press notice announcing that reconstruction was to take place. The essential point for all three men was functions not composition.

* * *

What, finally, can we say about the question: was Asquith *ousted* from power?

Mr. A. J. P. Taylor has argued that, when Asquith broke off negotiations and resigned, he was putting Lloyd George to the test of forming a government confident that Lloyd George would fail. As Mr. Taylor puts it:

> Asquith was not manoeuvred out of office. He deliberately resigned office as a manoeuvre to rout his critics. His complaints, when this manoeuvre failed, were those of an ageing heavyweight, who has been knocked out by a younger, more agile opponent.

This is a tempting and picturesque explanation, but not, I believe, the right one.

We shall never be certain what was in Asquith's mind, but we can observe some aspects of his behaviour and some influences which must have affected him. There is one sentence in a letter to a lady friend which gives us the key. Asquith wrote: "When I fully realized what a position had been created I saw that I could not go on without dishonour or impotence—or both." He added in a choice egotistical afterthought: "And nothing could have been worse for the country or the war."

Asquith did not at first equate the proposed new arrangements with dishonour and impotence. Why did he change his mind? Two factors have been suggested. The first was that a leader in *The Times* of 4 December 1916 exposed in an embarrassing and humiliating way how dependent Asquith would be on Lloyd George under the new organization. But Asquith himself described *The Times*' article as a misrepresentation of the real position; and we have seen Churchill's opinion about the merits of the arrangement from Asquith's point of view. It is also argued by some historians that Asquith changed his mind because of the advice of some of his other Liberal colleagues and promises of support from the Tory camp. However, a careful hour by hour analysis of the events makes it almost certain that Asquith reached his decision before he consulted any one else.

The solution is not to be found either in pressure by friends or, directly, in abuse from the press. The short answer is that Asquith momentarily lost his nerve. After 8½ years in office as Prime Minister, he was ageing rapidly and subject to fatigue and to bronchial sicknesses from which he had never previously suffered. With his sons at the front he suffered agonies of apprehension climaxed by the death of his oldest son Raymond in September 1916. Since May 1915 he had badly missed the sustaining companionship of Venetia Stanley. He had grown increasingly dependent, personally and politically, upon the support of his leading colleagues. Perhaps, too, he was more dependent than ever before upon the comforts of alcohol. With the war going badly, and his own administration being attacked in Parliament and in the press, he drew deeply on his stock of personal courage and willpower. He was not the kind of man who was discouraged by criticism; but a barrage of savage attacks and wounding comparisons with his colleagues could be withstood only as long as his physical strength and his self-confidence lasted.

For a very short time—long enough to commit himself to resigning—Asquith lost the desire to go on enduring criticism and attempting to control what he imagined was the insatiable power lust of Lloyd George. Perhaps only for a few hours he longed for release. He must have realised, as his Liberal friends did, that if he resigned, Lloyd George could certainly form a government. It was one way of salvaging his own self-respect, however, to hope that a Lloyd George ministry would soon crash and that he would be recalled in triumph.

*   *   *

There is abundant testimony that Lloyd George was not anxious to assume the supreme responsibility of the premiership. He and Bonar Law genuinely feared that Asquith's sway over Parliament was still substantially unimpaired. Until the moment when he was invited to form a ministry, Lloyd George was afraid that he would be outmanoeuvred and forced to go into the wilderness. He had secretly arranged private accommodation and a contract as a newspaper correspondent to replace the ministerial rooms and salary that he expected to forfeit. When he thought that Asquith had agreed to an acceptable compromise he was completely satisfied. When he discovered that Asquith was backing out, he urged intermediaries to press Asquith to keep to the agreement. There is no proof of any kind that Lloyd George tried to organise a personal following in the House of Commons or have a team in readiness to strike a coup in the Parliamentary Liberal Party. When he himself learnt that Asquith was declining to reconstruct the government as they had agreed, he sent his own resignation without bothering to check what sort of support he would be likely to command among the Liberal rank and file. Inspired by the conviction that the nation was in peril, he refused to parley any longer. Resignation, with all its personal dangers, was the only honourable course.

Any man as able as Lloyd George would not, if he were intriguing for total power, have been so careless in estimating and mobilizing his own forces. We can understand Lloyd George's failure to prepare his Liberal supporters for battle only if we discard the hypothesis that he had set his mind on the overthrow of his Prime Minister. Had Lloyd George tried to mobilize the Liberal back-benches the probability is that he could have secured a comfortable majority in his own favour. It is one of the continuing mysteries of the whole affair that so few people seemed to realize that Asquith's power was almost entirely based on an illusion.

What is even more disturbing to the historian is that, although he lost the parliamentary struggle, Asquith so triumphantly captured the history books of a generation.

Alfred Gollin: "A Governor of Men"[3]

The man who became Prime Minister in December 1916 was as devious and crafty as any politician of any generation. He was an expert in every device of the intriguer's art. Contemporaries often condemned him as a rabble-rouser. Even his closest colleagues could never be certain of him. Asquith spoke only the truth when he once said that Lloyd George did not inspire trust. Yet, at the supreme crisis of the war he became the King's first Minister. And, in the opinion of many, not one of his contemporaries was so well equipped to discharge the duties of that high office. . . .

In 1916 Lloyd George was in his fifty-fourth year. He had begun his political course as a Welsh Nationalist, as the champion of his people against the political and religious intolerance of their English neighbours. During the Boer War he enlarged his reputation. In that period he demonstrated moral courage and oratorical ability of such magnitude that he became a national figure. He was accepted by the Radical masses in Great Britain as their hero.

After Asquith became Prime Minister in 1908 he was recognised as his first lieutenant. He carried forward the Radical banner which had languished in defeat for nearly a decade. At the Board of Trade, and later at the Exchequer, he revealed administrative powers of the first class. He could get things done. In the sphere of social reform he stood alone, in a reforming Ministry. His National Insurance Act of 1911 carried the nation and the people whose lives were affected by it into the modern age. His speeches in the House and in the country roused the ardour of his friends, and the frenzied hostility of his enemies.

Unlike Winston Churchill or Asquith, however, Lloyd George contrived to maintain and even promote friendly personal relationships with a large number of Tories at Westminster during the high summer of the Asquithian Government. He was always prepared to discuss matters with his opponents. He could charm anyone and everyone. His public attacks were balanced by his private courtesies.

In 1910 he urged upon the Conservatives the formation of a National

[3] From Alfred Gollin, *Proconsul in Politics* (London, 1964), pp. 384–87. Copyright © 1964 by A. M. Gollin. Reprinted by permission of Anthony Blond Limited, The Macmillan Company, and the author.

Government so that the major objects of Liberals and Tories alike could be achieved, unhampered by the narrow restrictions of party tradition. Although his plan failed, many of the younger Conservatives never forgot the proposal and the broad outlook of its author.

He could be relied upon to place nation before party whenever a genuine crisis came. In 1911 at the time of the Agadir episode he astonished the Germans by publicly warning them that there were limits to the pacifism of Liberal England.

The coming of war tested Lloyd George more severely than any of the peacetime crises he had surmounted. For a moment, in August 1914, he hesitated. Should he seek to lead and guide the pacifists of Britain, or should he join the great mass of the nation in its desire to aid Belgium and France?

Once his mind was made up, Lloyd George never looked back. He threw himself into the struggle with every ounce of his strength. He soon saw that he was qualified to meet the test. He proved to be a better war leader than any other of his colleagues.

Moreover, at an early stage he realised that the generals, despite a lifetime of training, possessed no secrets that might equip them to control the supreme direction of the State in time of war. His great personal triumph as Minister of Munitions served to fortify him in his belief that he was fitted for the first place in the Government. The Radical orator disappeared from the political scene. In his place there now stood the man who was determined to win the war. . . .

Can we discover a red thread that links the aspects of Lloyd George's career together, that turns a series of episodes into a unity?

Lloyd George fed upon power. His qualities swelled in the exercise of it. He was a man who dealt in power. As a leader of the Welsh Nationalists, he fought his way to Westminster. As a reforming Minister he established himself upon an eminence in Whitehall. When he became Premier, he dominated the hopes and aspirations of an Empire. Essentially, he was not a Nationalist, or a Radical, or even a reformer. These were the phases of his course. He was a governor of men; one of those who is fitted to direct the lives and energies of his fellows.

Small of stature, Lloyd George throbbed with physical and intellectual energy. He was seldom at rest. Unlike Arthur Balfour, for example, he could never observe the political scene with the weary eye of the satiated aristocrat. In order to maintain his position he found it necessary to be in action constantly. At all times he felt obliged to prove himself.

He was inordinately proud of his large head. Such are the foibles of great men that he always measured his contemporaries by the size of their heads. Neville Chamberlain, for example was dismissed as a "pinhead" who would never amount to anything in the political world of Westminster. Lloyd George never abandoned this curious opinion, although he was to live to regret it after Chamberlain became the master of the Conservative Party. A handsome shock of hair, worn in a flowing mane that descended below his collar, was another curious source of pride. He wore a fairly full moustache for a different reason. Once, when he shaved it off, he was astonished by the aspect of the thin line of his mouth. The moustache was restored as quickly as nature allowed. Too much that was better hidden from the eyes of men was revealed by the absence of this facial adornment.

Although he took pride in these minor details of his physical appearance, no man was more of a realist than the new Prime Minister. The weakness, ambitions and idiosyncrasies of other men were qualities to be fastened upon for his own purposes. Flattery might work with one colleague, an air of honest purpose with another, the harsh demands of the man of power with a third. Lloyd George was a master of all these roles. He seldom made a mistake in dealing with men.

Loyalty was a political concept that he never understood. When a subordinate had served his purpose, he was jettisoned with ruthless speed. In the same way, if a political object could not be attained by frontal assault, there was always another way round.

Robert Blake: "An Enigma to the Historian" [4]

Haig had already met and disliked Lloyd George when the latter became Secretary of State for War in the summer of 1916. He was now to be thrown into the closest relations with him. The distinguished cavalry general, brought up in all the dignified assurance of the old order, was confronted by the brilliant orator who from an obscure and penurious origin had risen to the highest office in the land. Apart from their determination to beat the Germans the two men had not a single characteristic in common. While Haig had been proceeding by calm and consecutive steps along the path of professional advancement, Lloyd George had been delighting one half of the nation—and enraging the other half—with a display of political acrobatics unsurpassed since the days of Disraeli. Whether he was escaping disguised as a policeman from the patriotic fury of a Birmingham mob, or riding on the crest of the radical wave in the storms provoked by his own attacks upon the peerage, or floundering in the embarrassing depths of the Marconi Scandal, Lloyd George's whole political life had been a whirl of publicity and excitement. Haig, although he did not realise it, was meeting in Lloyd George the first portent of the new mass age, the first man to climb from the very humblest class in society to the summit of British politics. Such men do not and cannot be expected to obey the political conventions which govern the classes whose citadels they storm. In another land and at a later time Lloyd George, with his skill as a demagogue and his hatred of the aristocratic way of life, might have been an exponent of the new Caesarism, the creator of a dictatorship based upon the radicalism of the masses and directed against the established order of society. Yet—such is the all-absorbing power of the British political tradition—he who began as the bitter enemy of property and privilege was destined to end his days, like Haig, a landowner and an earl.

Haig did not dislike Lloyd George for social or political reasons. He was no snob. He got on well enough with men like Asquith, Haldane and Henderson, whose political views were very different from his own. Nor is it true, as has sometimes been averred, that Haig disliked clever

[4] From Robert Blake, ed., *The Private Papers of Douglas Haig 1914–1919* (London, 1952), pp. 41–42. Reprinted by permission of Robert Blake and Eyre & Spottiswoode (Publishers) Ltd.

men. It is true, however, that he greatly disliked men, clever or foolish, whom he did not consider straight. There was something in Lloyd George, a love of intrigue, a lack of fixed principle, a curious inconsistency, which at once puzzled Haig and aroused his suspicion. What lay behind the charm, the wit, the swift ripostes, the romantic oratory? Lloyd George's closest friends could not always tell. Was he a man of principle pursuing by devious means a consistent end, or was he an opportunist who relied upon his intuition to gratify at every turn his love of power and office? To this day it is not an easy question to answer. Lloyd George remains—and perhaps will long remain—an enigma to the historian.

Roy Jenkins: The Break-up of Liberal Unity [5]

      Asquith made some attempt to get back on to reasonable personal terms with Lloyd George. Margot and he even had him to luncheon at Bedford Square—with the Queen of Roumania, Desmond MacCarthy and Viola Tree—an event which would have seemed inconceivable five years before. But Asquith's heart was hardly in this rapprochement; and Lloyd George's certainly was not. His position had perhaps become the more difficult of the two. His fall from power had been more recent and more precipitate. His international fame was unparalleled, and his energy, at this stage at least, not only appeared to be, but was much greater than Asquith's. Yet he had to occupy the subordinate position.

      There was one respect, however, in which his position was far from subordinate. He had the money. The Lloyd George Fund far exceeded any sums which the Liberal Party as such was able to command. Lloyd George was determined to preserve this position, and the power which it gave him. He argued that the terms on which the Fund had been raised made it illegal for him to hand it over to the Liberal Party. At one stage the Liberal Shadow Cabinet proposed that this should be tested before a Chancery lawyer, but it would have required more than counsel's opinion to make Lloyd George hand over these resources to the Chief Whip.

      The issue naturally caused great bitterness within the Liberal Party. The separate existence of the Fund was a constant reminder both of the incompleteness of the Liberal re-marriage and of the profitable if doubtfully respectable past of the Liberal Coalitionists. Nor did Lloyd George try to use the Fund in such a way as to assuage the bitterness. At the 1924 election he had not hesitated to force a reduction in the number of Liberal candidates from a projected 500 to 343. The money was there, but he made only a relatively small sum (£60,000) available.

      Asquith responded with some impatience and more distaste. He disliked concerning himself with money, most of all political money. He believed that such matters should be left to the Chief Whip and not obtrude upon the party leader. But Lloyd George made the continuation of this old practice impossible. Asquith either had to raise a substantial

[5] From Roy Jenkins, *Asquith* (London, 1964), pp. 512–16. Reprinted by permission of Chilmark Press Inc. and Wm. Collins Sons & Co. Ltd.

sum under his own aegis or see his authority drained away by the pull of Lloyd George's money. Accordingly, in January 1925, he launched the so-called Million Fund Appeal. The sponsoring body was the National Liberal Federation, and the purpose was clearly to make Asquith and the party independent of the money which Lloyd George would only grudgingly and conditionally dispense.

The Appeal was not a success. Some money came in, but not nearly enough. Partly, no doubt, this was because of lack of confidence in the future of the Liberal Party generally. But it was also due to the existence of the Lloyd George Fund. This pervasive *cache* was responsible both for the launching and for the failure of the Appeal. Rich Liberal supporters did not see why they should subscribe when the leader of the party in the House of Commons had large sums of money—to which they had probably contributed—already at his disposal.

The failure of the Appeal weakened Asquith *vis-à-vis* Lloyd George. This was pointedly brought home during the autumn of 1925. Lloyd George had presided over a committee of enquiry charged with a review of Liberal land policy. The result was a controversial scheme, which was strongly opposed by a number of leading liberals, notably Runciman, Charles Hobhouse and Mond. They protested to Asquith against Lloyd George mounting a public campaign in favour of his own proposals before they had been accepted by the party. Asquith asked Lloyd George about his intentions. Lloyd George replied intransigently that he proposed to act in accord with "the whole tradition of independent Liberal initiatives . . . ranging from the anti-Corn Law League, through the Liberation Society to various campaigns for local option and even prohibition." Asquith then wrote one of the few letters of rebuke which he ever sent to Lloyd George. There was to be a conference to thrash the whole matter out. In the meantime he "strongly deprecated a great campaign led by the Liberal leader in the House of Commons on an issue which was not accepted as (party) policy."

The effect of the rebuke upon Lloyd George was negligible. He continued his campaign (supported by his own Fund); the conference broadly endorsed his policy: and Asquith had to come into line with a speech at a joint meeting in February, 1926. This incident did much both to disenchant Asquith with the terms on which he held the Liberal leadership and to weaken his always precarious post-1922 relationship with Lloyd George. It only needed one more incident to provoke a severance. This incident was quickly provided.

The General Strike began on May 3rd, 1926. On that day the Liberal Shadow Cabinet met, and there seemed to be no great difference of opinion amongst those present (including Lloyd George) as to what the party attitude should be. On the following day Asquith spoke in the House of Lords, unreservedly condemning the strike and supporting the Government's efforts to resist it, although adding some words of criticism of their handling of the coal dispute. In addition, he and Grey each sent messages in a similar sense to the emergency paper, the *British Gazette*, and Simon used the House of Commons to condemn the strike as illegal. But Lloyd George spoke, if not in a directly contrary sense, at least in a very different one. He condemned the Government more than he condemned the strike; and he wrote a syndicated article for the American Press (a regular commitment at the time), which was pessimistic about the Government's ability to win the day.

As a result of these differences, Lloyd George did not attend the next meeting of the Shadow Cabinet (on May 10th), and wrote saying that he was refraining from doing so on policy grounds. Asquith at first did not appear to take this defection too seriously: "When I came up yesterday morning to our 'Shadow Cabinet' at Abingdon Street," he wrote to Mrs. Harrison on May 11th,

> there was one notable absentee—Ll.G.—who was in the sulks, and had cast in his lot for the moment with the clericals—Archbishops and Deans and the whole company of the various Churches (a hopeless lot) —in the hope of getting a foothold for himself in the Labour camp. He is already, being a creature of uncertain temperament, suffering from cold feet. So much so, that I have a message this morning from Miss Stevenson asking me to arrange for a joint meeting in July at Carnarvon, which he and I are to address.

A few days later, perhaps because of the representations of colleagues, or because of reflection on previous difficulties, Asquith came to take a more serious view of the matter. On May 20th, he wrote Lloyd George a long and somewhat portentous letter. He rehearsed the events leading up to the meeting of May 10th:

> All my colleagues attended with the notable exception of yourself. The reasons for your absence, as set out in a letter dated the same morning, seem to me to be wholly inadequate . . . It was, in my judgment, the primary duty of all who were responsible for Liberal policy, and certainly not least of the Chairman of the Parliamentary Party in the House of Commons, at such a time to meet together for free and full discussion, and to contribute their counsels to the common stock. Your refusal to do so I find impossible to reconcile with my conception of the obligations of political comradeship.

After despatching this letter Asquith retired to Castle Howard in Yorkshire. While there he was pressed by his closest colleagues, including his host, Geoffrey Howard, to announce that he would explain his whole position in an early public speech. But he refused to do more than telegraph a peremptory instruction for the publication of his letter on May 20th. He greatly overestimated the degree of Liberal support which this would win. Nor did he allow for the obvious consideration that Lloyd George would respond by himself publishing a persuasive and subtle reply. This was issued on May 25th. The effect was made more damaging by the non-publication of Lloyd George's original letter of May 10th. It looked as though Asquith had started a largely unprovoked quarrel. . . .

On June 12th Asquith suffered a slight stroke and was incapacitated for nearly three months. He was unable to attend the annual meetings of the National Liberal Federation at Weston-super-Mare, at which he had intended to fight back. For his convalescence he went once more to Castle Howard. Slowly, over the summer he recovered his health, but not his political position. Back in London, at the end of September, he faced the end of the road. He attended a final, sad and hopeless "conclave of the faithful" at Edward Grey's house. When it was over he wrote to Margot:

> The alternatives are to lead a squalid faction fight against Ll.G. in which he would have all the sinews of war; or to accept his money and patch up a hollow and humiliating alliance. I am quite resolved to do neither.

Kenneth O. Morgan: "A Decisive Catalyst"[6]

His very career, with its dramatic ascent to power, seemed a personal vindication of the nationhood of Wales. He helped to preserve and strengthen a Welsh community. He failed to produce a self-governing Welsh state, but, as Tom Ellis found in the 1890's and as *Plaid Cymru* has found since, the demand for this was but intermittent. Finally, Lloyd George taught Welsh radicals that their programme rested implicitly on the links with England being preserved. He showed that the partnership of Wales and England did not mean that Wales could not attain a distinct national status. In this sense, his own career is a parable of the history of modern Wales.

In the wider history of Britain as a whole, Lloyd George's career was a decisive catalyst in the transition from Victorian Britain to the new society of the twentieth century. His faults were many—his ruthlessness in personal relations, his unpredictability in outlook and in policy. Yet surely his achievements make these seem trivial by comparison. More than any other man he laid the foundations for the modern welfare state, which "has brought warmth and glow to the grey lives of the people." More than any other man he was the architect of victory in the First World War. The recent torrent of denigration that has assailed his reputation cannot take these achievements away. Perhaps, however, his main significance for modern Britain rests in something more intangible—not what he did, but what he was.

His career symbolized a new social revolution, that "the day of the cottage-bred man" had indeed dawned even in the stratified society of Edwardian Britain. More, his rise illustrates the revival of an element which has been more and more in evidence in twentieth-century Britain, which we may perhaps call the growth of provincialism. It can be seen in the rise of the Labour Party, a revolt of the working-man of the provincial, industrialized North and West against the domination of the capitalist South and East. It can be seen in the re-awakening of provincial culture, in the search for a re-defined "common culture" from the days of Housman and Hardy to those of Raymond Williams and Arnold Wesker.

[6] From Kenneth O. Morgan, *David Lloyd George, Welsh Radical to World Statesman* (Cardiff, 1963), pp. 84–85. Reprinted by permission of the author.

167

Lloyd George's triumphs, and the way in which he attained them, impressed on contemporaries anew the rich diversity of their country, which consisted not of one national community but of several. A new and deeper appreciation, not merely of Wales but of British cultural life as a whole, has resulted. This has survived the fragmentation even of the divided, disillusioned world of the mid-twentieth century, poised in horrid fascination before the prospect of its self-destruction.

A. J. P. Taylor: "His Balance Sheet of Success" [7]

For Lloyd George, parliament was less important than the public meeting. He said: "My platform is the country." This was the time when all political leaders did a great deal of public speaking. The period opened in the 1880's, after Gladstone's Midlothian campaigns; it tailed off in the 1930's, perhaps because interest in politics declined, perhaps because of the radio. Lloyd George came just at the top of the wave. His style was all his own. Other statesmen spoke in formal terms, carefully prepared. Churchill, for instance, learnt his early speeches, word for word, by heart; and read his later ones. Lloyd George spoke with his audience, not to them, and snapped up phrases as they were thrown at him. "Ninepence for fourpence" was the result of one such interruption; making Germany pay to the uttermost farthing, the less happy result of another. Most public speakers seemed to be the contemporaries of Henry Irving or Beerbohm-Tree. Lloyd George gave a music-hall turn, worthy of Harry Lauder or George Robey, the prime minister of mirth; and the great days of the music-hall, roughly from 1900 to 1930, corresponded exactly with his. In 1923 Lloyd George was persuaded to use a microphone for the first time; and he accepted it ever afterwards. I suspect that it ruined his public style, as it certainly ruined the music-hall.

Speech-making was not Lloyd George's only instrument for projecting himself on the country, perhaps not even the most important. No public man has made more use of the Press. This was not new. Palmerston wrote leaders for the *Globe* and the *Morning Chronicle,* often reproducing the very words of his dispatches, and rewarding the proprietor of the latter with a baronetcy. Salisbury wrote in the *Standard,* and made his ghost, Alfred Austin, Poet Laureate. Even Sir Edward Grey briefed J. A. Spender, of the *Westminster Gazette.* Lloyd George approached the Press in a different way. He was never forthcoming to reporters. On the contrary, he was the first prime minister who employed a press secretary to keep them at bay, and even then often complained of their misrepresentations. Lloyd George went for the man at the top—the editor and, still more, the proprietor. Why bother to make a case when the proprietor

[7] From A. J. P. Taylor, *Lloyd George: Rise and Fall* (London, 1961), pp. 11–14, 33–37. Reprinted by permission of the author.

could make it more decisively simply by issuing an order? The most famous example came in 1918. Lloyd George, angered that the *Daily Chronicle* had enlisted his critic, Frederick Maurice, as military correspondent, got a group of Coalition Liberals to buy the paper and turned out the editor, Robert Donald, at twenty-four hours' notice.[8] This was not his first exercise in financial influence. As early as 1900 he persuaded George Cadbury to buy the *Daily News* and to turn it overnight from a pro-war to a pro-Boer paper. Usually he used less direct means. Common sympathy with the Boers established a deep intimacy between Lloyd George and C. P. Scott, owner-editor of the *Manchester Guardian,* an intimacy not really broken even when Scott was denouncing the behaviour of the Black and Tans in Ireland. Scott remained faithful even unto death: almost his last act was to swing the *Manchester Guardian* against the National government, and behind Lloyd George, during the financial crisis of 1931. Even more important for Lloyd George was his friendship with Sir William Robertson-Nicoll, editor of the *British Weekly,* a man now forgotten, but wielding decisive power in his time. It is hardly too much to say that Robertson-Nicoll was the man who first, by supporting Lloyd George, raised him up; and then, by withdrawing his support, cast him down.

Newspaper proprietors in the stricter sense were flattered by Lloyd George and often ennobled by him: Riddell, owner of the *News of the World,* the first divorced person to be made a peer; Rothermere; Beaverbrook. Lloyd George had a curious on-and-off relationship with Northcliffe, the greatest of them all, intimate at one moment, hostile at the next. The two men had much in common, despite their conflicts, both sprung from the people, both impatient with conventional politicians. There was in both the same mixture of impulsiveness and calculation, though Northcliffe was the less calculating of the two. When once asked to co-operate with Northcliffe, Lloyd George replied: "I would as soon go for a walk round Walton Heath with a grasshopper." A good analogy; but who more like a grasshopper than Lloyd George himself? Lloyd George did not court the newspaper proprietors merely as the makers of public opinion. He genuinely believed that they understood this opinion and could interpret it. How else had they achieved their enormous circulations? Hence he canvassed their advice before taking decisive action. He supposed also that they possessed executive ability of the highest order. When he filled his administration with "press lords," this was not only to "buy" them; he thought that the work would be done better by them than by anyone else, and it often was. Then, by an odd twist, he discovered the same abilities in himself. After all, if the inarticulate Northcliffe and the ponderous Rothermere had journalistic genius, how much more must

[8] This manipulation of "public opinion" proved useful to Lloyd George in another way. He put some of his private political fund into the *Daily Chronicle,* and sold out in 1926 at a fourfold profit. [A. J. P. Taylor's footnote]

Lloyd George have it too. I doubt if this were the case. Though he was highly paid by American papers after he ceased to be prime minister, this was rather for his name than for the quality of his contributions. But Lloyd George believed himself suited to a great journalistic post. In 1922 it was seriously proposed that a group of wealthy friends should buy *The Times,* then being hawked around after Northcliffe's death, and set him up as editor. Lloyd George was ready, eager, to resign the premiership for this purpose. No doubt he had other reasons for wishing to be rid of office. Nevertheless the affair is striking testimony that Lloyd George rated the world of journalism highly, perhaps even more highly than the world of politics. Editors of *The Times* have often believed that they were more important than prime ministers. Lloyd George was the only prime minister who apparently agreed with them.

Parliament, platform, press, one element needs to be fitted into place, maybe the key place: politics. Though Lloyd George was never a good party man, indifferent to many party doctrines and regardless of party discipline, he was first returned as a Liberal, and managed to call himself a Liberal of some sort or another throughout his political life. The peculiar circumstances of the Liberal party gave him his opportunity; later snatched it away again.

Few writers have noticed how peculiar these circumstances were. Historians of recent times assume, perhaps rightly, that the two-party system is a permanent feature of British politics; and they go on to assume, with less justification, that the swing of the pendulum follows inevitably from this. Hence, they find nothing surprising in the Liberal victory of 1906. On the contrary, it was against all the rules. When Lloyd George entered parliament in 1890, the Liberal party seemed clearly on the way out: sustained by Gladstone's great name, but then doomed to decline and disintegration. So it happened: defeat in 1895, and thereafter disruption into warring factions. This was not surprising. Historic liberalism was a *bourgeois* cause, inspired by the advance of *laissez-faire* capitalism and successful in the days of limited suffrage. It lost drive as individual enterprise diminished; and it offered little which could attract a mass electorate. This was the common pattern all over Europe. The National Liberal party in Germany, the Liberal party in Austria, the French opportunists, the moderate Italian Liberals who followed Cavour, all saw their greatness disappear. Old-fashioned British liberalism really ended in 1874, as Gladstone recognised by resigning from the leadership. The party was revived only by the freak controversies first over the Eastern Question and then over Home Rule. . . .

*　　*　　*

Of the period after 1918, A. J. P. Taylor writes:
Ramsay MacDonald, not Lloyd George, became the symbol, adequate or not, for the triumph of democracy. It is fascinating to watch how

Lloyd George missed the meaning of all this. He actually wanted to see 200 Labour members of parliament so that he could balance more adroitly between the contending "interests." But where was the base from which he could operate? During the war the "interests" could sink their differences in a common will to win; after the war this uniting principle disappeared. Lloyd George made repeated attempts to found a Centre party. This was possible only if it included representatives from both extremes. There would be none from Labour. Therefore the Centre party could only be another name for the Conservatives; and they preferred their own. Even the Coalition Liberals recognised this and refused to be swallowed up, clinging to the rags of their Radical origin—Free Trade and the Free Churches. Lloyd George's Centre party remained a one-man band.

Lloyd George had still one asset, achievement, and he worked it to the full. His balance-sheet of success after the war was remarkable, perhaps more so than during the war itself. It is possible to debate how much he contributed to victory. Lloyd George himself said that the war was won not by him, but "by the man in the steel helmet." What he did after the war was all his own doing. Peace with Germany. Lloyd George alone, against Clemenceau and Wilson, secured a moderate territorial settlement, which did not deprive Germany of any "ethnic" territory; he alone arranged reparations in such a way that they could be settled in agreement with Germany, as soon as the Germans wanted to agree at all. Peace with Soviet Russia. Lloyd George secured this not only against his French allies, but against the majority of his own cabinet including particularly Churchill. Peace with the trade unions. Lloyd George circumvented the challenges from the railwaymen and the miners until they ceased to be dangerous. Peace with Ireland. Lloyd George performed the miracle which had defied every British statesman for over a century, or perhaps for five centuries—the younger Pitt, Gladstone, Asquith, to go no further back; he settled the Irish question for good and all. There was hardly a problem where he did not leave success behind him. The inter-war years lived on his legacy, and exhausted it.

Yet it was all dust and ashes. Each success lowered his reputation instead of adding to it. What went wrong? What turned Lloyd George from the most admired into the most hated and distrusted figure in British politics? It was partly his method. He defined this method in classic words: "I was never in favour of costly frontal attacks, either in politics or war, if there were a way round." He was the leader of a predominantly Right-wing coalition; yet his instincts were all to the Left. He did not browbeat his followers. Instead he led them with much blowing of trumpets in one direction until the moment when they discovered that he had brought them to an exactly opposite conclusion. Conciliation of Germany was prepared under a smoke-screen of "Hang the Kaiser" and "Make Germany Pay." The Soviet leaders were Bolshevik untouchables until the day when Lloyd George signed a trade agreement with them. The trade-union leaders were a challenge to civilisation at one moment; and were being offered whisky and cigars at the next. Ireland was the supreme example. Lloyd George's successful peace was preceded by the Black and Tans, one of the most atrocious episodes in British history. The Unionists were told that Lloyd George had murder by the throat; and then found themselves called upon to surrender everything which they had defended for nearly forty years. Men do not like being cheated even for the most admirable cause.

Success ruined Lloyd George in another way. Confident in his own powers, he would tolerate no rival near the throne. During the war he had colleagues of equal, or almost equal, stature—Bonar Law, Milner, Balfour. He had formidable antagonists—admirals and field-marshals. He was the little man asserting the cause of the people against great odds. After the war he reigned supreme. He had no colleagues, only subordinates; men who, however distinguished, had pinned their fate to his, and had no resources with which to oppose him. He established with them "the relation of master and servant," which Churchill acknowledged even years later, when chancellor of the exchequer and Lloyd George a mere private member. Though Lloyd George reluctantly restored the full cabinet in place of the small war cabinet, he then disregarded it and settled policy on his own behind the scenes.

There was another terrible flaw in his position: the sale of honours. Lloyd George could plead that governments had notoriously been selling honours for the last forty years and, less directly, long before. He ran the system too hard. Not only did he sell more honours with less excuse. Lacking a party, he sold them for his own account, as the existence of the Lloyd George fund still testifies. It was one thing for him to maintain a personal dictatorship, based only on his individual gifts. The Lloyd George fund raised the threat that he would turn his disregard of party into a permanent system. Moreover, politics had to become more respectable with the advance of democracy. Corruption was an accepted necessity in the old days of a closed political nation. Appearances had to be kept up now that "the people" had a voice in government. The integrity of Labour finance was itself a standing reproach to the older parties. Most of all, the supply of buyers was running out. It was easy to be delicate about the sale of honours when few wanted to buy them. Those who had bought honours in the past wished to elevate their position by ensuring that no one did it again; and those who still aspired to honours wished to avoid paying for them.

Some of the forces which had brought Lloyd George to power moved away from him; others lost their strength. Independent Labour removed one prop. The retreat of the business-men from public life removed another. Some of Lloyd George's business ministers, among them the most successful, returned to their firms when the war was over; others were itching to go. Besides, Lloyd George had one great failure to set against his many successes: he could not stave off the decline of the old Liberal staples which had long been threatening. He came to power on a wave of industrial expansion which drowned financial scruples. After the war, "the penguins of the city" enforced deflation and unemployment. The self-made business-men who had prospered along with Lloyd George were now ruined. The Coalition Liberals vanished as abruptly as they had appeared. At the end Lloyd George was forced back on his origins. In 1922 he was hastily mobilising the Free Churches as his last line of defence. They were no longer a decisive element in British politics, now that education had ceased to be a sectarian question. He who had once seemed the man of the future was by 1922 curiously oldfashioned. He looked, and spoke, like a Victorian. His public speeches, though still effective, sounded like an echo from the past. His audiences often took his point before he made it. His support in the press also dwindled. The press lords moved from him. He quarrelled with Northcliffe in 1918; with Riddell in 1922. Beaverbrook backed away when Bonar Law left the government. There remained only his private organ, the *Daily Chronicle*.

The fall of Lloyd George was provoked by his attempt to resist the Turkish advance on Constantinople—an attempt incidentally which, like most of his enterprises, was largely successful. This was the occasion, not the cause. He was brought down, as he had been raised up, by a revolt of the backbenchers. The Conservative meeting which ended the Coalition was actually summoned by the leaders in order to break this incipient revolt; and the rebels thought, until the last minute, that they would be defeated. It is curious how Lloyd George repeated, in every detail, the mistakes which had destroyed Asquith. He, too, came to believe that he was "the indispensable man," safe from all storms. He, too, came to count solely on "the talents" at the top, and disregarded the other ranks of politics—the very men in the trenches who had made him prime minister.

Afterword

Lloyd George's reputation has traveled through three distinct phases. Before 1916 he was looked upon as their hero by those who were discontented with the state of society. He was the man who would sweep away the inequalities and mitigate the hardships which followed the industrial revolution. For those of wealth and comfort he was the reverse; a dangerous demagogue who would upset the natural balance of society and who, striking out in the name of equality, would create chaos.

After 1916 this pattern changed completely. The discontented no longer looked to him as their champion. They feared that he had fallen a victim to the lure of power and to the intricacies of political in-fighting. He seemed to have lost contact with the men whose belief in his reforming zeal had brought him to prominence, and who had benefited so much by his legislation. Conservatives, however, against whom he had fought for twenty years with all his massive energy, now turned to him as their savior. He was the man who would win the war; the man who would make a stern and lasting peace. He would protect and even extend the British Empire. Most important, he would provide, inside his Coalition Government, a safe place for Conservative retrenchment.

When the Conservatives finally abandoned him in 1922, Lloyd George could still not convince the dispossessed, the out-of-work or the underdog that he would once more be their champion. They had already turned to the Labour Party for salvation. Lloyd George spent much of his large political fund in trying to persuade the working man to give him another chance. But labour no longer trusted him. For the last twenty-five years of his career the man who had been so much admired, and had achieved so much, was looked at askance and denounced as an opportunist, a quack and a failure.

Now we are entering a third phase. Lloyd George is at last proving attractive to the historian. Perhaps this phase will also pass, but I doubt it. As evidence grows, his stature mounts.

In retrospect, it is possible to see the impressive nature of his genius and of his achievements. Lloyd George's career was dominated by his personality; a rich blend of imagination, enthusiasm, bluntness, and energy. He was one of the most hard-working, fast-thinking men who have held high political office in Britain. His career was full of many apparent inconsistencies. It is for the reader to judge whether he acted according to principles which were constant, or emotions which were contradictory. His outspoken attacks on the Boer War were followed by his dynamic leadership in a World War sixteen years later. His violent assault on the power of the House of Lords was followed almost simultaneously by his search for a Coalition with the very Party he was assailing. His enthusiasm for Hitler's achievements in building up the German economy and restoring German self-confidence was followed two years later by his vigorous denunciation of fascist methods. He conducted an eager search for a peace of compromise and conciliation after 1918, but was insistent on a more energetic conduct of both the First and Second World Wars. Mediation and ruthlessness were the two sides of a single coin.

Lloyd George was politically fearless, and also cunning. If he wanted to pursue a course of action he could do so regardless of the consequences to his reputation. He knew that effective action was possible only from a position of strength. Often, to obtain that strength, he trimmed his sails before the winds of popular pressure. But I doubt whether, in the long run, he ever compromised over crucial matters. Many of the apparent inconsistencies in his career are the result of tactical maneuvres. But his goals did not change. Lloyd George devoted the first part of his public career to improving the conditions of the unprivileged. By legislation, he led them out of despondency and toward a fairer, more comfortable life. He devoted the second part of his career to seeking international concord. From Versailles, where he helped to modify the terms of the Peace Treaty, to Genoa, where he fought to bring Germany back into the European family, his aim was conciliation. French fears and German resentment frustrated this aim. But he pursued it with tenacity throughout his peacetime premiership. In war he was a fighter. From 1916 to 1918 he revived and mobilized the spirit of the British people. Between 1939 and 1941 he was outspoken in his criticism of all feeble or incompetent conduct of the war. He urged Churchill to tell the truth to the British people when things went badly, as he himself had done twenty-five years before. Many interpreted his speech of May 1941 (pages 86–90) as a call for surrender, a defeatist moan, a pathetic collapse of stamina and moral fibre. This it was not, as the reader will see who studies it carefully.

Lloyd George's reputation is on the mend. It is for the historians now to reexamine the many complex problems of his career, and to interpret them. We have seen something of their range, and of how they have been interpreted so far. It cannot be expected that a man who was so persuasive an orator, so ruthless a politician and so outspoken an opponent can be dismissed in a few words, a neat phrase or a glib jibe. The years of denigration are surely past. Lloyd George was a man of diverse achievements and a mixed reputation. The reader must form his own opinions as to the final place of this bold, unconventional, imaginative man in British and world history.

Bibliographical Note

There is as yet no complete edition of Lloyd George's speeches or writings, nor has his private correspondence been extensively published. But he himself supervised the publication of several volumes of speeches and articles at different moments in his career. The most useful of these are:

The Lords, The Land and The People (London, 1909)
Better Times (London, 1910)
The People's Insurance (London, 1911)
The Rural Problem: What It Is (London, 1913)
The Great Crusade (London, 1918)
Is It Peace? (London, 1923)
We Can Conquer Unemployment (London, 1929)
Slings and Arrows (London, 1929)
Organizing Prosperity (London, 1935)
Spain and Britain (London, 1936)

In three important books Lloyd George not only put his own views forcibly, but also included much previously unpublished documentary material:

The Truth About Reparations and War Debts (London, 1932)
War Memoirs, six volumes (London, 1933–36)
The Truth About the Peace Treaties (London, 1938)

The principal sources of unpublished material on Lloyd George's political life are in the Lloyd George Archive, now housed in the Beaverbrook Library, 33 St. Bride Street, London E.C.4. Among the authors who have already made use of the material now in this Archive are:

Malcolm Thomson, *David Lloyd George* (London, 1949)
Frank Owen, *Tempestuous Journey* (London, 1954)
Lord Beaverbrook, *Men and Power* (London, 1956)
Lord Beaverbrook, *The Decline and Fall of Lloyd George* (London, 1963)

Each of these books contains important source material on Lloyd George's career. But as yet the Lloyd George Archive remains relatively unexplored.

Many books and pamphlets were written about Lloyd George during his lifetime. The four volumes of Herbert du Parcq, *Life of David Lloyd George* (London, 1914) are a major source for his opinions before 1914. Of interest are: G. E. Raine, *The Real Lloyd George* (London, 1913) and Harold Spender, *The Prime Minister* (London, 1920). Walter Roch, *Mr. Lloyd George and the War* (London, 1920) is bland but informative. A. Fenner Brockway, *Lloyd George and the Traffic in Honour* (London, 1922) puts the case against Lloyd George. J. M. Keynes and H. D. Henderson, *Can Lloyd George Do It?* (London, 1929) supports Lloyd George's "New Deal" economic proposals. Charles Mallet, *Mr. Lloyd George: A Study* (London, 1930) gives a hostile Liberal view. A short, useful biography of Lloyd George is Charles Loch Mowat, *Lloyd George* (Oxford, 1964). Of value for its understanding of the influence of Wales on Lloyd George is Kenneth O. Morgan, *David Lloyd George, Welsh Radical as World Statesman* (Cardiff, 1963). A most stimulating published lecture is A. J. P. Taylor's *Lloyd George: Rise and Fall* (London, 1961). A. J. P. Taylor, *English History 1914–1945* (Oxford, 1966) should also be consulted: it is rich in material and ideas on Lloyd George.

Among the books by those close to Lloyd George at different periods of his career are Countess Lloyd-George of Dwyfor, *The Years That Are Past* (London, 1967); William George, *My Brother and I* (London, 1958); Earl Lloyd-George, *Lloyd George* (London, 1960) by Lloyd George's eldest son, in part filial, in part hostile; Thomas Jones, *Lloyd George* (Oxford, 1951), a somewhat abbreviated biography by a former Cabinet Secretary; W. Watkin Davies, *Lloyd George 1863–1914* (London, 1939), sympathetic and useful; Sir H. Bunbury, ed., *Lloyd George's Ambulance Wagon* (London, 1957), the memoir of W. J. Braithwaite on the evolution of National Insurance; A. J. Sylvester, *The Real Lloyd George* (London, 1947), a secretary's reminiscences over thirty years; Sir Geoffrey Shakespeare, *Let Candles Be Brought In* (London, 1949), a lively account of work with Lloyd George; and Tom Clarke, *My Lloyd George Diary 1884–1939* (London, 1939), a journalist's jottings. A rich contemporary source is to be found in the diaries of the newspaper proprietor, Lord Riddell, a close friend and busy diarist, published as *More Pages From My Diary 1908–1914* (London, 1934), *War Diary* (London, 1933), and *Intimate Diary of the Peace Conference and After* (London, 1933).

There are references to Lloyd George in every book dealing with British politics between 1900 and 1945. Among the most important of these, for the information which they provide about Lloyd George's own activities and opinions are:

Christopher Addison, *Politics From Within,* 2 volumes (London, 1924)
———, *Four and a Half Years,* 2 volumes (London, 1934)
L. S. Amery, *My Political Life,* 3 volumes (London, 1953)
H. H. Asquith, *Memories and Reflections* (London, 1928)
Lord Beaverbrook, *Politicians and the War* (London, 1966)
Lord Birkenhead, *Frederick Edwin Earl of Birkenhead* (London, 1933)
Robert Blake, *The Private Papers of Douglas Haig 1914–1919* (London, 1952)
———, *The Unknown Prime Minister* [Bonar Law] (London, 1955)
Violet Bonham Carter, *Winston Churchill* (New York, 1965)
Robert Boothby, *I Fight to Live* (London, 1947)
Thelma Cazalet-Keir, *From the Wings* (London, 1967)
Randolph S. Churchill, *Lord Derby* (London, 1959)
———, *Winston Churchill: Young Statesman* (London, 1967)
Winston S. Churchill, *The World Crisis,* 5 volumes (London, 1923–31)
Duff Cooper, *Haig* (London, 1936)
Lord D'Abernon, *An Ambassador of Peace,* 3 volumes (London, 1929–31)
Frances Donaldson, *The Marconi Scandal* (London, 1962)
Blanche E. C. Dugdale, *Arthur James Balfour* (London, 1936)

Bentley B. Gilbert, *The Evolution of National Insurance in Great Britain* (London, 1966)

Martin Gilbert, *The Roots of Appeasement* (New York, 1966)

Alfred M. Gollin, *The Observer and J. L. Garvin 1908–1914* (London, 1960)

———, *Proconsul in Politics* [Lord Milner] (London, 1964).

———, *Balfour's Burden* (London, 1965)

Sir Keith Hancock, *Smuts, The Sanguine Years* (London, 1962)

Lord Hankey, *The Supreme Command* [First World War] (London, 1961)

———, *The Supreme Control at the Paris Peace Conference* (London, 1963)

Robert Rhodes James, *Lord Rosebery* (London, 1963)

Roy Jenkins, *Mr. Balfour's Poodle* [the People's Budget and the Lords] (London, 1954)

———, *Asquith* (London, 1964)

Thomas Jones, *A Diary With Letters 1931–1950* (London, 1954)

Basil Liddell-Hart, *Memoirs,* 2 volumes (London, 1965)

Arthur J. Marder, *From Dreadnought to Scapa Flow: The Road to War 1904–14* (London, 1961)

Lucy Masterman, *C. F. G. Masterman* (London, 1939)

Kenneth O. Morgan, *Wales in British Politics 1868–1922* (Cardiff, 1964)

Harold Nicolson, *Peacemaking 1919* (London, 1964)

———, *Curzon: The Last Phase* (London, 1934)

———, *King George V* (London, 1952)

———, *Diaries and Letters 1930–1939* (London, 1966)

Frank Pakenham, *Peace by Ordeal* [the Anglo-Irish Treaty of 1921] (London, 1935)

Sir Charles Petrie, *Life and Letters of Sir Austen Chamberlain,* 2 volumes (London, 1939–40)

The Marquess of Reading, *Rufus Isaacs,* 2 volumes (London, 1942)

Sir William Robertson, *Soldiers and Statesmen 1914–1918* (London, 1926)

Lord Ronaldshay, *The Life of Lord Curzon,* 3 volumes (London, 1928)

Lord Simon, *Retrospect* (London, 1952)

Leonard Stein, *The Balfour Declaration* [the Jewish home in Palestine] (London, 1961)

Dudley Sommer, *Haldane of Cloan* (London, 1960)

Richard H. Ullman, *Intervention and the War* [Britain and the Bolsheviks] (Princeton and London, 1961)

S. D. Waley, *Edwin Montagu* (Bombay, 1964)

Trevor Wilson, *The Downfall of the Liberal Party* (London, 1966)

Sir Llewellyn Woodward, *Great Britain and the War of 1914–1918* (London, 1967)

With the opening of the Lloyd George Archive in 1967, and the operation of a "30-year-rule" for all official British Government documents as from 1968, we may expect the publication of further detailed studies of Lloyd George's career. John Grigg is at present at work on a multi-volume biography. There will also be important new documentary material on Lloyd George in the forthcoming main and companion volumes of Randolph S. Churchill's *Winston Churchill.*

Index